ROAD FEVER

ROAD FEVER

A HIGH-SPEED TRAVELOGUE

TIM CAHILL

RANDOM HOUSE
NEW YORK

Library of Congress Cataloging-in-Publication Data

Cahill, Tim.
Road fever: a high-speed travelogue / by Tim Cahill.
p.   cm.
ISBN 0-394-57656-X
1. Cahill, Tim—Journeys—America.
2. America—Description and travel—1981–
3. Authors, American—20th century—Journeys—America.
4. Adventure and adventurers—United States—Biography.
I. Title.
PS3553.A365Z463   1990
917.04′539—dc20   89-42873

Manufactured in the United States of America

98765432   24689753   23456789

First Edition
DESIGNED BY DEBBY JAY

This One's for Karen Laramore

ACKNOWLEDGMENTS

A journey is best measured in friends rather than miles. Everywhere, in every country Garry Sowerby and I visited, people offered assistance, advice, and encouragement. We tried to sell Pan-American unity as a dream. The following friends made it a reality.

In Argentina: Jacques Crete, Monica Johnson de Escardo, Duilio DiBella, Oscar E. Barralia, Raul Oscar Capuano, Roberto O. Ducca, Hector O. Alberici, Horacio Zentner, Italo F. Delano, Jorge Fernandez, Roberto Nori, Daniel Leguizamon.

In Chile: Frank Chandler, Christian LaBelle, Gregory C. Nicolaidis, Daniel A. Buteler, Basil Drossos, Mario Archeta, Enrique Gutierrez.

In Peru: M. Dinev, Ricardo Cordove Freyre, Jesus Gonzales Marquesado, Carlos Gonzales Zuzunage, Noel Yriberry Lira, Mercedes Gotuzzo Balta, Dario Caamano Montero, Estuardo Melendez Hoyle, Carlos Garcia Salazar, Luis Zamudio Garcia, Norma Espinoza, Enrique Viale, Fernando Viale.

In Ecuador: R. Mora, Ralph Gillies, Dick Stead, Alejandro Penaherrera, Ivan Toro, Dr. Juan Herman Ortiz.

In Colombia: Perry J. Calderwood, Jaime Alberto Morales, Alan Carvajal, Elie J. Rezk, Santiago Camacho, Jaime Lopez Mendoza, Luis Eduardo Nieto Venegas, Captain Juergen F. Steinebach, Señor G. Giaimo.

In Panama: Ruth Denton, Luis Paz Cardenas, Jose Tapis, Manuelita del la Guardia.

In Costa Rica: James Lambert, Matthew Levin, Greg Cooney, Marco Antonio Pinto.

In Nicaragua: Chistita Caldera, William Vargas, Cesar A. Noguera Ch., Mayda Denueda.

In Guatemala: Thomas G. Cullen, Ricardo Pennington, Frances Asturea, William Gonzales.

In Mexico: Laurent N. Beaulieu, Mario Silva, Luc Javier R. Saucedo Renoud, Francisco Resendiz.

In the United States (lower forty-eight): Rich Cox, Tucker Willis, Pat Moore, W. Marvin Rush III, Bob Lake, Dave Fugate, Art Christy, and Paul Dix. We are especially grateful to Albert J. Buchanan.

In Canada: At Canadian Tire: Jim Miller; at GM Canada: Chris Douglas, Doug Terry, Gerry Gereski, Earl Weichel, Nick Hall; at Farmers: Barrie Reid, W. E. McLellan; at the Canadian Dept. of External Affairs: Anne Hilmer; at the Canadian Automobile Association: David Steventon.

In Alaska: Jim Messer, Bob Mills, Gordon Messer, Terry Tipoly, John Horn, Fritz Guenther, Phil Blackstone, Bob Lewis.

We are also grateful to the following individuals and corporations for special assistance in the U.S.:

At GMC Truck: John Rock, Rich Stuckey, Bill Hill, Steve Olsen, Al Walker, Russ Cameron, Frank Cronin.

At Detroit Diesel Allison: Jim Moloney, Wally Renn, Judy Kangas, Jack Blanchard.

At Stanadyne: Joe Boissonneault, Barbara Bartucca, Mary Seery, Lee Jannet.

At *Popular Mechanics:* Joe Skorupa, Joe Oldham.

At GMODC: Ron Royer, Fred Schwartz.

At Motorola: Dave Weisz.

At Delco Products: Dick Westfall.

Special thanks to those who provided invaluable letters of introduction: Alan Russell, former editor, *Guinness Book of World Records;* Ivan Toro, Automovil Club del Ecuador; Manuel Lissarrague, Automovil Club Argentino; Monica Figueroa Navarro, Automovil Club de Chile; Otto Jelinek, Minister of State, Fitness and Amateur Sport, Canada; Joe Clark, Secretary of State for External Affairs, Canada; David Steventon, Canadian Automobile Association; Deb Drummond, Canadian Automobile Association; Laurie K. Storsater, Canadian Embassy, Peru.

Finally, the author wishes to thank Barbara Lowenstein, a professional agent and personal friend. Thanks also to David Rosenthal, a gifted editor with a whole lot of patience and faith.

ROAD FEVER

IT'S HOT HOT HOT
(BOOM, BAM,
KA-POW)

January 1987 · Las Vegas, Nevada

THERE WERE ABOUT three thousand of us for dinner that night at the Bally Casino Resort in Las Vegas. We were seated at large round tables accommodating ten people apiece, and each place setting bristled with flatware. There were at least ten separate utensils per person: knives and forks and a few mysterious surgical-looking devices with shiny sharp points. I counted almost four hundred tables in the cavernous convention hall. During the meal an odd group of musicians played understated dinner music on a raised stage at the front of the hall. There was a bass, an accordion, and ten women playing violins. They played "Hava Nagila" and "Roll Out the Barrel." They played "Tie a Yellow Ribbon Round the Old Oak Tree."

An army of waiters and waitresses, moving with military precision and import, delivered the food so that everyone—all three thousand of us—got his or her melon simultaneously. Next we were served a dish in a shell-shaped chalice that contained small pieces of shrimp and lobster in a cream sauce. The following course, designed to clear the palate, was a frozen peach cut in half, hollowed out and filled with sherbet, which was followed by steak with sautéed mushrooms. Broccoli with cheese sauce. Baked Alaska.

The women playing the violins wore green empire-waist shoulderless dresses and they produced "symphonic" polkas, with their eyes closed in feigned ecstasy.

As the waiters whisked away the gummy remnants of the baked Alaska, Nashville comedian Minnie Pearl took the stage and told a lot of jokes about the knee-slapping problems of the elderly. She gave the impression that she herself was too old to enjoy anything much and that the audience, a reasonably flamboyant collection of auto dealers and their spouses from the Western states, should find this amusing. Minnie Pearl remarked upon a female acquaintance of certain years who wanted female pallbearers at her funeral. No men. The acquaintance saw this as a form of revenge for disappointments suffered regarding heterosexual romance in her latter years.

"If they won't take me out when I'm alive," Minnie Pearl quoted the embittered woman, "then they ain't gonna take me out when I'm dead."

Minnie Pearl wore a large garish bonnet with a price tag hanging off one side and said that a few years ago, in her hometown of Grinderswitch, there was a fad called streaking, in which people ran around naked as a means of self-expression. One of these erstwhile streakers was yet another older woman, who, Minnie Pearl suggested, was revealing her body in order to arouse men who might make her life a garden of sexual delight. Concerned onlookers pointed out the spectacle to an older gentleman known as Grandpa, who didn't see so well.

"She's streaking, Grandpa," they said.

"What's that?"

"Why, Grandpa," the concerned onlookers explained, "she's wearing her birthday suit."

Grandpa squinted his eyes and said, "Looks like it needs ironing."

Three thousand people laughed heartily at this and there was a smattering of applause.

Exit Minnie Pearl. Enter John Rock, the general manager of GMC truck, a forceful and solid-looking man who appeared to be well named. Rock said that he wasn't going to waste a lot of time, but that the audience, which included a healthy sampling of the automotive press, should know that he was pretty excited about the new truck GMC was introducing. The Sierra pickup had been designed from the wheels up at a cost of $2.8 billion. It was the first redesign on the old workhorse in fifteen years. It was a tough truck. It was easy going on the road. It was hot.

The trucks, we were given to understand, would sell like hotcakes. The typical buyer, Rock thought, might be defined as an "upscale cowpunk." The way Rock pronounced the words, he seemed to think upscale cowpunks were some pretty fine fellows completely aside from the fact that he expected them to make him and everyone in the room fabulously rich.

"Our typical buyer," Rock said, "he's an easy guy. He comes to a meal like this one, he's going to have about four forks and a couple of knives left over." Everyone laughed because we all had a bunch of gadgets left over, inexplicable little scalpels and picks scattered about, marking us all as easy guys, likable upscale cowpunks.

The easiest thing about the easy guy, John Rock said, is that he only wants the best. That would be how one ad for the new truck might read: "I'm an easy guy, I only want the best." Rock thought GMC dealers would be in fine fettle vis à vis the easy upscale cowpunk buyer in that they had a product that was, in his opinion, clearly the best pickup on the market.

Another thing about the easy guy, Rock said, is that he would like this show, and he'd love the next act: "Ladies and gentlemen, the fabulous Mr. Roy Clark."

Later, at a booth near the entrance to the dining room, several attractive young women handed out free clothes that the dealers might want to wear at tomorrow's test drive. Members of the automotive press in attendance snapped up the easy-guy gear: leather driving gloves, Levi's jackets lined in something like sheepskin, and 4x Beaver Stetsons. There were parties that night in various private suites—lots of Tanqueray, goblets of Wild Turkey, laughter, and the sound of tinkling ice cubes behind closed doors.

A few of the dealers, their spouses, and the automotive press in particular looked a bit musty the next morning at six. There were lots of hung-over clones in denim jackets and cowboy hats; it was the dawn of the dead upscale cowpunks. We were bused to a large convention center on the outskirts of Las Vegas. GMC had booked the center's parking lot for a demonstration of its rear-wheel antilock brakes. The parking lot, aimless acres of concrete, had been cordoned off from the general public and was sprayed with a mixture of oil and water. A mechanic disabled the antilock brakes in one of the trucks, and a stunt driver pushed it into the water and oil at top speed. The truck made a sweeping turn and the driver hit the brakes at the apogee of his arc, the point where centrifugal force wanted to send the vehicle spinning out of control. There was a bucking motion, the tires lost their grip in the oily water, and the truck spun off at an odd vector, doing doughnuts and tossing up oily rooster tails in the early-morning desert sun. The falling sheets of water had that vague multicolored rainbow effect characteristic of petroleum products and water.

The antilock brakes were enabled, the stunt driver powered the truck into the same arc at what appeared to be the same speed, and, at the same point, he hit the brakes and the truck stopped, bam, like that. It wasn't very exciting or colorful, though GMC executives explained that losing the back end of a pickup on a slippery road was the sort of excitement they felt easy guys could do without.

"We found," a GMC executive told me, "that half the time a guy is going to be driving around without a substantial load in the bed of the truck. It's pretty easy to swap ends that way and these antilocks take care of the problem." He nodded in such a way that I felt obliged to nod back my approval. "These brakes," the man said, "are going to save some lives." We nodded at each other. "Lots of lives." Antilock brakes were right up there with Mother Teresa in this guy's book.

Later, we all drove to a resort on the slopes of nearby Mount Charleston, where the dealers and the automotive press were given a chance to drive these new trucks over some pretty rough terrain. Shining new Sierra pickups were lined up in the parking lot. I chose a half-ton gasoline-engine vehicle and sent it pounding over one of the rougher off-road courses. The truck had plenty of guts—it was actually fast—and I beat the crap out of it; had it thumping over high-desert moguls in B-movie-chase-scene mode.

"Uh, Tim . . ."

My partner and friend, Garry Sowerby, a professional endurance driver, was getting uncomfortable.

"Tim, tell me what you're doing."

"Trying to get all four tires off the ground," I explained. "Give this thing a workout."

We were rocketing down a gravelly wash at perhaps fifty miles an hour. There was a small hillock at the bottom. It sloped upward at a gentle angle and appeared to drop off sharply on the far side. Garry was talking reasonably about keeping everybody happy on our upcoming odyssey. The vehicle was actually "somebody," indeed, "she" was the third member of the expedition, and the way we treated "her" would influence "her" attitude toward us. The truck could be our best friend or our worst enemy. The truck deserved respect.

"They want us to beat these trucks up," I argued. "It's our duty. Like with a rental car."

We hit the hillock hard and I discovered that the slope was not entirely gentle. Quite suddenly the desert ahead dropped below the hood of the truck so that we were looking at the peaks of various mountains and blue sky beyond. There was a momentary sense of weightlessness, then gravity shanghaied the engine and we found ourselves staring down at the desert floor. All this happened very fast. Mountains and sky, then sand and gravel, followed by an instantaneous and walloping jolt. The steering wheel twisted in my hands and we went into a gravel-spitting skid, which I corrected and then lost to the other side. We were careening over the desert floor at various forty-five-degree angles to our actual direction of travel. There were no obvious obstacles in sight and, purely out of curiosity, I hit the brakes full on. Unexpectedly, the truck straightened up and stopped right.

"Antilock brakes," I commented.

"We are definitely going to have to have a talk," Garry said mildly.

IT WAS A PRETTY GOOD TRUCK, tough on the rough cross-country course and unexpectedly smooth on the road. In the resort dining room, John Rock again spoke to the dealers. He said that GMC would do a lot to promote this truck: it would be a pace car at certain important automobile races, there would be "Easy Guy" television ads emphasizing that the truck was in fact "not just a truck anymore." I wondered what that meant. Was it a boat? An armadillo?

John Rock assured the dealers of GMC's support. There were television promotions and print ads scheduled—something new for every month. "In September," he said, "Garry Sowerby will drive a virtually stock Sierra truck from Tierra del Fuego at the tip of South America to Prudhoe Bay, Alaska. That's as far north as you can drive, on the longest road in the world." The trip would be a test of the new Sierra's speed and endurance. "Garry," Rock said, "will set a world speed record for this drive."

Rock explained that Garry had set a recognized world record for driving a GMC Suburban from the tip of Africa to the most northerly point in Europe. During that trip, Sowerby had been fired on by bandits in northern Kenya. There were some holes in the Suburban but Garry had escaped intact. Sowerby also held the current speed record for driving around the world. It took him seventy-seven days, and Rock neglected to say that he did it in a Volvo sedan.

"Stand up, Garry."

There was much applause for Sowerby and his accomplishments. "Garry's codriver is Tim Cahill," Rock said. "Tim's gonna keep Garry out of trouble on this one." There was a smattering of applause and some curious looks. Rock had meant the comment as a joke—no one was going to keep Garry Sowerby out of trouble—but I got the feeling that people suspected I was a dangerous fellow, a bodyguard type, handy with a gun and knife. I touched an index finger to the brim of my new Stetson, *Gunsmoke* style, and surveyed the room with fierce secret-service eyes.

BACK AT THE BALLY, several thousand truck dealers milled about in a hangar-sized room off the dining hall. Various models of the Sierra were on display. Truck dealers, I noticed, actually kicked tires just like ordinary people. Garry and I were on display, available, I guess, for publicity photos. We stood next to a one-ton Sierra painted black and white, with a green map of the Americas, north and south, that covered the entire hood of the vehicle. There was a thick red line pretty much bisecting the map that was supposed to represent our route on the upcoming Pan-American record run. Our names were painted on both doors. The press and various dealers stopped by and took pictures because that's what they were supposed to do.

Some of the dealers asked a number of informed questions.

"What about Nicaragua?"

"It's a problem."

"What do you do about the Darien Gap?"

The gap is an eighty-mile stretch of roadless area extending from northern Colombia into Panama.

"The rules," Garry told people, "say that we have to drive to the end of the road in Colombia and Panama. We can have the truck shipped, but no airfreighting it."

"Who makes the rules?"

"The editors of the *Guinness Book of World Records.*"

"Why them?"

"They represent the only credible institution that could certify a new record."

"What's the old record?"

"Months."

"Can you beat it?"

"Yeah. But there's a guy about to give it a try pretty soon. Some European prince. He's taking six Land-Rovers."

"Kick his ass."

One of the dealers asked me what engine we were using.

"Six-point-two-liter diesel," I said. The guy popped the hood. "What's this?"

"What?"

"Gasoline engine in here."

I stared at a big gleaming hunk of metal for several seconds exactly as if I knew something about automobile engines. Then I bailed out.

"Garry, tell this guy about the engine."

"It's a prototype," Garry said. So. It wasn't our truck at all. It was a prototype. Just a Sierra with a special paint job and a gasoline engine inside.

"Prototype's a gasoline engine," I explained.

The dealer smiled tolerantly.

"Garry," I said, "is the mechanic on this team."

After that I avoided dealers who kept asking pesky technical questions—"size tires you guys using?"—and hung out by the bar with the press and a very credible Marilyn Monroe impersonator.

We discussed Marilyn Monroe and various other subjects that fired the reporters' imaginations: who was canned at what four-wheel magazine, who was getting divorced, which auto company put on the most lavish launches and provided the most drinks. They didn't talk much about the new Sierra, easy guys, or the fact that these trucks were not just trucks anymore. A GMC executive I was chatting with couldn't stand it anymore. The company had put up a fortune and here these guys were, standing around like ordinary people, men and women who had not just driven the new GMC Sierra.

"What's the matter with these guys?" the man asked me.

I understood, suddenly, that this was a very nervous time and that these executives were rather like actors waiting for opening-night reviews. They were, most of them, big hardy men, and there was an odor of ego and anxiety in the air. It wasn't just business or money as I saw it. These guys genuinely identified with the new GMC Sierra, which wasn't just a truck anymore. When I told one executive that I wasn't particularly in love with the dashboard layout, a look of hurt bewilderment crossed his face, and this was followed by a quick flush of anger. I might have said, "Gee, you sure got some butt-ugly kids."

"Most of the reporters I talked to really like the truck," I said. "You just don't go around gushing about anything if you've been in the business for a while. It's bad form. Makes you look like a patsy. Your colleagues think you're a jerk."

"I thought you were a driver."

"On this trip."

"You talk like a journalist."

"That too."

I WAS IN MY ROOM at the Bally, watching closed-circuit TV psychodramas that showed GMC dealers how to sell trucks to easy guys. Garry called just as an actor portraying a GMC dealer said, "Dodge makes a fine product, all right, but maybe you'd like to see a few of the features we think make this vehicle an outstanding . . ."

Garry said, "They're nervous about you. They wonder if you'll say bad things about the truck."

I knew I wasn't going to like this conversation. "We have an agreement," I said.

"I know."

The arrangement was simple enough. I would not endorse or participate in advertising the truck. I would accept no money from any sponsor, and Garry would pay my expenses. Because the rules called for a codriver, he'd figured those expenses into his original proposal to GMC. If the truck fell apart on the record run, I was free to write about it.

"They're thinking about the two-point-eight billion they put into the project."

"Look, Garry, if they want a book that's an advertisement for the truck, maybe they should send some ad guy with you."

"I'm just telling you what they told me. As far as I'm concerned you're my codriver. But it's their money."

"Because there's no way I'm making them any promises."

"I'll talk to them, try to calm them down."

"Tell 'em it's smart business. Advertising costs money and no one believes it. The truth is free."

"We might have a problem is all I'm saying. I'll tell you what they think tomorrow."

AT NINE THE NEXT MORNING, the final day of the launch, GMC put on a two-and-a-half-hour show about the 2.8-billion-dollar vehicle. Four women in tight golden pants danced erotically around a couple of gleaming trucks. Three video screens above the stage kept flashing the word "HOT" at us in feverish stroboscopic bursts. Several executives spoke, one after another, and then there was a grand finale with explosions and sparky fireworks—"it's hot hot hot"—and the women in gold draped themselves lasciviously over protruding bumpers and sang about how it wasn't just a truck anymore so that any nincompoop could tell what it was—every easy guy has one—and green laser beams swept over our heads, preternaturally bright in the lingering smoke from the fireworks, and Garry leaned over and said, "They want you to tell the truth."

THE END OF THE ROAD

April 1987 · Ushuaia, Argentina

THESE ARE THE LAST five road signs in the world: CONSERVE SU DERECHA, followed closely by a yellow diamond-shaped warning featuring an arrow snaking upward; a few miles later there are two more closely spaced yellow warning diamonds, both with the same schematic drawing of rocks dropping off a cliff onto a rather boxy-looking car; the last road sign in the world is posted on the last bridge in the world and it reads, 20 T MÁXIMO PESO. After that, there are no more road signs.

You might imagine that beyond the last road sign there would be a warning or legend such as ancient mapmakers placed on unexplored portions of the globe: "Here there be dragons." But no, the last messages civilization imparts to drivers seeking the end of the world are: keep to your right, watch the curves, don't let rocks fall on your car, and, finally, twenty tons is about all the last bridge in the world can handle.

A MONTH BEFORE GMC launched the new Sierra in Las Vegas, Garry Sowerby had visited London and hammered out the rules for the trip with Alan Russell, the editor of the *Guinness Book of World Records*. "The clock starts when you start and ends when you get there." That was it. Simple.

Garry and Alan Russell were eating in an Italian restaurant on Southampton Row. They were on their coffee when Russell said, "It might interest you to know that we have two parties attempting the record." One, a Frenchman, Prince Pierre D'Arenberg, would start from Prudhoe in February. Another fellow, a Canadian, had started in early November. Russell gave Garry a hastily scribbled note. Jerzy Adamuszek was driving a Cadillac, alone. "Which is one reason people should contact us," Russell said. "We would, on this trip, require a codriver. A driver attempting to set a record could easily push himself

past the danger point. Complete exhaustion can have bloody conse-
quences. I don't want to be responsible for accidents to anyone, the
would-be record setter or someone standing alongside the road. For this
reason, for safety's sake, we require a codriver."

Garry looked at the note from Adamuszek and didn't give the guy
much of a chance anyway. A lot of people attempt this particular trip.
Some are stymied by mechanical problems, or fear, or exhaustion, or
a simple failure of will. A fellow who had neglected to inquire about
rules at the outset, Garry guessed, was most likely to be crushed under
the weight of some peculiarly baroque border-crossing formality.

The prince, however, could be a problem. You can never tell about
French princes. They're always breaking records on wind surfers or
skiing down entirely vertical mountains. A prince is likely to get better
treatment at the border. The prince could be trouble.

"What about the Darien Gap?" Garry asked.

After some consideration, Russell made a decision. "You have to
drive to the northern end of the road in Colombia, then to a port and
ship your vehicle. Once in Panama, you have to drive to the southern
end of the road there."

"Can we airfreight over the gap?"

"No," Russell said, "I don't think so. If the road is ever completed,
and somebody makes that drive, including the gap, you'd have done
eighty miles of your trip by air. This doesn't seem fair. Boats, however,
are slow. Shipping is the only fair way to do it."

"Let's say we set the record."

"Yes."

"Then the road is completed, someone else comes along, they drive
the gap but they don't beat our time. Do they get the record?"

"It's a judgment call."

"I keep hearing," Garry said, "about groups that have driven the
whole way, gap and all. Some guys with a whole corps of engineers to
build bridges across the river in the gap. Stuff like that."

"Those groups have never contacted us."

"What if someone does it all, including the roadless area of the gap,
but they take, say, a year more than we did. Does that count?"

"It's a judgment call," Alan Russell said.

Several people, Russell said, had claimed the record, but he had not
seen fit to recognize any of them for a number of reasons. Some claim-
ants to the Pan-American record had failed to provide any very con-
vincing documentation. One person had started his trip from
Anchorage, Alaska, and Russell was adamant: distance and speed rec-

ords had to be set from geographic point to geographic point, and in this case from one end of the Americas to the other; from the Beaufort Sea to the Beagle Channel; or vice versa. "Otherwise," Russell explained, "you'd have people claiming a record drive from, say, London to Shropshire, or Columbus, Ohio, to Detroit. You'd have someone claiming the world record for a drive from his house to his girlfriend's apartment. Where does that stop?"

The geographic points for the purposes of the Pan-American record, however, were those that could be reached by road. Prudhoe Bay, for instance, isn't as far north as Barrow, Alaska. On the other hand, there was no road to Barrow. It seemed ludicrous to airfreight a vehicle over the roadless tundra. The road ends where the road ends. Provided it ends at a geographic point. Like the Beaufort Sea at Prudhoe.

"I've been doing some research," Garry said. "I think the end of the road in the south extends a bit beyond Ushuaia, the last town."

"Are you going to scout the area before you start?"

"Of course."

"Send me a report. I'll give you a ruling."

And so, in April of 1987, Garry and I flew to the town at the end of the earth. Ushuaia, Argentina, at the extreme tip of South America, on the island of Tierra del Fuego, the land of fire, is considered to be the southernmost town in the world. Founded a little over one hundred years ago, the town has a population of about 23,000 permanent residents. They are descendants of English missionaries who stayed on as farmers, of Yugoslavian and Romanian miners, of sailors from Spain and Italy, of Chileans who came looking for work, of a few Germans, and of the minuscule sad remnants of the native Indian population. The people are miners, fishermen, farmers, sheep ranchers, builders, construction engineers, cannery workers, and shopkeepers. A large number are involved in tourist services, an industry that seemed, in April of 1987, to be booming.

In the lower-latitude competition, Ushuaia is the clear winner. Port Elizabeth in South Africa is 33 degrees 58 minutes south; Hobart in Tasmania is 42 degrees 54 minutes south; Invercargill on New Zealand is 46 degrees 26 minutes south; and Ushuaia is 54 degrees 48 minutes south.

More than likely, many tourists are drawn to Ushuaia precisely because it is the town at the end of the earth. The settlement is a scant 760 miles from Antarctica, specifically from the Antarctic peninsula, a section of the icy continent that stretches up well above the Antarctic Circle. Even so, the weather in Ushuaia is surprisingly constant and mild. The record winter low is 10 Fahrenheit degrees above zero. The record high is just above 80 in the summer, with an average summer day coming in at 51 degrees. The town of graceful frame houses is set on a hillside overlooking the Beagle Channel to the south. A spectacular range of mountains, the Cerro Martial, rises behind the town, to the north. Those tourists who come to see the end of the earth often return because Ushuaia is beautiful, serene, and temperate. The Argentine government has recently upped the ante on tourism as well: Ushuaia is now a duty-free port and there are a number of elegant shops selling expensive goods at a discount. A visitor can now buy Calvin Klein jeans and shirts with alligators on them at the end of the earth, an idea with all the charm and grace of a mugging.

Chile claims to have the most southern city on earth, Punta Arenas, at 53 degrees 9 minutes south, and there are Chileans who will claim that the settlement of Puerto Williams, on Isla Navarino, a mile or so across the Beagle Channel from Ushuaia, is the southernmost town in the world. But Puerto Williams is a Chilean navy base. Even the tourist hotel on the island is owned by the navy.

And there are Argentines who contend that military installations don't constitute an actual permanent and entirely voluntary population. In Ushuaia, there is a government tourist agency, Turismo, where a spritely young Argentine woman named Veronica Iglesias argued that her town had to be considered the last in the world. It got down to splitting hairs, really, Veronica felt. There were scientists and workers who overwintered in Antarctica, after all. Were they a true "permanent settlement"? Did any of them own their own houses there? Or expect to live out their lives there? Be buried there? And how about Puerto Williams? Wasn't it really a military base? Not really a civilian settlement where men and women lived as a matter of choice?

Garry and I told Veronica we were looking for the end of the road, and she was equally adamant. There was a road, after all, on Isla Navarino, but it "wasn't a national road." I gathered that Veronica meant the road existed on the island and for the island. It was not part of a larger national and international system. Veronica believed that the road we wanted was even now being built east and south of Ushuaia. It branched off of Argentina Route 3, was part of the national system. It was called Route J, though when it was first being built about twenty-five years ago, the governor of the territory felt it was such a poor excuse for a road that he called it "Ruta Cero," Route Zero, and the name has stuck.

The next day I ran into an American, Mark Eichenberger, who understood the search for the end of the road. He had driven down from the States over the winter of 1977–78. He too had felt compelled to go to the end of the road, which at that time was at Lapataia, a bit west and a few miles south of Ushuaia. Mark had stayed on in Ushuaia: for three-and-a-half years he worked for the American National Science Foundation as deputy director of ITT Antarctic Services, and was relief captain of a research ship, *Hero.*

Mark, clearly, knew his way around the southern tip of South America, and, as an American, he wasn't blinded by national pride in regard to assessing precisely where the road ends. Mark pointed out that Tierra del Fuego was an island, separated from the mainland by the Strait of Magellan. The true end of the continent was Cape Froward, a hundred miles north, in Chile.

Still, Tierra del Fuego looked like the end of the road on the map, it felt like the end of the road, and there was emotional resonance to the idea. A regular and frequent ferry service, for instance, across the Strait of Magellan (it runs twelve hours a day), connects the island to the mainland, and Mark felt that such a ferry was a de facto bridge. "Looking for the end of the road," he said, "is an exercise in banging your head against the wall." He mentioned a road he knew of on King George Island, just off the Antarctic Peninsula. The road runs from the Chilean air force base there to the Uruguayan base to the Chinese Great Wall Station. It is two-and-a-half-miles long. Did you include these little bits and pieces of roads?

No, Mark thought Route Zero had to be the end of the road, the last place you could reasonably drive to if you left Des Moines and turned south.

I stopped back in at the tourist agency and asked Veronica if there was a regular and frequent ferry service from Ushuaia to Puerto Williams. Yes, she said, there was a ferry that runs on Sundays only, but "he is broken." Veronica spoke English with the most delightful accent. In any case, the broken boat wasn't a car ferry. Veronica did mention that Garry and I would pass Harberton Ranch on the way to the end of Route Zero and if I was interested in car ferries, I might talk to the manager who, she said solemnly, "has a boat that carries ships."

The more I thought about that special boat, the more intrigued I was. A boat that carries ships? Wasn't that like a car that carries trucks? And why would you put a ship on a boat anyway? Why couldn't you just pull the ship along behind the boat?

There were three places in Ushuaia that rented cars. Two didn't answer their phones. At the third place, I got their last available vehicle: the last car at the last rental station in the last place on earth.

SATCHEL PAIGE, the great and ageless major-league pitcher, once described the secret of his longevity thus: "Don't look back, something might be gaining on you." I couldn't look back because the last car on earth—a cruel, clattering, two-cylinder beater—didn't have much in the way of a defogging fan or heater. Occasionally, there was a strangled huff from the one vent under the driver's side of the windshield. "Uhhhh," the fan said, and, sometime later, I'd smell, rather than feel, a feeble fetid sigh from the vent. Each breath promised to be the last. It was like waiting for someone to die of halitosis.

April, in the Southern Hemisphere, is genuinely cruel, the beginning of winter, and we were driving through a steady-falling rain that wanted to be snow. The first snow of winter would be brilliant and joyous, but the temperature was recalcitrant, and it continued to hover inconveniently. Consequently, the rain was sullen and angry, gray, desolate, and moody.

"Nice day," Garry said. He was sitting in the passenger seat with his knees bunched up around his chest, and I could see his breath as he spoke.

There was a fog bank in the backseat that obscured the back window, and, because there were no side mirrors on the last car on earth, I couldn't tell if anything was gaining on me. I wiped the windshield with the sleeve of my jacket.

The road was earthen, puddled, and potholed. To the left, mountains rose four thousand feet and more above the Beagle Channel. They were capped with snow, and icy skeins of white ran down the couloirs. There were streams, swollen in the steady rain, that ran alongside the road. Deciduous trees along the creek bottoms were deep into their fall colors of crimson and gold, so that the evergreens among them stood out in bold relief. There was an occasional small lake. The landscape was reminiscent of the Olympic Peninsula in Washington State except for the New England intensity of the foliage. In all, this strip of land along the Beagle Channel was a strange mix of those things that are beautiful across the entire northern part of the United States.

At a place called Rancho Hambre, I turned off Route 3 onto Route J. In Argentina, an *estancia* is what Americans would call a ranch, and a *rancho* is a shack. It seemed appropriate to hit Route Zero at a place called Hungry Shack.

Along the river bottoms, the grass was golden, but, rising up over a hill, we found ourselves in a strange and spectral forest of leafless trees and hanging moss. Farther on, there were areas of pasture where great flights of geese and ducks were massing for the migration north. Cattle, fat as any in Iowa, grazed among the ducks. Sheep wandered along the road and scattered as the car passed them. They were so robust and heavily wooled that they ran in a comical bow-legged fashion.

This was all part of Estancia Harberton. Established one hundred years ago, Harberton is the oldest ranch in Tierra del Fuego. We stopped to talk with the manager, Tom Goodall. He was a young-looking fellow with a weather-reddened face and an anomalous gray beard.

It was like talking to any rancher. Prices were down. Times were tough. Because the ranch was a piece of history, Tom had started tourist trips to the place. Out in the bay, I could see a few small boats and a large flat-bottomed barge. I wanted to ask about the amazing boat that carries ships, but Tom started telling me about the barge. It was handmade. He used it to carry his sheep to pastures on nearby islands owned by the ranch.

"Don't you have another boat," I asked, "one that carries . . ." And then it occurred to me that the "ships" Veronica mentioned were, in fact, sheep. Sheeps, ships. A boat that carries ships. The barge.

Tom said the road had been finished to Harberton in 1962. When tensions between Chile and Argentina began rising several years ago, it was thought that a road to the military base farther east and south along the Moat Channel would be of strategic significance. There were three islands just to the south of the base—Picton, Lennox, and Nueva—that were in dispute. Fortunately, a few years ago the pope settled this disagreement between these two largely Catholic countries. The road, Tom said, was no longer a priority. Tensions had eased and work was going slowly. It was about twenty miles to the end of the road.

I had gotten wet in the cold steady rain and now, approaching the last road sign in the world, the heat from my body had combined with cold, sopping clothes to produce a fog bank that encompassed the entire interior of the car.

"Uhhh," the dying beater gasped, flatulently.

Nineteen miles past Harberton, we passed the military road-crew camp, drove over the last bridge in the world, and pushed on through the ungraded soggy mud. Three miles later, the road ended on a hillock, in a ridge of black mud. We stepped out of the car and sank up to our calves in cold mud. Wind-driven rain stung my face. I calculated the road ended at 54 degrees 52 minutes south.

There was a bulldozer that looked defunct, a small trailer, and a ridge of mud. Nobody was working on such a foul day. Sowerby and I were alone at the end of the road. Directly below the hill, dead ahead, was the sea, roiled and gray. To the right, I could just make out Picton Island through the mist. Beyond Picton, seven hundred and some miles across the gray sea, was Antarctica.

Garry and I stood shivering at the end of the world. There was nothing to say. Our calculations suggested that we could drive the entire Pan-American Highway in about a month. We'd been to Chile, Peru, Ecuador, Colombia, and several other South American countries. In a few months we'd visit Central America, where conditions were changing from day to day. The more recent our knowledge of those countries, the better off we'd be. The politics were volatile, but the distances were compressed. (Three days from Nicaragua to Texas, the president said, to hoots of derision. I thought, Three days, huh?)

So: we'd let winter come and go in the south land, and then, in five or six months, in the southern spring, we'd return.

I thought about the drive back from the end of the road in the last car in the world. It wouldn't matter that there were no side mirrors or that I couldn't see out of the back window. It's the one thing you say about going to the end of the road: when you start making your way back to civilization, you don't need the rearview mirror. Ain't nothing gaining on you.

Or so I thought.

THE DEAD COAL CAR'S COUNSEL

June 1987 · London, England

ALAN RUSSELL passed a statue of the world's tallest man, which was across a hallway from a statue of the world's heaviest man, which was around the corner from a statue of the world's smallest person, who, judging by the life-sized replica, was about the size of your basic bust of Beethoven. Mr. Russell and I were strolling through the Guinness World of Records, an amusement arcade of sorts located in The Trocadero Centre in London's West End.

There were exhibits graphically depicting the jumping ability of fleas (stupendous), kangaroos (don't hold a candle to fleas), and men (pretty punk in comparison). There were videotapes of various incredible human sporting achievements (let's see a flea—any flea, any five fleas—backlift 2.8 tons off trestles, as Paul Anderson of the United States did on June 12, 1957).

I had wanted to meet Mr. Russell at the Guinness offices: I had envisioned an oak-paneled boardroom, a library of maps, perhaps a pint of Guinness stout. Unaccountably, the idea seemed to make Alan Russell uncomfortable. He preferred to meet at Guinness World.

Russell was a sturdy man of fifty, impeccably dressed in a blue pinstriped suit. He carried an elegantly battered leather briefcase and his manner was exceedingly precise. I had the agreeable sense that he was the sort of Englishman whose precision masked an underlying balmy eccentricity. Indeed, London entertainments and tourist attractions generally suggest that the English habit of polite understatement is a rigid necessity, a last-ditch defense against the danger of a great nation falling forever into the abyss of wretched excess.

Outside, on the winding cobblestone streets leading to a large pedestrian mall outside Guinness World, there were people lining up to buy cut-rate tickets to that night's performances of the hottest plays in town: *Chess* or *Les Misérables* or *Starlight Express.* The latter was an extravaganza performed entirely by actors on roller skates who represented train engines (and smoking cars and dining cars) from several different nations. The American engine was played by a guy in a leather jacket with greasy black hair and an attitude. He was supposed to be a diesel. There was a full orchestra sequestered under the stage, and the performers sang inspirational songs about striving for railroad excellence as they rocketed through whirling colored spotlights over twisting ramps that snaked through the audience.

Near the cut-rate-ticket vendor, men of all nationalities could be seen skulking into the LOVE shop, where someone had scrawled the words *you pathetic little wanker* under a sign on the door advising passersby that the establishment provided entertainment for adults. News shops sold London tabloids that all seemed to feature headlines about plucky grandmothers foiling "sex beasts." Inside small kiosks lining the mall, British citizens from Pakistan and Jamaica and Hong Kong made change for people from America or Germany or Switzerland: they took dollars or francs or marks and turned them into pounds. People from all over the world used these pounds to enter the Guinness World of Records.

Alan Russell said he had been editing the *Guinness Book of World Records* for just over a year. The job was "fascinating and challenging," though, of course, Russell admitted, "there is always the danger of becoming a record bore." For instance: "If there are potato chips at a party, you hear yourself reeling off the most stupendously dreary statistics regarding potato-chip consumption. You can become a monotonous pomposity."

Mr. Russell said that, in many cases, he personally certified various records. "If a sport or event is governed by an international body, such as in track-and-field events," he explained, "then that body lays down the rules and ascertains what is a record and what is not. In those cases where an event is not sanctioned by a recognized governing body—such as eating baked beans with a cocktail stick—then we lay down the rules. In this case, the record is held by Karen Stevenson, who, on the fourth of April 1981, ate two thousand seven hundred and eighty cold baked beans in thirty minutes. We do not accept hot baked beans because we have to have a standard. Hot beans can shrink or expand. The beans must be stuck on the cocktail stick and eaten one at a time."

Mr. Russell and I contemplated this achievement for a few moments. "That would be, what, about ninety baked beans a minute," I said, striving for an English sense of precision in excess.

Alan Russell allowed that Karen Stevenson must have had a very fast hand indeed. "It works out to one point five four baked beans a second. You see, we no longer accept duration gluttony records. We have established time limits for eating events."

Mr. Russell said that there were many records that he knew about that didn't make the book for one reason or another. "Sometimes we don't have the space. If I put every record I knew about in the book, I'd be writing twenty-four volumes every year. To be included in the book, a record must be interesting and preferably based on some sort of international competition. Another reason is pure subjective opinion, which is a writer's and an editor's choice. It's your right to omit, oh . . ."

"The loudest fart," I suggested.

"Precisely. I wouldn't approve it. Another one, a supreme example, is the world's youngest mother. I won't even give you the details on this one. Tragic, tragic. This is the sort of fact that is fascinating in a medical journal, of course, but a lot of children worldwide read the *Guinness Book of Records*. I do not want to encourage some child to break that record.

"And today I turned down a record from America. Someone wanted to see how many grapes he could put in his mouth without swallowing them. I refused that one. There are many reasons. First, it's medically dangerous. Grapes could get stuck in the throat. Secondly, who is going to measure the grapes? Should it be done on weight or on the size of the grapes? One has got to find a universal standard. Third, the person has got to spit them out afterward and someone has to actually count them. A pretty horrific job."

As we strolled through the exhibits, Mr. Russell said that "people should realize we very often have to change the rules and invent new rules in a category. We have to anticipate problems. Very often, records change because of changes in the world that are beyond control. We have, for instance, a record for driving across America, coast-to-coast. There is, of course, a nationwide speed limit of fifty-five miles an hour, so there is a limit to how fast the drive may be done. We will not accept anybody who gets a speeding ticket. I will not require people to break the law to get into the *Guinness Book of Records*. That is ethically very, very wrong indeed. But what has happened in America recently—I just got a telex from my American editor—is that federal law now says that

people may drive ten miles an hour faster in certain areas. So rules
change.

"Sometimes, in fact, we change the rules ourselves. Just in the past
year, for instance, there has been a very serious competition for a
record in rope jumping. Skipping rope with a team of ninety on the
same rope. How many turns can the team do? Now, I don't know
whether the concept started here in the UK or in Japan, but Japan is
a very big skipping country. They hold a lot of skipping records. And
battle was waged between Japan and Britain over this team of ninety.
I was speaking to some Japanese recently, trying to analyze this from
a physiological point of view, and I realized that some of the teams are
now so disciplined that they will be able to push this record further and
further, depending on the strength of the people turning the rope. Very
strenuous. And it occurred to me that soon they'd be changing the rope
turners. So I've specified that the rope must be turned by the same two
people for the duration of the record attempt."

"There is a Japanese edition of the book?"

"At present," Mr. Russell said, "we have editions in thirty lan-
guages. I write the book in London. A team of editors decide what we
will and will not accept as a record. Now, we put two types of records
in the British edition: world records and British records. Americans
may not be interested in some of the British records. Say, records set
in the sport of cricket. But they will be interested in baseball records.
The Japanese will also be interested in baseball records, but with an
emphasis on baseball as played in Japan.

"Foreign editors have the right to put those categories in their own
books because their own national records are of interest to them. They
also have the right to leave out a record they feel is not appropriate to
them. But if any country wants to claim a world record for something,
it must be authenticated in London. We are the only people who make
that final decision."

"So people all over the world read the book," I said.

And Alan Russell, who knew the dangers of becoming a record bore,
simply couldn't help himself. "It is," he said, "the largest-selling book
in the world. Actually it is the largest-selling 'copyrighted' book in the
world. We do bow down to the Bible, which is the largest-selling book
in the world. The Bible, however," Mr. Russell said, with his customary
regard for accuracy, "is not copyrighted."

The book itself—or at least the incipient idea for it—was born in
Ireland, on a place called the North Slob, near the river Slaney. On the
afternoon of November 10, 1951, the late Sir Hugh Beaver raised his

shotgun, fired at a passing golden plover, and missed. Beaver, a good shot, declared that the plover must be the fastest game bird in Europe. That evening, Sir Hugh ransacked his reference library and discovered that it was impossible to ascertain which game bird flew the fastest.

Nearly three years later, in August of 1954, the argument arose again, this time in relation to grouse. Sir Hugh was the managing director of Guinness, the makers of a black and ambrosial stout bearing that name. In this capacity, he was familiar with social interactions in the 81,400 pubs of Britain and Ireland. These were places where people sometimes disagreed about the velocity of bird flight and other subjects of note. There was, however, no book with which to settle arguments about records. Guinness, Sir Hugh decided, might publish such a book in the interest of public relations.

On September 12, 1954, Sir Hugh asked Norris and Ross McWhirter to produce the first *Guinness Book of World Records*. The brothers were former track-and-field athletes who had published a sports magazine. The first *Guinness Book* had a plastic cover to protect it from the sort of spills that happen frequently in pubs, especially toward closing time. The 198-page edition was a number-one best-seller in six months. By 1986, worldwide sales amounted to fifty-three million, which, the *Guinness Book* itself proclaims, is equivalent to 118 stacks of books, each as high as Mount Everest.

Ross McWhirter died in 1974, and Norris edited the book until 1986, when Alan Russell, who had been producing a TV series based on the book, took over. In the course of his work at Guinness, Alan Russell has had reason to celebrate the honesty of people worldwide. "Very few try to cheat their way into the book," he said.

"You mean it never happens?" I asked.

"Oh, occasionally," he said. "I suppose the biggest group of fakes are people claiming to own old cats. You have someone who tells you that she owns a cat that is fifty-seven years old. But she has no documentation to back up the claim. Well, I'm not an expert on cats, but I'm an expert on experts, and the ones I consulted in this matter told me they would not accept a fifty-seven-year-old cat, no matter what."

Those who cheat are so few and far between that Mr. Russell remembers them well. There was, for instance, an individual in Spain who claimed to be 120 years old, which would make him the world's oldest man. In an attempt to authenticate the record, Russell discovered that the man was using his father's birth certificate: an eighty-five-year-old geezer who, to his shame, thought he could put one over on the world.

Russell said that those who would like to legitimately break a record should check the rules very carefully. If they have an idea for a new record, or if the rules aren't clear, prospective record breakers can write for clarification.

"Well," I said, "that's what I wanted to talk to you about. Clarification."

"You know, then, I have told Garry that two people have now completed the Pan-American trip."

"Right. The prince. I think we can beat him."

"The documents on his trip seem to be in good order."

"What about the Canadian, Adamuszek?"

"I'm still not certain whether he obeyed the rules."

"The news report we read in Argentina had him coming in twenty-four days. Later we tried to figure it out."

Garry recalled that the note Adamuszek had sent to Guinness was dated the day he left: November 2. The tourist magazine said he arrived in Ushuaia on November 27, at 7:45 P.M. to be exact. That was twenty-five days, no matter how you cut it.

In Ushuaia, we talked to Veronica at Turismo, and she sent us to see the man Adamuszek had stayed with when he reached the end of the world.

Miguel Zaprucki, an Argentine of Polish descent, lived in a neat, newly painted wood-frame house in a neighborhood of neat, newly painted frame houses set on a rise above the main street of Ushuaia. A gentleman in his sixties, Zaprucki wore a comfortable-looking cardigan and stood on his front porch, chatting with us. He said Adamuszek was thirty-two, that he left from Prudhoe Bay, and that he had been stopped for two days at some border. Nicaragua or Colombia. Finally a soldier had accompanied him through the country. (Had to be Nicaragua, I thought, an afternoon's drive, as opposed to Colombia, which would take several days.) Zaprucki said he couldn't be more specific because Adamuszek didn't speak Spanish.

I asked how a man who didn't speak Spanish could possibly talk his way through borders in at least ten Spanish-speaking countries. Zaprucki said that Adamuszek was very determined, and that determination seemed to amuse him in some secret way.

How long had the trip taken?

Zaprucki said that Adamuszek was claiming twenty-six days.

"Twenty-six days exactly?" I asked.

"Más o menos," Zaprucki said. More or less? This phrase, in most of Latin America, is often a throat-clearing exercise, like saying, "you know." More or less? How much more? How much less? Zaprucki didn't know. "Twenty-six days, and then a little more," he said finally.

I think Garry and I amused Mr. Zaprucki as much as Jerzy Adamuszek had.

"So," I told Alan Russell in London, "we aren't certain whether Adamuszek is claiming twenty-four, twenty-five, or twenty-six days."

"It's twenty-six and a few hours," Alan Russell said.

"You're sure?"

"I'm sure. Though, as I said, I'm not certain he obeyed the rules. For instance, when Garry came to me and said he'd like to do this drive I researched backwards through our files to see how his concept compared with other long drives. I decided that this was something very comparable. You see, it's very nice for people to come to us in advance and say, 'What will you accept?' "

My $120-a-night hotel room was clean enough, and there was a view of the crenelated roofs of Covent Garden, but it was small. Eurosmall. I took one of my dirty shirts, measured out what I supposed was the length of a cat, tip of the nose to tip of the tail, and swung it about. I could find no position at all in which the shirt did not hit at least one wall. Yep, not enough room to swing a cat.

Everything was white, hard plastic Eurowhite, and there was a gadget in the corner that would press your pants for you, and a teapot. There were three television channels, and one of them consistently featured endless ceremonial events: guys in florid Elizabethan uniforms walking around stiffly, and commentators who elucidated the action in the hushed reverence usually reserved for golf.

For an American, the room was claustrophobic. Worse, the hotel catered to the theater crowd, a well-dressed group, so that occasionally a house detective, noticing a man in a leather jacket and jeans, saw fit to check my room key. Who would want to break into the place: it was like a prison.

So I sat at a café called the Pelican, eating venison with a tangy raspberry sauce—the Pelican saw itself as a French bistro—and perused the British version of the *Guinness Book,* which Alan Russell, not surprisingly, thought superior to the American edition.

My impression was that Russell was inclined to not accept Jerzy Adamuszek's claim. I, on the other hand, was fairly certain that Jerzy Adamuszek, a Polish Canadian from Montreal who didn't speak Spanish, had driven a black 1981 Cadillac from Prudhoe Bay, Alaska, to Ushuaia, Argentina, alone, in twenty-six days. More or less.

It seemed wise to set that as the time to beat. Jerzy probably wasn't going to get the record, but as Garry had pointed out in Argentina, if he did it—if he really did it—we were honor bound to consider his time the standing record.

No forty days, no thirty-five days: didn't matter if those times would give us the record. "It's a matter of morality," Garry had said.

And just in case, just to cover all possibilities, I thought, privately, that it would be nice to bring it all in under twenty-four days.

No questions that way.

Those would be our rules.

I studied the book for a time and worked on my bottle of wine.

"Many people," Mr. Russell had said, "think some of these records are trivial."

Hmmm?

The duration record for continuous clapping (sustaining an average of 160 claps per minute audible at 120 yards) is 54 hours by V. Jeyaraman of Tamil Nadu, India from the 13th to the 15th of December 1985.

"We cannot consider anything trivial," Mr. Russell had said. "The person actually doing it is likely to be someone who will never be the fastest runner, never be Mark Spitz or Billie Jean King. Nevertheless, they are deadly serious in their endeavors and for this reason, we must treat them seriously."

It occurred to me, over my second glass of Beaujolais, that what Alan Russell was saying is that while certain records may seem a little silly—duration drumming, cucumber slicing, prolonged sermonizing, continuous showering, billiard-table jumping—the person attempting the feat is motivated by the same soaring human desire for excellence that puts a man on the moon or creates a da Vinci. Over the third glass of wine, I began to imagine that the *Guinness Book of World Records* is about striving and desire, about courage, nobility, and the human soul.

The record distances in the country sport of throwing dried cow chips depends on whether or not the projectile may or may not be molded in a spherical shape. The greatest distance achieved under the "nonspheri-calization and 100 percent organic" rule (established 1970) is 266 feet by Steve Urner at the Mountain Festival at Tehachapi, California, on August 14, 1981.

Aside from cow chips, there was a lot more nobility in the book. Arthur Rank was sixty-nine in August of 1984 when he set the stone-skipping record ("fourteen plinkers and fifteen pitty-pats"); Chris Riggio completed a 28.5-mile marathon in four hours and thirty-four minutes while carrying a fresh egg on a dessert spoon for the official egg-and-spoon-racing record; a Mr. Shriv Ravi stood on one foot for thirty-four hours—the rules in this one require that the disengaged foot not be rested on the standing foot and that no object be used for support. Mr. Ravi is from Tamil Nadu, India, and would have been able to hire his neighbor, Mr. V. Jeyaraman, the human applause machine, to give him a hand for a couple of days.

I BOUGHT A TICKET for that night's performance of *Starlight Express*. In the final scenes, the railroad engines, who were actually actors on roller skates, massed for one last final race, and, as I recall, the old rusty steam engine (named, of course, Rusty) was inspired by a song sung by his old coal car, now sadly deceased but alive in soul and memory. The part of the dead coal car was sung by a black man, whose soaring and spiritual voice seemed, in a spectacular effect, to light up the backdrop night sky with brilliant and glittering stars.

> "Only you have the power within you
> Just believe in yourself,
> The sea will part before you
> Stop the rain
> And turn back the tide."

I had a vision of human striving and the dignity of trivial pursuit: a vision of Mr. Ravi swaying on one sore leg, of Mr. Jeyaraman clapping hysterically. A tingling sensation shot up my spine and ran along the tops of my forearms.

So: twenty-three days, más o menos.

A matter of morality, más o menos.

THE ADVENTURE-
DRIVING BUSINESS

[FEATURING AN AMBUSH IN AFRICA]

July 1987 • Moncton, New Brunswick, Canada

I WAS EN ROUTE from my home in Montana to Moncton, New Brunswick, Canada, to work out the final details of the drive with Garry Sowerby. I made some notes about pursuing a phantom Caddy propelled by the spiritual advice of a defunct musical coal car and tried not to think about the flight. Airline travel fractures my equanimity. Delays. Lost baggage. Overworked and consequently curt personnel.

I have lost my temper in airports. It's embarrassing. People staring at you as you scream and gibber, hands in the air. People moving away from you in the lounge as you fulminate. It is, I am sure, merely a personal quirk.

I wasn't going to lose it again. This falling onto the ground and pounding my fists on the cold tiles simply wouldn't do. Time to put myself in a defensive mode. I jotted down some notes for an imaginary book about an airline crash in the wilderness. Everyone survives, but a large grizzly bear, as if directed by the hand of God, singles out and savages airline employees only. Call it *Furry Fury.*

Flights out of Montana serve what are called "snacks." A stewardess tossed a bag of nuts on my tray, like peanuts at the ballpark. She was very busy, flinging nuts, this stewardess, but my companion, Karen, took the opportunity to ask a question.

"Could you arrange for one of those carts to meet us at the gate? We have a tight connection and I'm on crutches."

Karen had been experiencing pain standing for any length of time. She could outrun me for a mile or so before her feet began to hurt, hurt badly, and the doctors said it would only get worse. They told her that

28

they could fix her up in two simple operations. It was a painful matter of breaking and rearranging a single bone in each foot. Karen opted to get it all over with at once: the same operation on both feet and then six weeks on crutches. We imagined that the decision would be an exercise in the conservation of misery.

Our flight attendant said she would make the call later, after she had finished tossing out the rest of her nuts. It looked, I thought, like dinner in the monkey house. There were, by actual count, eight nuts in my bag. Was I supposed to eat them all myself?

The flight into Minneapolis was late, no great surprise. Seasoned travelers, in 1987, had begun referring to the airline as Northworst. Passengers suspected that the company routinely delayed flights—sometimes claiming mechanical difficulties—when in fact they were waiting for delayed connecting flights in order to fill all seats on any given flight. Disgruntled ex-Northwest employees insisted that this was the case.

Indeed, most of Northworst's current employees seemed disgruntled. Flight attendants worked planes full of passengers who had been kept waiting for hours and who were certain to miss connecting flights. There was a feeling of antagonism that pervaded most flights. The attendants themselves had some labor-related gripes with the company, and were not inclined to simple pleasantries. They had begun to develop a kind of homeroom high-school-teacher attitude toward their passengers.

This was par for the course: I wasn't going to steam myself into any kind of tantrum.

An announcement was made about the captain and how he had instructed us to put our tray tables up and to return our seats to the full and upright position. As the flight attendant passed my seat I attempted to ask again if she had arranged for the cart. The woman was overworked—Northworst could have provided a couple more attendants on this flight—and the exertion of firing nuts at the passengers had dampened her hair so that moist ringlets framed her face. She appeared to be in her early forties, and wore a fatigued expression that said something about what I imagined were twenty years of professional glamour and fun at thirty thousand feet. With frequent stopovers in Minneapolis.

"Excuse me," I said as she strode by my seat.

The woman treated me as she might treat a flasher on the street. No recognition: all these perverts want is attention. Don't encourage them.

"Miss?"

But she was gone.

I reached up and punched the attendant call button. Nothing. Once more.

Bing, bing.

And the attendant was standing there, towering over me, glowering. "Yes," in a tone that meant "now what?"

"Did you arrange for that cart?"

"Sir," the woman sighed, "I said I would call and I did." A dozen passengers within earshot now knew that I was the kind of guy, he's got a friend on crutches, he's gonna ask for help not once but twice. Twice! I felt my face flush with anger and consoled myself with *Furry Fury.*

So, of course, when we had collected Karen's crutches and deplaned, there was no cart. We stood there, at the boarding gate, while the scheduled time for our connecting flight came and went. Karen could not walk more than fifty yards on her new feet. We were stymied. The other passengers were gone and the area was devoid of people. Presently, our crew deplaned, the pilots carrying their square flight bags, the attendants pulling suitcases on leashes behind them. When the woman with damp hair passed, I did no more than catch her eye.

She stared at me coldly and in her best homeroom teacher's voice said, "Sir, I made the call. If the cart isn't here, it's not my fault."

And off she went to have sex with animals.

ALL RIGHT, I'm sorry. That was a little tantrum right there and it was uncalled for. Time has passed. I'm better now. I can say nice things about the airline industry if I really want to.

For instance: the flight out of Montreal to Moncton, New Brunswick, left smack-bang on time, and the Canadian attendants seemed to enjoy their work. It was a pleasant flight and no surprise at all. Over the past six months, in preparation for the long drive, I'd flown to nearly a dozen countries in South and Central America. Not one of my flights originating from a Latin destination—not one—had ever been delayed. No bags were lost. The flight attendants had been professional and pleasant. Even American carriers were on time out of South America. Small Central American carriers—companies that might be called Firecracker Airlines—had been on time. Professional.

And now a Canadian flight was proving as pleasant and professional as a flight out of El Salvador.

I just want to know how it is that the United States of America suffers *the worst airline service in all of the Americas.*

No, wait. A pleasant upbeat attitude is said to prolong life. I'm going to take a deep breath here, count to ten, and try to see it from the industry's point of view.

So:

Air travel, in the United States, is no longer the option of the privileged few—as it is in Third World countries—and what passengers experience is the result of a kind of economic egalitarianism. That's the way to look at it. The airports are crowded because more and more people can afford to fly; which results in more scheduled flights; which results in delays; which results in crowded airports; which results in seatmates who know, and can recount with enthusiasm and startling endurance, the plot of the latest *Star Trek* movie.

Better conversation, I'd say, than the kind of things you hear from ticket agents.

When I'd gone to London to talk with Alan Russell, my flight out of Kennedy in New York had been delayed. Natch. "It'll be about three hours," the ticket agent said. A line formed and several people changed flights. After a half-hour wait, I had my audience with the man behind the counter.

"Can you tell me," I asked, "how long we'll have to wait?" I thought I could cab over to see a nearby friend.

"You mean exactly?"

"Sure."

The man smiled one of those you-poor-fool smiles: the kind of merciless grin you might see on the face of a Marine drill instructor hectoring a naive recruit.

"Sir," the ticket agent said, "we could leave in two hours. We could leave in five. There is no such thing as 'exactly' in the airline business."

It's the kind of attitude you expect from bureaucrats in failing countries all over the earth, and the nicest thing I can say about the airline corpocracy in the United States is that it is not precisely evil. Odd that mismanagement and inefficiency should breed such arrogance.

NEW BRUNSWICK, bounded by the Bay of Fundy and the Gulf of St. Lawrence, lies on Canada's eastern seaboard, just north and a bit east of Maine. It is one of Canada's Maritime Provinces along with Nova Scotia and Prince Edward Island.

Prior to the treaty of Utrecht in 1713, which ceded the region to Great Britain, the area was known as Acadia and was French. During the American revolutionary war, British Loyalists settled the Maritimes. The Acadians, a French-speaking minority, however, have preserved their identity and have increased in population. The sense of struggle that Acadians live with has toughened them, and Acadian men, especially the younger ones, are regarded as tough monkeys: "Hey, Bobby Choquette, he can scrap, eh?"

Many of the Acadians live on the Atlantic coast and are fishermen. You meet men of forty who recall the shame of going to school every day with a bag lunch that was the mark of their poverty. The rich kids had peanut butter and jelly. Sons and daughters of Acadian fishermen had to make do with lobster sandwiches.

New Brunswick was once famous for the quality of its ships and the men who sailed them. Today, it is the eighth most populous of Canada's ten provinces, and per-capita income lags behind Canada as a whole. The best and the brightest of New Brunswick's young people often see little opportunity, and there has been an exodus to the more dynamic provinces to the west. On the other hand, forest covers over 80 percent of the province, and the moose population is increasing.

Maritimers who stay in the provinces are often great travelers, adventurers of a sort, the kind of people who venture out to see the big world, absorb all they can, and return to commune with the moose in what they consider to be the finest place on earth in which to live.

Maritimers, and Canadians in general, generally suffer a beneficent affliction that the Canadian writer Marian Botsford Fraser has forthrightly and fearlessly labeled "niceness." An American who spends too much time engaged in a corrosive harangue about a bad airline flight falls into line soon enough. Persist in your ill temper and people begin looking at you as if you're wearing a leather mask and carrying a chain saw.

Garry Sowerby picked the two of us up at the airport in his family car, and older-model Oldsmobile 98 with ninety thousand miles on it. On the way into Moncton from the airport I believe I said that the land was inspiring and the people seemed, well, nice.

"It's a national trait," Garry said sorrowfully. "We can't help it. It's like, well, you know why Canadians say 'eh?' at the end of the sentence?"

"I thought it was a lingering French habit, like saying, *'n'est-ce pas?'* "

"No. It's this niceness. This Canadian niceness. You say, 'piss off!'

and then add 'eh?' What does that mean? It means piss off but, uh, you don't have to if you don't want to. I mean, look at your national symbol. You've got a bald eagle. Fierce eyes, a snake in its talons. What do we have?" Garry bit down on his lower lip, thrust his face into mine, and widened his eyes so that he looked moronically eager. "Beaver, eh?"

Sowerby, who had the slightest of Canadian accents—"aboot" for about—was a connoisseur of great "ehs?" but he himself never eh-ed except in jest. "Remember when we came back from Panama?" he asked. "We flew out just before the riots. And then you got back to the States, what were the big headlines there?"

"Iran-contra," I said.

"The big scandal here, front page across the country, somebody found out the prime minister owned forty pairs of shoes."

"Yeah?"

"That was it. That was the scandal." Apparently, Canadians felt that the prime minister was about thirty-five pairs of shoes to the dark side of nicety. Garry, like any man who deeply loves his country, purely enjoyed complaining about it.

"You know who our prime minister is?" he asked.

"Uh, used to be Trudeau. Now it's, who, Mulroney?"

Niceness doesn't make headlines. Americans don't know anything about Canada. We read about Noriega, or Qaddafi, or Khomeini. We respect Canadians, we like them, but the great mass of ordinary Americans somehow missed the big northern footwear exposé. Virtually any Canadian could tell you the name of the American secretary of state. I didn't even know what you called his Canadian counterpart.

The two-lane road ran through the forest and into Moncton where Garry Sowerby was born and raised. It is a town of sixty thousand, an old railroad center where the streets run parallel to the tracks and the homes are generally well maintained and newly painted. The nearby Bay of Fundy, an inlet of the Atlantic Ocean between New Brunswick and Nova Scotia, surges with the highest tides in the world—up to seventy feet—and at their highest, these tides produce a kind of tidal wave that runs up the Petitcodiac River, so that, in Moncton, the river runs backward twice a day. I think this is called the tidal bore.

"We've got the biggest tidal bore in the world," the nice people of Moncton will tell you. Or they say that the finest eating lobster in the world is processed at a nearby plant at Cape Bimet. Research on my part reveals that this brag is, in fact, an indisputable fact. Or they tell you about a rise outside of Moncton where a car in neutral appears to roll uphill. "I'll take you out to Magnetic Hill," Garry said, full of false portent, "and you will be sore afraid." Research on my part reveals the mystic powers of Magnetic Hill are an optical illusion.

The railroad has recently pulled out of Moncton in a big way, so the housing market is depressed, and Garry's $35,000 (American) home is a large two-story affair, neatly painted, like all the other houses on the street. There are a backyard, alive with flowers, a garage, and two vehicles parked in the driveway. One was our truck. The other was a GMC Suburban, riddled with bullet holes.

I KNEW that bullet-ridden truck. I had driven it a couple of thousand miles through Canada and Alaska with Garry. That was in 1985 when he was competing in a five-thousand-mile road race—a rally actually—through Alaska and Canada. The event was called the ALCAN 5000 and I had been assigned to cover it and Garry for a magazine.

There were three of us in the big truck—Garry, myself, and Glen Turner, from Moncton, Garry's codriver. Sowerby explained that he made his living as an "adventure driver," and I thought, as we barreled down the Alaska Highway, that if I could learn all there was to know about the bullet holes in the Suburban, I would begin to understand this rather unique occupation. I had never heard of a professional adventure driver before.

So, start at the beginning:

In 1977, Garry Sowerby and his friend Ken Langley began working on a project they conceived in college, nearly a decade earlier. The boys were Maritimers, they liked road trips, and the idea, as originally hatched, was posed as a question: Wouldn't it be great to drive around the world? What began as a lark took almost three years to organize and cost $300,000 in money raised from various sponsors.

Sowerby and Langley formed a corporation, Odyssey International, Limited ("We're in OIL") and borrowed $25,000 from friends and relatives to launch the project. They studied bus schedules from various countries to estimate the driving time from point to point. They produced a slick professional proposal, and spent years pitching the project, called Odyssey 77, to various companies.

Garry is always a little amused when people, noticing his success—he is something of a Canadian national hero—suppose they can simply approach a sponsor with an intriguing proposal.

"Nothing's easy," Garry likes to say. "Nothing's free."

Of the three years the round-the-world project took, the vast majority of the time was spent raising money.

"You have to understand," Sowerby told me, "we weren't kids. We were twenty-nine when we started this. Ken was a lawyer. A great organizer and planner. I had a lot of experience with vehicles."

Garry, in fact, had a degree in physics, had flown jets in the Canadian air force, and had sailed as an officer on destroyers. In the service at Camp Borden, Ontario, Sowerby had taken an extensive automobile engineering course and was posted to a five-hundred-acre vehicle-testing ground. He designed tests devised to take vehicles to their failure limits. He drove armored personnel carriers over swampy tundra and frozen muskeg, and rolled more than his share of Jeeps. On purpose.

This background was invaluable in the struggle to fund the project. "Kenny and I," said Sowerby, "had some credibility."

The trip would take them through four continents and twenty-three countries in both the Northern and Southern hemispheres. At every coast, they had to have planes waiting to airfreight the vehicle to the next country or continent. Guinness, at that time, required that the circumnavigation entail "an equator's length of driving (24,901.47 road miles)." Sowerby drove; Langley navigated. (The previous record for the fastest trip around the world by land had been 102 days.) The Canadians completed the drive (26,738 actual miles) in seventy-four days one hour and eleven minutes.

THE ADVENTURE had left them deeply in debt. The thought of paying off $80,000 on their income—the pair were each driving taxis in Toronto until they settled on a plan—was intensely disturbing. The only way to avoid personal and corporate bankruptcy was to launch another project, financed by more generous corporate donations. It was this financial problem that forced the two into the adventure-driving business. Unfortunately, projects kept falling through. In 1983, desperate, the partners traveled to England and met with Norris McWhirter, the editor of the *Guinness Book of World Records.*

"We were looking for a new record," Sowerby said, "but we couldn't think of anything, so here we were, two adventurers without an adventure. We met with Norris McWhirter in this typically British boardroom with big oak tables, lots of books and maps on the wall. Norris was wearing a blue pinstriped suit and drinking a mug of stout."

It took only an hour and a half and three mugs of stout apiece to come up with the project: a two-driver automobile traverse of Africa, Asia, and Europe, the world's largest landmass. Sowerby and Langley would drive from the southern tip of Africa to North Cape, Norway, over four hundred miles above the Arctic Circle. "The rules were that we both could drive," Sowerby said. "Norris told us, 'The clock starts when you leave and stops when you get there. Everything in between is your problem.' "

So: a new project. Now the partners had to secure a proper vehicle, convince some giant automotive corporation that the adventure would be both successful and a good promotion, then recruit enough other sponsors to foot part of the bill, pay back their debts, and give them some margin of profit. GMC was a major sponsor, and John Rock was especially enthusiastic about seeing one of his tanklike Suburbans set a world record. Other subsidiary sponsors included companies that manufactured mobile telephones, one that made tires, and one that issued traveler's checks. Because of the success of the around-the-world trip, and the partners' growing sophistication in pitching their ideas, all major sponsors fell into line in about a year's time.

"The effort that went into planning the trip was enormous," Sowerby told me. "We spent fifty thousand dollars on telephone and telex bills alone. I mean, it took a year or so to set up. We started in January with the idea and signed the last contract in November. Then Kenny and I went on a reconnaissance to meet with people on the way: meet the auto-club people, the sponsors; meet with people from the Canadian government and the host governments; meet with the press people in various countries. There were two separate six-week recces. We wanted to make friends all along the route. Because time is the enemy, you have to make sure you're expected when you arrive. You don't want to have to spend two days at some remote border outpost.

"The diciest bit of politics had to do with the fact that we were starting in South Africa. No African country is going to let you in if you've been to South Africa. We figured the straightest approach was to tell the governments in the countries above South Africa exactly what we were doing. We made a deal: no press conferences at the start of the trip. No mention at all of South Africa. The first press conference would be in Nairobi, Kenya." Press conferences in the midst of a record attempt were a financial necessity: the sponsors wanted maximum exposure for their products.

Sowerby had planned to drive through the Sudan, north and east of Kenya. The timing was critical. "The road in the Sudan," Sowerby said, "floods out, and they close it about mid-March. That meant we had to start from South Africa on the first of March. But if we went any earlier, the road to North Cape, in Norway, would still be snowed in when we got there."

A week before the trip was to start, Sowerby and Langley learned that the Sudan road was closed because of an outbreak of civil violence in the southern part of the country. With a year's work and several hundred thousand dollars hanging in the balance, Sowerby and Langley began working feverishly on an alternate plan.

It turned out that there was a road that led due north, from Nairobi into Ethiopia. "Nobody had used that border in ten years," Sowerby said. "Well, we contacted the Canadian ambassador in Kenya who went to the president's office and asked if we could use that road. He was told that the Kenyans had had problems there for the last twenty-five years. Problems with ambushes and bandits. The Kenyan officials said we could use the road only if they could provide a military escort."

Meanwhile, the Canadian ambassador to Ethiopia was securing clearance in that country. "This was before the famine broke," Sowerby said. "Our ambassador convinced the Ethiopian administrator of tourism that what we were doing was a goodwill trip and that it would be good for tourism." In order to stress the point that Ethiopia was a terrific travel destination, Sowerby agreed to hold a press conference in the capital, Addis Ababa.

With permissions secured and a new route mapped out, Sowerby and Langley left Nairobi in the Suburban. "We picked up the military escort about three hundred miles south of the Ethiopian border," Sowerby said. "Four guys with machine guns. They told us there hadn't been an attack in six months. We get out on this road, this rough washboard road, and there is no traffic at all. It's all desert out there: all this burning rock and scrub. That's where we got shot up.

"Kenny was driving, and there were two soldiers sitting beside him, another one in the jump seat, and one in the bunk in the back. I was dozing in the alleyway between the two front seats. Kenny was playing a tape: Eddy Grant singing "Killer on the Rampage," honest to God. We came around this tight turn, and one of the soldiers flipped his gun from lock to automatic. It must have been a famous ambush corner.

"All of a sudden I hear *pop-pop-pop*. Then all hell broke loose. Two of the soldiers had their machine guns out the window and they were just spraying the area. I could see them hiding behind the door pillar, not aiming, just firing for effect. And all of them were yelling at Kenny: 'Faster, faster, faster!'

"There were six bandits out there firing single-shot bolt-action rifles. They had been hiding behind some scrub on the right-hand side of the road. Kenya is a former British colony, and they have right-hand drive there. The bandits must have thought they would be firing at the driver, but our truck was equipped for left-hand drive. That single fact may have saved our lives. Instead of firing at someone who was trying to drive and dodge bullets at the same time—which would have been pretty much a piece of cake for them—they were encountering automatic-weapons fire.

"I'm lying there, and these thoughts are going through my head. I have a new daughter. I brought her home from the hospital in the Suburban. We named the vehicle after her. Lucy. We thought it was such a tank that we added a last name: Lucy Panzer. But it wasn't a tank, and I could hear the bullets tearing through it. And in a way, I felt like they were firing at Lucy. At my daughter. Because if I was gone, what would her life be like? And my wife, Jane? You think it will never happen to you, and then it does. There's a moment of complete disbelief.

"Anyway, they shot out one of the back tires, and they hit the front fender and the roofline in a couple of places. Kenny had it floored and we were doing seventy with a flat tire, over this bad, rutted road."

Garry lay on the floor, between the seats. They had warned him about this road. Told him this could happen. Now he was going to die because he couldn't listen.

It occurred to him that it was going to be a particularly nasty death. He was fairly well protected from the bullets and would survive the initial stages of the attack. What would happen, he figured, was that everyone else would be shot dead. The vehicle would go careening off into the desert and bog down in sand. The bandits would find him there, the only living witness. Garry figured they'd cut his throat. What did Shiftas do to people? Why didn't he know that? His mind was filled with visions of Lucy and Jane.

Jane—Garry had heard it often enough—was beautiful. Tall and slender, with long flowing hair and a model's fine high-cheekboned face. Smart. Organized. And she had guts: Garry figured that anyone who married him—a guy who made his living as an adventure driver—would have to have guts. She had talents that sometimes seemed at odds with her beauty. She was, for instance, a licensed commercial helicopter pilot. And now she was going to have a corpse for a husband. Just some bones bleaching in the desert.

That didn't seem entirely right. Garry's mind began to function practically. He realized that if the truck broke an axle they'd be out in the desert for days, at the mercy of Shiftas.

"We gotta change the tire," he shouted.

The soldiers said, "No. Faster!"

And Garry made it a command.

"We gotta do it *now!*"

Langley stopped and the Kenyan soldiers covered the Canadians as they worked. "Naturally," Sowerby said, "we couldn't find the jack. It hadn't occurred to us that we'd have to change a tire under attack. The bandits were on foot, probably three miles back, but I was thinking, 'If I were these guys, I would have another five men down the road to pick up disabled cars or wounded drivers.' "

The jack sunk into the sand under the weight of the Suburban. Sowerby and Langley didn't have a shovel, and they fell to their knees, digging in the sand under the wheel, digging like dogs until their hands bled and their air burned in their throats. Two of the soldiers spelled them. Sowerby and Langley took the guns and covered the tire change in progress. Sowerby's military training kicked in then, a kind of bitter instinct that rolled over his fear and regret, even the visions of his family. He stood braced, the weapon on rock 'n' roll, full auto, and he thought, "C'mon you sons of bitches."

Nothing. No one. Just the scrub and sun. The Shiftas had had enough of Lucy Panzer. The tire was finally changed, but because the bandits had hit the tires stacked on the roof, the Suburban jolted over six hundred miles of the worst roads in the world with no spares. "It was," Sowerby said, "like waiting for a bad telephone call. One blowout and a year's work and all that money would be wasted. Luckily, the tires held out."

"Anyway," Garry Sowerby told me, "we got to Addis Ababa, and they told us we couldn't drive the road to Djibouti because two weeks before thirteen trucks had been blown up there. The Ethiopian government wasn't going to let us take that road: it would have been bad press for them if we were blown up. What they did instead, they provided a special train for us. Put the truck on a flat car. We had twenty-six soldiers with us. It was only one hundred fifty miles, but that train had been blown up three times in the three previous months."

"Who was blowing them up?" I asked.

"Ahh," Sowerby searched his memory, "the, uh, Somalia Liberation Army. It was the war of the week out there on that trip. Anyway, we made it: Kenny and I were just sitting on the hood of the truck as we pulled into Djibouti, past these French Foreign Legion barracks, and all those guys were amazed that we had made it. We had been front-page news in Africa, and now we had the French Foreign Legion saluting us. It was one of the proudest moments of my life."

Getting the truck across the Red Sea was a problem, but Sowerby—through the Catholic bishop, one of the contacts he'd met on the first reconnaissance trip—found a known smuggler who agreed to ferry the boat for $5,000. "The guy's boat was a forty-foot wooden dhow, and we had to put the truck on sideways, with the bumpers hanging off either side just below the sail. We had no insurance, of course, because pirates don't register their boats, but this guy was the only game in town."

Sowerby and Langley arrived in Saudi Arabia and drove north, into Iraq. "The last thing the first secretary told us when we left Kuwait city was, 'Keep your eyes open to the east because the Iranians do strafing runs on that road.' "

In Turkey, border guards demanded a $50 bribe to clear the Suburban. "They wouldn't take the money at the police compound there," Sowerby said. "The guy had us drive him about two miles to this hovel. I walk in and it's all dim candlelight and these thieves are all sitting around, cleaning their weapons. The guy says, 'Things have changed. It now costs you one hundred dollars.' I told the guy it wasn't fair, and he told me life wasn't fair. I said, 'Do you take traveler's checks?'

"I always thought this scene would make a great commercial. Thomas Cook Traveler's Checks was one of our sponsors. The guy asked, 'What kind of traveler's check?' I said, 'Thomas Cook.' And all these guys with scars on their faces and eye patches look up and say, 'Thomas Cook, yes, those are good.'

"I took out five twenties, and I did something that was pretty stupid, but it made me feel good. I signed the first one and the guy looked at the signature, but I knew he couldn't see, it was so dark in there, so I signed a false name on the rest."

Sowerby, in fact, was getting a little sick and tired of being ordered around by guys with guns. "About three that morning," he said, "I'm driving up on the crest of a hill and I see two guys with machine guns standing in the middle of the road. Now, if these guys are bandits and you stop, they're going to shoot you. If they're soldiers and you don't stop, they're going to shoot you. I decided to stop. Turned out they wanted a ride. Ordinarily, a guy with a machine gun asks you to do him a favor, you say, 'yes sir.' But at this point, I said, 'Naw, no riders.' Just slammed the door and left them standing there in the middle of nowhere with their machine guns."

The rest of the trip went smoothly, and the Canadians reached North Cape—they actually followed the first snowplow through—twenty-eight days after starting in South Africa. The record still stands, as does Sowerby's around-the-world record.

*   *   *

GARRY AND I examined Lucy Panzer for a moment. I put my little finger into one of the bullet holes, and then started to tell him about my latest travel adventure but thought better of it. They don't actually shoot at you on Northworst.

THE BUSINESS OF ADVENTURE DRIVING

[OUR DIRTY LITTLE SECRET]

July 1987 · Moncton, New Brunswick, Canada

SO I GOT MY FINGER out of the bullet hole in the Suburban and followed Garry into his house. He was going to come clean, to show me the documents that outlined, in what I hoped was obscene detail, the fine points of our dirty little secret.

The floors were hardwood, newly sanded and waxed. There was a fireplace set into a new stone wall, and all of the rooms had been painted very recently. A door from the kitchen led to the darkened basement, a good place for dirty secrets. We walked through a long, dark, concrete-floored hallway flanked by a furnace and water heater. Heating ducts snaked about overhead and there was a dim light at the end of the tunnel. Two lights, actually.

The room to the right was "the bunker," a research room containing an IBM Selectric typewriter, a dictating and transcribing system, and a copying machine. The walls were lined with files—House Insurance, Sponsors in General, Correspondence (In and Out), and others with the names of several African countries: Uganda, Sudan, Botswana, Kenya. On one wall was a framed commendation from the mayor of Moraine, Ohio, presented to Garry and Ken, in honor of their Africa-to-the-Arctic run. The engine they used, a Detroit Diesel 6.2-liter job, had been built in Moraine, Ohio. Next to the commendation was a picture of the Suburban, caked with mud and scarred with bullet holes. It was the vehicular equivalent of the unshaven jungle tough guy.

Next to the bunker was another room Garry called "the pit." It was decorated with a giant picture of the Volvo bursting through a big paper banner reading: "Start Odyssey 77," and prominently featuring the word "SHELL!" There was one desk, littered with papers, all held down by a globe and a telephone which was flanked by a number of paper-filled wire baskets. Two chairs, one defective. A single overhead light.

The bunker and the pit: these were the offices of Odyssey International, Limited.

Stuck to the globe, somewhere in the mid-Pacific, was a yellow Post-it note reading: "sunglasses, coffee holders, windshield clipboards, secret document place, moose whistles." Driving necessities. A moose whistle is a small upright plastic flutelike gadget mounted on the upper front fender of a motorized vehicle. A car traveling at speed generates enough wind through the flute to generate a high-pitched scream, inaudible to human ears. The sound is supposed to clear the road ahead of any lingering moose. In New Brunswick, the animals can weigh up to one ton. Enraged moose have been known to charge and overturn beer trucks.

The uppermost sheet on a pile of papers a foot deep read: "Review tools, test jack, spare parts. Thermos, safety triangles, water . . ."

"Have you got that stuff I wanted to see?" I asked.

Garry lifted the globe and there it was, a great stack of papers, several hundred pages thick. I liked Sowerby's touch: our dirty little secret lay under the weight of the world.

ADVENTURE COSTS MONEY. Whether it's a surly stewardess or an African ambush, the point is to put your equanimity or your life on the line using *other people's money*. It is an insight that occurs very soon after one discovers that he or she has drifted helplessly into a life of travel and/or adventure. My friend Rick Ridgeway, the first American to climb the world's second-highest mountain without oxygen, said that the essential OPM insight occurred to him with particular force during the successful American ascent of Everest in 1976. "I was up at the magic twenty-four-thousand-foot level, feeling very good, strong," he said. "There was someone filming what I was doing, and suddenly I realized that this guy was having every bit of the adventure that I was. The only difference in our situations was that someone was paying him for it." Ridgeway has since written several well-regarded books, a screenplay about mountaineering, and has designed his own line of backpacking gear.

There are dozens of opportunities and scams in the adventure business. Just lately, large corporations have begun paying adventurers big money to motivate employees by describing various against-all-odds escapades. These talks are thought to be a source of cost-effective inspiration.

Colleges pay for lectures. Money from foreign governments is often available to would-be travelers, and likely targets of opportunity include various ministries of tourism or national parks administrations worldwide. Companies that manufacture beer or cigarettes sometimes sponsor expeditions. There is a growing market for professionally produced videos shot in exotic locations.

Alternately, a writer, photographer, or video artist approaches an airline, generally a foreign carrier—for instance, Garuda, out of Indonesia—and offers to document the beauties of, say, Java. Garuda assumes that the project—a photo essay, film, or article—will appear in the United States and inspire tourists to fly to Java on Garuda.

There is a obvious problem here. The essence of travel is discovery, and if you are going to Java for the first time, you have no idea whether it's your kind of place. Java could be a hellhole—I've been there, it isn't—and, having been financed by Garuda, you are obligated to expound on the island's beauty.

Consequently, I finance my own travels so that I don't feel obligated to write glowing accounts of destinations that I may find dismal or dull or desperate. This policy makes me feel upright, even sanctimonious, so I should hasten to add that picking the source of your OPM is also good business for someone who wants to stay in the low-rent travel biz. Write too many puff pieces out of the Sheraton and editors begin to doubt your commitment to the truth.

My travel money comes from magazine assignments or advances on books. Any extended stay usually requires that I piggyback assignments. An airline magazine doesn't usually pay well, but tickets are considered part of an article fee. Since I spend a lot of time at my destination walking around with a pack on my back and eating gummy freeze-dried dinners, airline fees are often my largest single expense. With a ticket to some exotic location in hand, I can approach any number of magazines and propose a story. (Magazines, sad to say, are not nearly so free with expense money as most people think.) Pitching my stories—gorillas in Africa, lost cities in Peru, river running in India, drunken diving for poison sea snakes in the Philippines—is important, of course, but editors can sell almost any project to their financial officers if it looks like a bargain. An author also needs a fairly respectable track record in such endeavors. Virtually no one will issue expenses to an unpublished writer.

"All I need," I tell an editor, "is in-country expenses." Sometimes,

I'll pile another article on top of that, consulting with editors at three magazines to be sure that the stories I want to do don't conflict. A three-story piggyback, in my experience, is good for a couple of months' worth of hard traveling.

I do not take junkets provided for travel writers. A junket is a tour group and that is all. People on junkets never get to go anywhere interesting. They stay in four-star hotels and end up in the bar talking to the other travel writers about previous junkets.

Given my profession, such as it is, I am constantly reading between the lines of the most recent adventure or travel book: how did the author finance this saga? Do we have an airline ticket scam here, a generous book advance, an articles piggyback, a cigarette company advertising expedition? Some journeys are clearly self-financed and they often result in the best books. A tight budget is the mother of adventure. It generates tense situations, confrontations with unsavory characters, hysterical desperation, and uncomfortable sleeping arrangements.

Self-financed travel books are generally written by previously unpublished writers driven by an immense love of the subject matter and a deep desire to prove that every editor who turned down the initial proposal is an idiot. Sometimes, reading a particularly good travel-writing debut, I can hear the sound of disembodied and distant applause as editors all over New York slap their foreheads in chagrin. But editors are not complete idiots, and if the book is good enough, or if it simply made money, the author can expect an advance on the next project.

I know of no author of a successful self-financed adventure-travel book who put his or her money on the line for the second effort. You don't get rich writing these books—most of us don't—because they are generated out of some timeless human desire that has little to do with remuneration. But, hey, why not get someone else to pay us to do what we'd be doing anyway? In the past half-dozen years, my travel expenses have exceeded my income, sometimes by a factor of two or three. That's the business of the adventure-travel business. It's not a bad life.

Happily, travel and adventure has recently become a hot publishing item. The best writers travel to provocative destinations to explore the interior as well as the exterior landscape. Writers freely discuss their fear or fret over subtle racist attitudes that they didn't know they possessed. Some of them admit to cowardice, or extraordinary moral lapses. You read of writers, alone in the forest, masturbating in homesick loneliness.

But no one ever writes about the money. It is, as D. H. Lawrence said about sex, our dirty little secret.

And yet the quest for financing is often a story in itself. Like travel itself, there are setbacks, victories, and plenty of moral lapses to be considered.

When Garry Sowerby and I began planning our Pan-American run, I asked him to take notes on the fund-raising process, to read his thoughts into a tape recorder. The transcripts of those tapes were the documents under the globe.

Here's our dirty little secret, just under $350,000 worth of it:

In May of 1985, John Rock, the manager of the truck-bus group at General Motors—the man who had been principally behind sponsoring the Africa-Arctic Challenge—asked Garry if he would be interested in setting a new record on the Pan-American Highway as a way of promoting the all-new designed-from-the-wheels-up Sierra (It's not just a truck anymore).

Interesting, I thought. Finding sponsors for the first project, the around-the-world run, had taken three years. Sponsors for the bullet-ridden Africa-to-Arctic run had fallen into line in less than a year. By 1985, sponsors were coming to Sowerby.

The new truck was scheduled to be introduced in 1988, which meant, in Detroit terms, late 1987. Documents in Garry's files seemed to suggest that John Rock was completely behind Garry, but that other executives, somewhat down the chain of command, saw the professional adventure driver as a particularly adroit con man. However, there seemed to be no doubt that GMC would love to prove that their pickup could handle anything the real world could throw at it. They wanted an advertising hook, press coverage, something to exhibit in auto shows ("It conquered the Americas," or some such), and even a book. But, some suspicious execs wondered, why not do the project in-house?

Sowerby asked GMC to consider what their internal costs would be. It was always cheaper to contract someone than to do it in-house: a corporate fact of life. Furthermore, he had a proven record of success in similar projects. Who else did they know who held two world records? There were other advantages: ventures billed as Odyssey events rather than GMC undertakings would come across more as a legitimate adventure than a corporate advertising scheme. Garry asked his critics in Detroit to consider the ramifications of failure, especially—a worst-case scenario—equipment failure. How could your easy-guy buyer see himself as an upscale cowpunk in a truck that had crapped out in Peru? In public.

There were other advantages: in face-to-face meetings, executives could see that Sowerby was articulate, a storyteller. Tall and fit, with a pleasantly self-effacing sense of humor and the requisite adventurer's beard, he was also a man who saw clearly the main chance, and could name reporters all over the world whom he counted as friends. People reported on Garry Sowerby because he was Garry Sowerby, completely aside from his association with GMC. Every person who had ever interviewed him was on a list, and Garry sent off a newsletter on his activities so that reporters knew when he was likely to be in their area for a personal interview. They only had to review the last few letters and make a phone call to churn out a quick feature in a pinch. Garry was a great interview, full of good stories: ambushes and pirates.

"And what I'm selling is good news," Garry told prospective sponsors. He generally wore what he called his automatic-man suit, an expensive pinstriped affair, and he could sell the logistics of the event like a general briefing his troops. Sowerby had hated the military when he was in it, but the experience had taught him to set goals and achieve them. His wife thought he was a workaholic.

Even so, he could appear completely relaxed: sit with his feet up, shoot the crap, join the boys for a drink and regale them with stories. "Ultimately," Garry would tell the executives, "the trip is about international cooperation. About products that work. About a dream and how that dream became a reality."

Sowerby thought of himself as a dream merchant: the shabby basement office of Odyssey International was "the dream factory."

Better yet, Sowerby wasn't asking GMC to foot the entire bill. Garry himself would bring on additional sponsors. In all of his projects, the major sponsor—in this case GMC—provides the vehicle and service requirements and enough money for Garry to pay himself a modest wage and run Odyssey's operations. Sowerby argued that budgeting the project involved many variables, including logistical arrangements such as flying or shipping the truck to South America, communications costs, and research trips to the various countries. It was impossible to honestly estimate how much the drive would cost. GMC, however, would not be liable for any of Sowerby's financial shortcomings.

The actual expedition costs would be raised through associate sponsors. Garry did not approach potential associate sponsors—tire companies, oil companies—until he had secured a contract with the major backer. According to Garry's records, it looked as if he made or lost money on the associate sponsors.

So Garry would put it all together as he always had. There was one major problem: Ken Langley wasn't interested. The young lawyer had had the adventure of a lifetime on the around-the-world trip. He'd had the adventure of a lifetime in Africa. It seemed to him that all he'd had was adventure, and no lifetime. It was time to settle into his law practice. "It was very emotional," Garry said. "I knew exactly how he felt. Still, it was like we'd been married, and this was a separation. It was hard. But I understood what he wanted to do and why he wanted to do it."

Five months after talking with Rock about the Pan-American run, I met Garry in Alaska on the ALCAN 5000, and we hit it off immediately. We both worked out of home offices, lived out of the mainstream in country-and-western sorts of towns, and traveled for a living. I spent a lot of time patching deals together, financing those travels, and I sure wasn't rich. In fact, Garry and I both spent the same amount, about $50,000, for our respective houses, well less than half of what the average new house costs in the United States. We had both gotten good deals because, in both places, at about the same time, the local railroad had abandoned the town. Garry listened to country-and-western music and classic rock as I did. He didn't complain about the Bach and Vivaldi tapes I popped into the cassette on waking. We were both a little over six feet tall, we both had beards, and more to the point, we both liked to tell stories. Garry's tales of corrupt Turkish border guards gave way to my descriptions of what it's like to be interrogated by the Peruvian Investigative Police.

Better yet, I spoke some Spanish. Garry had only a smattering. And I could write a book about our Pan-American run, sell it to a publisher, and Garry could use that contract to attract the associate sponsors he needed to realize a profit on the venture.

We shook hands on our collaboration at the end of the ALCAN 5000. That was the only contract we ever had.

BY DECEMBER OF 1986, Garry had put together a proposal out of his basement office: a press kit that emphasized his experience, the backing of GMC, and the public-relations benefits that would accrue to potential sponsors. According to Garry's notes, Firestone, Uniroyal, and Goodrich had declined sponsorship. He made a note to hold off sending out another fifty proposals until the first of the year. The proposals were glossy, professional, and they cost twelve dollars apiece. Six hundred dollars.

Which meant, in essence, that Lucy would get a lump of coal in her stocking for Christmas, and Jane, pregnant with their second child, would get a tender hug. On the other hand, why send out the proposal so that it arrived three or four days before Christmas when it was likely to get buried? Why not get it to the various offices first thing into the new year, when the executives were fresh, more likely to look favorably on a new venture.

And that decision generated a trip to the bank, which was not in Moncton but two hundred miles away in Halifax, Nova Scotia. It was the bank Garry dealt with on his other projects. Garry had met Jane there in the late seventies. For Maritimers, Halifax had been something of what San Francisco was to American young people a decade earlier.

The long drive to Halifax was a good time for reflection. Garry spoke into a tape recorder he'd brought along for the purpose. "There's Amherst, Nova Scotia, where I used to go as a kid. My dad installed windows in storefronts there and he used to take me and my twin brother, Larry, with him when we were kids. It's the first town in Nova Scotia, Amherst, and you come over a rise, it's just sitting out there, like a fried egg on a marsh. I saw my first blacks there. We didn't have any in Moncton, and they seemed terribly exotic and exciting."

Years later Garry would find himself traveling through places where everyone was black and few had ever seen a white man. Children wanted to touch him, and he let them examine him as if he were an animal on the sales block. He understood the impulse.

Garry Sowerby "grew up with this story about how one time my dad was working in Amherst and these guys came at him and he decked three of them on Main Street. I don't know if the story got stretched or not, but the word around Amherst was, 'Don't screw with glaziers from Moncton.' " That's what travel was about: strange exotic people to meet, new friends, and a hint of danger. "Now that I think about it," Garry said, "those runs down the windy twisting road to Amherst in my dad's fifty-three Mercury two-ton glass truck were my first road trips."

Garry's mother worked at a department store in Moncton, "which was great for Christmas because she would do all the shopping on Christmas Eve, after the store closed and the prices on everything dropped to rock bottom." Garry and his brothers always had nice gifts.

And now Garry was driving past Amherst to Halifax, to borrow money so that he could provide proper gifts for his own family on his way to setting a world record.

An officer at Sowerby's Halifax bank, Sue Bain, understood his operation and considered him a bona fide and secure investment. With the GMC contract in hand—the automaker owed him a $42,000 retainer—Sowerby negotiated a loan for $25,000, Canadian.

It was enough to send out his proposals, take care of Christmas, buy tickets to Peru and Bolivia, fly to London to confer with the *Guinness Book* people, and still have a bit left over to fly to New York or Chicago or Los Angeles in case someone liked his proposal. It was tight but not impossible.

Less than a month later, January 10, 1987, Sowerby needed another $20,000, and he flew to Detroit to talk with GMC. He had accounting fees of $5,000, insurance premiums to pay, legal fees, telephone bills, telex fees, and he wanted me to accompany him to South America to research the roads, the border formalities, and the security situation. Airline tickets, once again, were a major expense.

In his money-raising capacity, Garry has no illusions. He considers himself an honest "huckster." A "dream merchant."

January 13, in Detroit, Michigan, according to Garry's notes, had been a good day:

"Ten-forty-two. Just left Ron Royer's office. He works for the General Motors Overseas Development Corporation and for the International Export Division. What a great guy. Ron was involved in the last project, Africa-to-the-Arctic, and he met us in northern Finland and rode to the finish line with us. He's about six three, Midwestern boy, talks about 'bidness' instead of business. Got a big flat-topped wooden desk about the size of a football field. Off in the corner there's a big floor-standing globe of the world with a light inside it, so the thing's glowing off in the corner. Pictures of the granddaughters, the daughter on a credenza.

"Ron can't get involved in this because his end is marketing North American vehicles built overseas. In South America, they do a lot of the actual assembly themselves. But he said he'd hook me up with some contacts.

"So he's going to call the people who handle Central American sales and service who can help us with contacts. Mexico is handled by Canada Chevrolet-Pontiac Division and that can be sorted out through John Rock's group.

"We went to see Al Buchanan, who is the vice president of General

Motors Overseas, and basically what Al can do, he can provide service and contacts in Argentina, Chile, Peru, Ecuador, and Colombia. Al's office was more in the couch–coffee table mode. Some jazz playing on the radio and a perfectly clean desktop. Al travels a lot in South America and his suggestion was to go the west coast all the way. Forget the Amazon. Too many question marks."

Garry's notes became a rhapsody. "I'm in a great mood about all this. I've got the support of John Rock, the guys that doubted me at GMC have fallen into line, and I walk into this vice president's office on a two-minute lead time and he's already keen on the idea. If I were trying to plug into GM on my own, well, it just wouldn't happen."

On the same day, Garry met with GM advertising. "I told them we weren't looking for an end on their stuff. No money for testimonials, no payment for using my image. Oh, Tim, I told them you didn't want to be involved in the advertising in any way. So for giving up any possible money on the back end, they approved another twenty thousand dollars for the recces. It will pay for our trips to Central and South America."

Later the same day, Sowerby drove to the Detroit St. Regis hotel and met with Joe Boissonneault, from Stanadyne, a company that makes diesel fuel pumps and had recently introduced a new diesel fuel additive. "Joe's a good guy and we're friends. Stanadyne sponsored the ALCAN 5000. I asked for thirty thousand dollars up front and he gave me fifteen thousand. Said the appearances and advertising royalties after it's over should come to maybe ten thousand. Joe said, 'Don't plan on retiring on this.' I thought that too, but it's just another building block. He wants to push the new fuel additive."

That evening—"Oh man. Come to America. Drive around Detroit. Score thirty-five thousand dollars American, fifty thousand Canadian. Got the bank paid off. I can tell Jane, it's okay, go ahead and have the baby anytime. Yeah."

Garry's made some notes on follow-up:

"Get a letter of agreement off to Stanadyne re sponsorship.

"Letter to Al Buchanan, recap our talk.

"Letter to Ron Royer, thanks.

"Letter to Alan Russell at Guinness, recap parameters.

"Talk to Art Christy tomorrow, Pontiac."

Christy was a retired executive at Detroit Diesel, "a bit of a godfather of all these projects," Sowerby explained. "He first introduced me to John Rock. I think he can help me figure out how to approach Detroit Diesel." Over breakfast, Christy told Garry that $25,000 from Detroit

Diesel might be possible. Sowerby left that meeting and flew to Toronto. He made some notes on the plane:

"Letter to Detroit Diesel with a modified proposal about getting involved for twenty-five thousand dollars.

"Letter to Bruce Goodsite, retired director of public relations for Detroit Diesel, help on the above."

In Toronto Sowerby met with GM Canada and a group called CanExpo that ships vehicle components off to different factories all over the world, including South America. Later he stopped to see his friend Finlay McDonald, who had taken some of the videotape that was shot on the Africa-Arctic run and pieced together a credible half-hour adventure film. The ambush wasn't on film but the audiotape had been running, and you could hear Eddy Grant singing, and then there were a few isolated pops, followed by automatic-weapons fire and shouting soldiers. Garry sometimes showed the video to prospective sponsors. It caught their attention.

Finlay McDonald introduced Garry to a man who hosted a Toronto business show called *Venture.* Sure, Garry said, he would love to do an interview, talk about his sponsors.

FEBRUARY 19: "I'm in suite 302 in the Delta Hotel in Ottawa. Jane's with me and she's been on the phone for the last few days, calling all the foreign embassies in Canada trying to figure out what I need to go on the recces: visas and the like. I've been trying to get the government in gear in terms of giving me some letters of introduction from the prime minister, secretary of state, and from the minister of sport. My meeting yesterday with Senator Finlay McDonald certainly got things rolling."

On previous trips, Sowerby had dealt with other government officials, but Senator McDonald was the father of Garry's friend Finlay McDonald, who made the video Garry uses to sell his proposal. It all fit together.

"Finlay's got an office in the east block of the Parliament buildings," Sowerby said. "It's a couple of hundred years old and very pleasant: muted yellow walls, high ceilings. The senator himself is a bit of a character and moved very fast. I sent him a letter last week. I went to meet him and he started dictating letters to his executive assistant to get things in gear. Basically I want to be able to meet with high-level diplomats in South and Central America. I want them to be informed that I'm coming. I'd like them to get that information from the ministerial level. I want to get a letter translated into Spanish on a ministerial letterhead. You never know when you can use a letter like that to impress some bureaucrat, especially if Canada is helping to fund a dam project or build a school down there."

Later the same day, Sowerby met with Janet Connor, an old friend of his who is an assistant to the minister of sport, and they talked about a letter of introduction from that ministry.

Sowerby and I had agreed early on that it would be best if the expedition was perceived as a Canadian effort. The United States has an unfortunate history south of the border and Latins have long memories. There were entirely understandable antagonisms. Canadians, on the other hand, had never invaded any nation south of the United States and were, predictably, considered *simpático*.

Late on the evening of March 3, Garry sat in his office and read off the contents of his "In" basket:

"I've got a spare-parts list and a service plan. Instead of having a service depot of spare parts and engine assemblies and transmission assemblies, which we did in Saudi Arabia, what we do is develop a good communications system and know exactly where the parts come from. Clutch parts, water pump, fuel injector, lines, glow plug controller, about twenty-five more essentials.

"Under the service plan is a newspaper headline: KILLINGS CONTINUE IN GUATEMALA.

"A letter to Senator Finlay McDonald thanking him for his help.

"The addresses and numbers of two contacts at the Department of External Affairs.

"The plan for the first recce that I did in Peru, Colombia, Ecuador, and Bolivia.

"The plan for the second recce we've got to do in Argentina and Chile next month.

"Under that is a copy of the contact letters I sent to all the South and Central American contacts: the Canadian embassies, the auto associations, and the GM people. It's about fifteen pages, got a couple of maps.

"Next is a list of things I have to do to get the baby's room together. Getting some heavy pressure on that. Jane's just about due and I recognize this phase from the last time: pregnant women seem to develop a very intense nesting instinct.

"She's in Halifax for a checkup. Lucy's with her. While she's been gone, I've managed to get the floors done anyway. Verathane."

Garry was sitting home, alone in the basement pit, talking into his tape recorder. "The house smells a bit. I don't know: last summer we talked about getting pregnant and we both wanted to do it. But this spring is madness. Jane having babies in the middle of all these recces. We've both got to be strong. Can't stop the baby. Imagine being born between Dad's two recces to South America.

"Let's see: under that I've got my corporate year-end report.

"Under that is a list of lists: stuff for the house, media contacts, GMC contacts, associate sponsors . . .

"What else?

"A bill for the copy machine.

"A note to myself to work up a contract for Canadian Tire. They've come on as a sponsor. Motomaster tires. I love that name. Motomaster. I figured I'd just copy the legalese off the Firestone contract for Africa to Arctic. Save some legal fees on that.

"Under that note is a list of things for Cars and Concepts, the company that will be putting the camper shell on the truck. We need driving lights, a tach, plug outlets for tape recorders, and stuff." Sowerby did not believe in modification, "after-market" changes to the basic truck. The vehicle had been tested, but modifications were always someone's best guess. Besides, driving a stock vehicle right off the assembly line somehow seemed more honest. Part of the dream. Buy one of these vehicles and there is no road in all the Americas that you can't drive. "The only thing we'll do to the basic vehicle," Garry noted, "is beef up the shocks. I want to see if we can get Delco involved in that. Also I'd like to upgrade the sound system."

Under the Delco notes, Sowerby found some of Lucy's artwork and he began telling a story about it. "She comes down here to play at night sometimes when I'm waiting for calls. The other day she was coloring. She's got her tongue hanging out of the side of her mouth. So she gives me this flower she colored, and I put it through the copier. My plan was to put the original on the refrigerator, keep the copy for my office. The copy comes out of the machine and I thought Lucy would be thrilled. And she started to cry. She thought the machine had sucked all the color out of her picture."

It wasn't difficult to begin reading a mood into the transcript. It was late at night, Sowerby was alone in his house, thinking about his wife and child, but there was something else bothering him.

"I don't know if I can talk about this now, but I met with Kenny last night. And it was sad. I knew he wanted to get on with his life, but I didn't know how he felt. He looked at me . . . like he wanted this. It was like a divorce. We had been separated, and now we were getting a divorce. Yesterday we signed the papers. He gave me a little over two thirds of his shares, and I think it was fair.

"But it was Kenny, man. We had a dream together and we made it work. He was there. He was always there. You think about those times. Getting shot at: we went through that together. You could depend on Kenny. Just stupid things: the first drive, we're in India, the steering wheel is on the wrong side, just like Kenya, and Kenny is leaning out his window telling me when I can pass. I trust him, he trusts me, and our lives were at stake on his judgment and my driving. We trust each other with our lives.

"Or—you know how you get silly after a long time, laugh at stuff that isn't really very funny?—In India Kenny and I notice that Indian men stand on the street with their hands over their privates. And we spent a long time trying to figure out why. Were they advertising? Or was it a defensive thing? Was it a way of constantly telling themselves, yep, I'm a man all right. And we talked about this for hours, different anthropological and psychological theories. And we couldn't figure it out. Now, I'm not proud of this, really. I know it's wrong. I know these guys standing on the corner grew up in a different culture and it's not for me to judge. We're just silly, Kenny and I. Goofy. And he leans out the window as we're going around the corner, he screams, 'Get your hand off your dick!'

"And the guy waved at us. With the other hand.

"I suppose it's not funny in the telling, but we had tears in our eyes from laughing. Couldn't stop.

"And once we were in a plane on our way from Pakistan to Athens with the Volvo. Cargo plane. We were over the coast of Iran. It was the beginning of the Iran-Iraq war and there were oil refineries burning below. Kenny said he was having some trouble. We were badly fatigued and he couldn't sleep. He said, 'It's like a hallucination.' He was seeing something he didn't want to see, like something that was going to happen in the very near future. And finally he told me that he had a very clear vision of himself popping the emergency exit and jumping. 'I have to be restrained,' Kenny said. So I told the captain and we looked around and found some rope, and that's the way Kenny went to Athens, tied to the fuselage."

The transcript ended there, on that bittersweet note.

Few people who know Sowerby, I thought, understand how hard he works. I suspect Jane is right: Sowerby is a workaholic. He spends sixteen hours at a crack shuffling between the pit and the bunker, or he's on the road, traveling to Detroit or Toronto or Los Angeles to make deals. His parents shrug off his life-style: he's thirty-seven years old, he keeps his family fed, and he's not hurting anyone. They refer to him, affectionately, as the orangutan. Jane's parents are supportive, though her father, a prominent physician, isn't sure why Garry doesn't simply go into some legitimate business. With his capacity for work, persuasive personality, organizational talent, and drive for success, he could be a very wealthy man in a very short time. Work in a real office with fluorescent lights.

After Kenny bowed on the Pan-American run, Garry made some notes about what keeps him in the adventure-driving business.

"I never set out to become an adventurer. The money we owed after the around-the-world trip forced us to do the Africa-Arctic trip, and by the time that was done I was hooked. I like taking a concept that involves travel and making it a personal, political, and technical challenge. The job involves conceptualizing, planning, financing, public relations, writing, and lots of wheeling and dealing. I like the fact that I can move through different elements of the job, which keeps the boredom factor at a low level.

"The glossy image is a nice bit of frosting on the cake. I think the reaction I get from people thrills me more than the fact that I am the guy that's done it. And dealing with the unusual, sometimes in stressful situations, has forced me to be more capable, to manage things more responsibly. This carries over from my business to my family."

We were in the pit from eight that morning until seven-thirty that night. Garry did a phone interview for CBC radio. He assembled another package to be sent south to Canadian embassies, to the auto clubs, GMC dealers, and other contacts in Latin America. "Let them know we're coming in a couple of months," Garry said.

The day before, Garry had registered the truck, which had been built in Canada's new GM plant. It had New Brunswick plates that read: B4 NE1. "That was Janet's idea," Garry said. Janet Shorten had been working for Sowerby as an aide-de-camp. Garry had wanted a personalized plate, "but I didn't want it to be a word, like 'further' or something. I thought the plate ought to have numbers and letters. Prevents confusion at the borders that way."

In the time that it took me to read over the transcripts, Sowerby also arranged for a kind of loan, a $75,000 letter of credit from GMC in Pontiac, Michigan, to cover the Carnet de Passage, a document required to take a vehicle across borders in South America. (Central

American countries do not operate on the carnet system.) "The carnet itself is one of the largest obstacles for a novice endurance driver," Sowerby said. "When you tell people that in order to get a carnet you need to submit a letter of credit to your national automobile association for three hundred percent of the value of the vehicle, they think about it."

Foreign automobiles are heavily taxed in most South American countries. The idea is to stimulate the local economy by forcing people to buy locally built or assembled cars. These nations do not like the idea of North Americans driving comparatively cheap cars to their countries and selling them at an outrageous profit to wealthy locals who consider such vehicles a bargain. The carnet is a small book, and each page is perforated into three sections. The first section is taken by a customs officer when a vehicle enters the country, the second section is taken when you leave. If you don't have the vehicle when you want to leave—if it has been stolen, for instance, or demolished in an accident—you forfeit the entire letter of credit, say, 300 percent of the actual value of the vehicle.

"The carnet situation scares people," Garry said. "They realize that they may need to back the letter of credit with their house. By the time you paint the picture of the truck being stolen in Colombia and the insurance only covering the vehicle and not the markup, they realize they would lose their house to cover the letter of credit. So the carnet is a problem. Tomorrow I'm going to see if I can have the truck insured at approximately the amount of the letter of credit."

"I wonder how our pal in the Caddy handled the carnet," I said.

"I suppose we'll never know," Garry replied. "I wrote him at the Montreal address he gave Veronica in Ushuaia. No answer. I asked a reporter friend there to look into it. Guy went to Jerzy's place, no one there ever heard of him."

"So what do you think?"

"I think he did it and we have to do this drive in under twenty-six days."

When the local paper, *The Times-Transcript*, came out that night, there was a long feature story about our upcoming trip. Garry had managed to name every one of his sponsors: GMC truck, Canadian "Motomaster" Tire, Stanadyne Auto Products, Delco Suspension Systems, Detroit Diesel Allison, GM Canada, and something I'd never heard of called Farmer's Milkshakes.

"Who's Farmer's Milkshakes?" I asked.

THAT NIGHT, about eight o'clock, Garry and I walked down the beach at Cape Bimet, about a twenty-minute drive outside of Moncton. He had rented a beach-front cottage for a month. "Our vacation," Jane said mildly as we walked in twelve hours after we left. Lucy, three and a half, was watching a video featuring Rainbow Bright, who was, apparently, a chubby white horse who could fly. Or maybe Rainbow Bright was a little girl who could ride the chubby white horse. I never figured it out.

Karen and Jane had had the kids all day, so Garry and I took them for a walk. Sowerby gently picked up Natalie, who was three months old, born between Garry's first and second reconnaissance trips to South America. Lucy came out of her bedroom wearing a T-shirt and nothing else.

"Put your swimming suit on," Jane said. Lucy stared up at the assembled adults with the contemptuous disdain of the true sophisticate. "I like to air my bum," she said.

It only took a moment before Lucy was decently dressed and we were walking down the brown sandy beach. The waters there were shallow, surprisingly warm, and it would be another two hours until dark. The Canadian sun was dithering about above the western horizon on this long summer day, and every little cloud it touched burst into flame so that our shadows fell red-orange on the sand. Lucy was looking for shells, which she pronounced "fells." When I squatted down to examine one of her prizes, she said I looked almost exactly like the Magic Bunny. This creature, I learned, was Lucy's imaginary friend who unaccountably lived in Key West, Florida. Lucy showed me how to hop like the Magic Bunny. I was to squat with my hands balled into fists and placed precisely between my feet. The Magic Bunny hops as high and far as he can and lands back in the proper position, with his balled fists between his feet.

"Do the Magic Bunny!" Lucy screamed, and I hopped down the beach followed by my red shadow and Lucy's hysterical laughter.

"Farmer's Milkshakes," Garry said, "is a Canadian dairy. They make these shakes that come in little square boxes, Tetra Packs, and they have a nine-month shelf life. Don't have to be refrigerated. Little seventy-five-cent milk shakes and they want to come on board for five thousand dollars."

"How did that come about?"

"Do the Magic Bunny!" Lucy demanded.

I hopped down the beach in my magical way. Garry said that on a flight out of Montreal, he had met a man who represented Farmer's. They had talked a bit and the Farmer's representative came to see the Pan-American run as a good way to promote his product. Farmer's Milkshakes: from the Antarctic through the tropics to the Arctic: the quality never varies. "They're going to give us about a thousand shakes to take with us," Garry said. "Three hundred thirty-three vanillas, three hundred thirty-three chocolates, three hundred thirty-three strawberries."

"What's in line for tomorrow?" I asked.

"We've got three more people coming in." Joe Skorupa was the outdoor and boating editor for *Popular Mechanics*. The magazine was planning a feature story on the Pan-Am run and Skorupa would ride with us for the Peru-to-Colombia leg of the trip, then meet us at the finish line. Jon Stevens was a Canadian photographer Garry had met in Barcelona, and he was coming to take some photos for Skorupa.

Graham Maddocks was a police officer from Vancouver, Canada. Garry had asked him to be our security consultant. Maddocks had some impressive credentials: he was a hostage negotiator, a member of the Emergency Response Team (SWAT) in Victoria, and had been a bodyguard to British royalty. It all sounded good, but I wondered if the guy knew South America.

"I met him in Peru," Garry said. "I should tell you that story."

"What I mean is, does he have any idea about what we're likely to run into down there?"

"He thinks of things that never occurred to me," Garry said.

"Like what?"

"Like: we're driving through some little town on the Pan-Am Highway. You know how those places are, narrow cobblestone lanes, no curbs, houses that front the street, people all around. Okay, we're at a stop sign. It's hot. The windows are open. Somebody runs up, throws a pail of gasoline on us. Sticks his arm in the window, he's holding a Bic lighter. Graham asked me: 'What do you do?' "

I thought about it as the sun ignited another cloud and the waves came in like pale blood. Natalie was sleeping peacefully in Garry's arms.

"What do you do?" I asked finally.

"Do the Magic Bunny!" Lucy squealed.

ZORRO MEETS THE GASOLINE BANDITS

[HAND-TO-HAND COMBAT 101]

August 1987 · Moncton, New Brunswick, Canada

REGARDING THOSE PESKY gasoline and lighter bandits, Graham Maddocks thought it best if we didn't let ourselves get into such a situation. Which was rather my idea to begin with, though Graham insisted there was a benefit in understanding that it could happen. He wanted to examine every possible worst-case scenario, in detail. The record attempt, he said, should be run like a military operation. A soldier does not encounter problems he has not trained for, or at least considered. A soldier should know all his options. I had a lot of trouble thinking of myself as a driver, much less a soldier.

Graham Maddocks was a dark-haired, handsome fellow with an ingratiating smile and a polite manner. He was not overly tall, nor did he seem, at first glance, to be heavily muscled. An average sort of guy. Except that after listening to him for a while and examining the way he held himself, I began to see that he was as solid as a chunk of chiseled granite. You could peg a golf ball into his chest and it would come zinging off as if it had hit a brick wall. He was, I thought, a concealed weapon, in and of himself.

Garry had met Maddocks in January, in Peru, drinking Pisco sours at the bar of the Hotel Gran Bolívar in Lima. Graham was taking a break from his duties on the Victoria, British Columbia, Emergency Response Team, which was basically a special weapons and tactics squad. In order to avoid burnout or the suicidal depression that plagues some cops, Graham took long climbing vacations in South and Central America. Risking death on solo climbs in the high Andes gave him a sense of control over his life that police work tended to erode.

60

Aside from his work with the Emergency Response Team, Graham had served as a bodyguard for British royalty in the Bahamas. As a hostage negotiator, he knew something about the terrorist's motivation and aspirations. Significantly, he had trained with the British SAS, a force whose antiterrorist squads are considered the most skilled in the world.

At the Hotel Gran Bolívar, Garry found himself grilling the policeman about various South American scams. Maddocks was fascinated with the various schemes crooks had devised to separate inattentive gringos from their money. He was a professional officer who collected crime stories in the way an entomologist might collect butterflies. The more brightly colored and flamboyant the scheme, the more skillfully executed it was, the more Graham Maddocks treasured it. Scams were his hobby.

Maddocks didn't have a lot of respect for the practitioners of the simple dodge. Climbers, for instance, were continually losing their packs on bus rides to the mountains. "What happens," Graham said, "is that the overhead rack is filled and the climber will put his bag in the rack several seats back." He assumes that anyone trying to steal his gear will have to walk past him, with the pack, to exit. But when the bus stops to pick up and disgorge passengers, someone in the back simply hands the pack through an open window to a confederate on the street.

Not much skill involved in that modest crime of opportunity. There were better examples of the art of thievery in the larger cities, Lima, for instance, where highly skilled teams of pickpockets could create a diversion while a master razor man slashed open the bottom of a woman's leather purse and caught the contents.

A less remarkable method of picking pockets was the ubiquitous dirty diversion. Someone who looks fairly presentable poses as a helpful local. As you walk by he notices some dirt on your shirt, generally on the upper arm, just below the point of the shoulder. He wipes it off for you—actually he is wiping the dirt on as he pretends to wipe it off—and someone else picks your pocket. "The dirt," Graham said, "is the diversion. It takes your mind off your wallet. But, consider: what does a person who is scrabbling on the street care if some gringo has dirt on his shirt? Anything unusual, anything that doesn't make sense is a likely diversion."

Garry sipped his Pisco sour and expressed some doubt that these scams were all that widespread. Maddocks suggested they take a stroll around the Plaza San Martin. "Keep your eyes open," he said. Minutes

later, in a crowded alleyway, someone actually made the mistake of
rubbing dirt on Graham Maddocks. "Señor, you have . . ." Garry was
flummoxed: here was the dirty diversion in the flesh. There was a
momentary blur of action, then a frozen tableau: Graham staring down
the dirt wiper, his right hand behind him, gripping the wrist of a second
man who had his hand in Graham's back pocket. The first man turned
and ran. Another blur of action. Graham was now facing the pickpocket. Somehow he had gotten hold of both the man's wrists and was
holding them just at chest level in an iron grip. Maddocks stared at the
fellow, smiled sadly, and shook his head.

"Uh, Graham," Garry said. Maddocks glanced over at Sowerby,
dropped the pickpocket's arms, and let him go running off into the
crowd.

"Yeah?"

"Have you ever worked as a security consultant?"

GRAHAM MADDOCKS had prepared a twenty-page report regarding
security on our drive, and we went over each recommendation in detail.
We were sitting on lawn chairs in Garry Sowerby's backyard. Fat bees
buzzed among the flowers and there was a symphony of birdsong in
progress. It seemed as if bandits and terrorists belonged to a distant
and probably fictional world.

Graham said that one option regarding gasoline bandits was to keep
the windows closed when passing slowly through towns. And for those
gasoline-minded persons inclined to break windows in order to indulge
their predilections, Graham suggested heavy-gauge chicken wire on
the outside of side windows and on the windscreen. Bulletproof glass
was okay, though it wouldn't stop certain kinds of rounds, and was so
heavy it would affect the performance capabilities of the truck. Graham thought we would be protected from bullets fired from the front.
The engine block would stop just about anything. If they were firing
from the front, just duck down and accelerate. Piece of cake. On the
other hand, it takes only a minute or so until futile front firing becomes
somewhat more lethal and problematic side firing. Light bulletproofing
in the doors was a good idea, though it wasn't impervious to certain
high-powered rounds. And we were, Graham thought, most vulnerable
to shots fired from behind. What we needed was a big slab of tempered
steel set behind the extended cab.

All of this—it's not just a truck anymore, it's an armored vehicle—
would cost us in weight and performance. I found myself sinking deep
into a kind of glowering paranoia. How about one guy, he's not driving,

he locks himself up in a little metal egg? How about maybe we just stay home and watch TV?

A less costly armor option was bulletproof vests. Biker's goggles in case someone breaks the windshield. Garry, having been shot at previously, was furiously taking notes. I began to wonder why I had never had a problem in Latin America. Not once. My experience was that people invite you into their homes and stuff you full of food for days at a crack.

Graham's perception was much the same, though he attributed his good fortune to forethought and awareness. Likely we would have little problem, but if we expected everything to run smoothly, we were literally asking for trouble. People who don't expect to encounter obstacles encounter obstacles. It was the way of the world.

In his job, Graham had spent a lot of time consoling victims of violent crimes. "The one thing I hear all the time is, 'I couldn't believe it was happening to me, I never thought it could happen to me.' " Garry nodded vigorously. That's what he thought. Never heard of Shiftas before and suddenly there's six of them firing guns at him. It had taken minutes—minutes!—before he had been able to react.

We, Garry and I, decided against turning the truck into a tank. We'd take bulletproof vests and goggles. Graham said that we should conduct some ambush drills and have several options in mind in case of ambush. He thought it most likely that an ambush would occur at night. The first option was the back up and drive away. Simply stop some distance from the obstruction on the road. Maybe it would be a fallen tree, or a staged accident. Examine the situation from a distance. Graham had heard of several cases in which people had stopped to render help in such circumstances. When they got out of the vehicle, they were kidnapped, robbed, beaten, killed.

If the obstacle looked dangerous in any way, back up and drive away. In any case, check the mirrors. Is there a car following? Armed men on foot? If so, consider the second option: the drive around. With our four-wheel drive and high clearance, we could probably escape quite easily. It was unlikely that anyone would have a vehicle with the off-road performance capabilities of our truck. I had a vision of upscale cowpunks cruising over the desert, leaving the bandits in the dust. I liked that scenario. There was a certain romance to it.

"Naturally," Graham said, "smart bandits are not going to set up an ambush in a place that allows you to drive around. In a mountain environment, you may have a cliff on one side of the road and a rock wall on the other. In the desert there may be deep irrigation ditches lining the Pan-Am, and a jungle ambush would probably occur in thick forest."

So: the third option in an ambush scenario was the ram and drive through. As an illustration of what not to do, Graham told a story about Princess Anne. One day in London, years ago, her limo was blocked by a compact car. The driver of the compact, a mental patient, shot the limo driver dead when he got out to investigate. The mental patient fired five rounds into the limo. He said later that, for reasons that seemed inexplicable to all, he needed to frighten the princess. "And it turned out," Graham said, "that the limo driver had little or no training in ambush and abduction. He should never have stopped for a compact. He could have simply pushed it out of the way."

That was our final ambush option and there were two methods. The first involved simply pulling up to the blocking vehicle and pushing it out of the way. That was if we felt that an abduction would take place only if we got out of the truck. The second method was more spectacular. If we felt that the ambush party was armed, if there was no way to turn and run, no way to drive around, then we could, at our discretion, floor it and crash through. "I like the heavy crash bar you have on the front," Graham said. "Get up some speed and hit the blocking vehicle at its lightest point. Hit it where the engine isn't."

Aside from ambushes, we could very well run into a riot or two. We knew there were civil disturbances every couple of weeks in Panama, not to mention a tense situation at the border of Peru and Chile, and another at the Peru-Ecuador border. What would be happening in Central America when we got there was anyone's guess. Riots could be vexatious and Graham suggested, quite sensibly, that we flee the scene immediately. "The longer you stay as a riot develops, the less you look like an innocent bystander."

Graham had once found himself in just such a situation. There was a crush of people behind him and police lines were forming in front. "I just walked toward the police and they parted to let me through. It was fairly obvious that I wasn't involved and just wanted to get out of there."

Most Latin American civil disturbances, Graham felt, were pretty ritualistic in nature. They generally happen in some major square, a gathering place, usually the site of past riots.

The ritual of the riot, in Graham's experience, went something like this:

People gather.

The police form lines.

There is a period of mutual provocation.

The police overreact and beat the hell out of everybody. Or they gas the demonstrators. Hose them down. Sometimes they fire into the crowd.

So it was best to avoid the ritual riot square. "You see reports on television—people getting clubbed or throwing rocks at police—and you assume that the entire country is in turmoil. But usually it's just one specific area—a square, a plaza—and three blocks away, nothing is happening."

Urban riots were one thing, but in rural areas the major road through the country often takes on political significance. Dissident groups sometimes halt traffic in an effort to prove that the government does not control the country. In Chile, for instance, striking labor unions sometimes throw "tire busters" on the Pan-American Highway. These were, Graham said, sharp, pointed nails twisted like children's jacks and thrown onto the road by the handful.

"So," Graham said, "you should be aware of the political situation."

Neither Garry nor I considered ourselves political, and I had been assigned the dirty job of trying to comprehend the situation in each country. "For the past six months," I told Maddocks, "I've read *The Miami Herald.*" The paper seemed to have the best and most comprehensive coverage of Latin America. I also read the *The Times of the Americas* and the *Tico Times* out of Costa Rica.

Garry and I had also talked to people who drove the roads we expected to travel. In Honduras we met a truck driver who explained that leftist rebels in El Salvador often cut off the road in the southeast portion of that country. "They put announcements in the paper," the man said. "Traffic will be interdicted between this date and that." Interdicted means that drivers get killed. "I was driving through on a free travel day," the guy said, "and I got stopped anyway. They said they needed my battery to make a bomb. Left me there with a completely disabled vehicle. But they apologized profusely for inconveniencing me. If it had been an interdiction day they would have killed me."

In addition to political danger, we could encounter drunken pedestrians or deadly drivers. "If there is an accident," Graham said, "if somebody runs an intersection, something like that, assume all the blame immediately and ask them how much. Pay them whatever they ask and run for it. If anyone is hurt, same deal. If, God forbid, someone darts out in front of the truck, and you hit him, assess the injuries and offer big money. Maybe a thousand dollars. Do it quick and get out."

Garry and I passed a look that wasn't lost on Graham. "You kill someone," Graham said, "it's awful. It's tragic. But it happens. People walk in the middle of the road. They don't look. It's not going to be your fault and I say, run. Just run."

I started to voice an objection, but Graham said, "Most South American countries don't have radio cars. They don't set up roadblocks. The first thing you need to do is get out of the immediate vicinity. Running is the best way . . ."

"It's not that," I said.

"Forget about the record," Graham said. "You want to face a murder charge in Peru?"

"Nobody is getting hurt," Garry said.

"It happens," Graham said. "No matter how careful you are, it can happen and you better be prepared."

"Nobody is getting hurt," Garry said again.

To that end, Graham thought we should take pains to be especially alert, drive defensively. He had designed a series of exercises that could be done in a car seat, exercises to rest the eyes and to keep feeling fit. He thought fitness was important.

"Are you taking any drugs?"

"Stay-awake drugs?"

"Yeah."

"No," Garry said. "We don't need them." When Garry and I drove the ALCAN 5000 we had discovered that each of us fell easily into a kind of bug-eyed keyed-up wakefulness. A twelve- or twenty-hour stint at the wheel wasn't uncommon. We liked it.

"I'm not talking about illegal drugs," Graham said.

I didn't think he was. I said, "We'll be driving for a month. Taking any kind of speed is just a bad idea. Somewhere along the line, the drug is going to catch up with us and we'll crash."

"What about sleep?"

"We'll just pass out," Garry said reasonably.

Graham didn't like it.

"Of all the dangers you face, the most insidious will be the danger you present to yourself. Specifically, I'm thinking about lack of sleep." Almost every time Graham goes out on an emergency—a hostage situation, a man with a gun—it turns out later that the central figure in the drama hadn't slept in days. "You try to figure out what went wrong, where their wires crossed. Ask the family what they were doing before they blew up and almost invariably they say, 'He was pacing all night, every night.' They say, 'He didn't sleep for days.' Or, I pick people up on the street, they're acting crazy, they pose a danger to themselves or others. And these guys, you find out, had just gotten out of some mental institution where they had been doing fine. But they stopped taking their medication. They stopped sleeping. Every time."

Graham suggested that we "monitor" our "stability."

"I did one hundred hours at the wheel once," Garry said.

"All right. But just because you did it before doesn't mean you can do it again."

"I'll keep my eye on Garry," I said.

"Guns?"

"No," Garry said. "We don't carry guns. We aren't trained, and they could cost us days at every border."

Graham took us on a tour of other, more external dangers. Drug and rob, long a favorite of crooks in Southeast Asia, was becoming more prevalent. A friendly stranger offers a drink from his own flask or perhaps some food. These con men prey especially on good-hearted travelers.

"Ah, señor, I am shamed at my poor offering. I understand why you won't drink with me. I am a poor man and have nothing better." Anyone who would like to think of himself or herself as an ambassador of goodwill will crumble, take a deep breath, and drink of a new friend's humble offering.

"No, really, it's very good," the would-be ambassador of goodwill hears himself saying and wonders why there is a slight interior echo. The victim wakes up six hours later, missing his cameras, backpack, possibly his clothes and nursing what feels like the worst hangover of his life.

I told Graham that we wouldn't be eating local food at all. "I've ordered fifty man days of freeze-dried food. We buy bottled water."

"And we've got milk shakes," Garry pointed out. "We won't be hurting for milk shakes on this trip at all."

Graham asked how we expected to heat the water. "One of those electric coils people use to heat tea," I said. "There's a kind that plugs into the cigarette lighter."

Graham nodded in approval, though, in point of fact, I hadn't considered drug and rob when I bought the food. Freeze-dried meals, I thought, could be made in a moving car: turkey tetrazzini at seventy miles an hour.

Since we wouldn't have to worry about drug and rob, Graham suggested that we spend some time fretting about choke and rob, a more traditional technique. The bad guy comes up behind your back, throws a rope or chain over your neck, and pulls tight until you hand over your wallet. "Watch your back," Graham said. "When you stop for diesel, watch your partner's back."

In regard to the dirty diversion, Graham suggested that whenever either of us noticed something unusual, we should yell "diversion" and move to a back-to-back position. "When you yell," Graham advised, "point at the person causing the diversion. He is usually the most presentable of the team and is not used to being fingered. This confuses pickpockets."

Graham didn't think that money belts were a good idea. Pickpockets and robbers expect them. A purse worn around the neck and inside the shirt is often suggested in guidebooks. "Some people put a guitar string inside the neck loop," Graham said. He didn't recommend the idea. "Sometimes thieves come screaming by on motorcycles and they grab the bag, hoping to tear it off your neck, rip the fabric. Better to lose the bag than suffer a broken neck." In Graham's experience, Latin American crooks didn't often look for a leg pouch, which is a pocket fastened to the calf with elastic bands. Graham himself kept his passport and larger sums of money in a leg pouch.

If all else failed and we found ourselves in an abduction situation, Graham said we should not get out of the truck. We were much safer in the cab. We should stay together. "They will try to separate you."

Abduction scenarios usually happen when an official—a real officer or a imposter: uniforms are easy to come by—asks to see your passport. If this happened in a city and we were not sure whether the man was a real police officer, we were to insist on going to the nearest police station. We should not surrender the passport to a suspicious official, ever. "That's the first step in an abduction," Graham said. "The confrontation usually happens in public. What they want to do is get you to a place where there will be no witnesses. The first move is to get your passport. Now they have something you want. You have to follow them. It's a situation that starts with a minor hassle and then gets worse and worse by degrees until you find things becoming very ugly very quickly. They lead you into an alley, for instance, and there's men there with knives."

The last ditch defense was physical force. A fight.

"Each situation has its own logic," Graham said. "Think ahead. If it looks like they want your truck and need to take it somewhere, try to ride with them, inside."

"Even if they have guns?" Garry asked.

"Especially if they have guns," Graham said. "A knife is a much better weapon in an enclosed space."

We, Garry and I, expressed some doubt about this.

Graham said, "Well, first of all, riding with your captors in the cab of the truck gives you more time to examine the weapons. I've heard of people being robbed or abducted with toy guns. You have to think. Don't be so panicked you forget to notice whether it's a cheap plastic replica. Look down the barrel. Does it have an obstruction like a lot of toy guns? Is it a revolver? Then you should be able to see the tips of the bullets staring at you from the cylinder. Sometimes the guns are real, but the perpetrators have no ammunition. It's expensive and illegal for locals to buy in many places."

If push came to shove, there were ways to disarm assailants. You could simply grab the gun, and get the webbing between the thumb and forefinger in between the hammer and shell.

That sounded a bit iffy to me.

There was another way: with hands up you create a diversion, something as simple as looking to the side as if you see something. When the gunman glances in that direction, you slap-grab the gun to one side and bring the other hand up to the barrel, twisting the weapon over the top of his hand and, hopefully, breaking the assailant's finger in the process. There was a way to continue this maneuver and disable the assailant, though Graham thought we didn't need to know that. We weren't going to arrest anyone. "You just want to get the gun and get out of there."

I knew that technique. I had practiced it years ago in a self-defense class. We used squirt guns. About every second attempt, I got a faceful of water. "Okay," Graham said, "but the guy with the squirt gun was expecting a diversion. He knew you were going to go for his weapon. In any potential situation you face on this trip, you'll have the element of surprise going for you. And besides, it's worth your life. You remember that Air Afrique hijacking last week? A French citizen was brought to the first-class cabin, they put a blanket over his head and shot him. That's ludicrous. It's so easy to disarm people at close quarters. When the French flight attendant went for the gun, he was shot but he got it. He's still in critical condition. But he's alive. Think about that."

And so, there in Garry's backyard, on a bright summer afternoon, we practiced taking guns away from people. There I was, standing with my hands in the air like some terrified dude in a western movie. My stomach was knotting up. On the other hand, the idea of doing this, of learning these techniques, seemed romantic and macho. It was a strange combination of sensations.

"You guys," Graham said after a few exercises, "are really hopeless. Tim, how long did you study karate?"

"Maybe a year."

"How long ago?"

"Fifteen years, I guess."

"What you know is only going to get you in trouble."

I told Graham that I fully intended to avoid situations where I might feel obliged to kick someone in the groin.

"Those kicks of yours," Graham said, "are easily blocked anyway. I teach a self-defense course for women and I think that's what you guys need to learn."

A comment which made me feel considerably less macho. And then, all at once, completely assured. If a woman could learn these techniques, I could probably pick them up pretty well myself. Another macho attitude, disagreeable, I suppose, but there it was.

"The first thing I'd say about hand-to-hand combat, having seen you guys," Graham said, "is to avoid it at all costs."

Good thinking there, Graham, I thought.

"But if you do need it to get out of some situation, forget everything you thought you knew about fighting and go for the eyes. Poke, scratch, anything. This isn't the movies and it's not a fair fight. Do it fast, do it unexpectedly, and inflict pain. People can't focus on hands coming for the eyes. Even you guys might have a chance."

Maddocks turned his back and asked me to grab him around the neck. I figured he'd throw me, and came in with my knees flexed, ready to straighten him up, pull him backward, use my weight to keep him off balance. Almost as soon as my forearm touched his Adam's apple, I noticed a knife at my raised elbow. It was a double-bladed survival knife, with a four-inch blade. The handle was black and the blade glinted in the late afternoon sun.

I let my arm drop, very carefully, and stood back.

"Where did that come from?" I asked. I hadn't seen him pull it.

Graham lifted up his cotton shirt, which he wore outside his pants. There was a sheath, no thicker than a pocket penholder, and it was clipped inside his pants so the knife was out of sight.

"I teach my students to slash," Graham said. "Don't stab, slash." The idea was to surprise and hurt the assailant, then run like hell. A slash across the face, especially the forehead, should stop just about anyone. Forehead cuts were especially bloody. People bleeding profusely from the face generally forget what they were doing and become intensely self-absorbed.

So we stood among the flowers and practiced the technique involved in slicing up people's faces. "Z" strokes were good: zip across the forehead, slice sideways over the nose, gash across the cheeks and mouth. I recalled doing something similar years ago at St. Mary's grade school. We called it "playing Zorro."

The summer afternoon was sweet and moist, heavy with the odor of flowers and grass, and we stood there for an hour or so, playing Zorro.

THAT EVENING, at Garry's summer cabin on Cape Bimet, I came across a disturbing item in the local paper: "AP, Mexico City: At least thirty people were killed yesterday when a Boeing 737 cargo plane slammed into a busy highway outside Mexico City in the evening rush hour, plowing into cars, houses, and a gasoline station, Red Cross officials said." I wondered why that eventuality was not in the security briefing: planes falling out of the sky on us.

Jane was going to bed and asked Garry to lock the door.

"You have here," Garry said in a Clint Eastwood whisper, "two guys who just had two, three hours of training in hand-to-hand combat."

"Lucy," Jane said. "Natalie."

And Garry Sowerby walked to the door. I heard the dead bolt snick into the secure-locked position.

"Let's get into tropical time," Garry suggested after Jane went to bed. "We could make ourselves a couple of gin and tonics." He motioned me into the kitchen and we sat at the table there, talking softly so Jane couldn't hear us.

"Nobody gets hurt," Garry said.

"What if they do?"

"You want to run?"

"We stop."

"Damn right," Garry said. "I never really thought about this much on the other drives. I think I'm nervous about it because of my kids. You know what my biggest fear is? The nightmare? It's not gasoline or abductions or even getting shot at again. It's hitting some kid. Killing a child. How could anyone claim a world record that represents the death of a child?"

"This was supposed to be a lark," I said. "It was supposed to be fun."

"So," Garry said, "nobody gets hurt."

"First priority."

"First priority," Garry said.

We sipped the gin and tonics in silence. Garry said, "Two more months."

"In Ushuaia."

"Look at it this way: we're aware of the dangers, we have our priorities straight, and we're going to have fun."

"Smiling planes falling out of the sky," I said, "giddy gasoline bandits, riots, tire busters . . ."

"The open highway," Garry said. "The song of rubber on the road."

I looked out the kitchen window to our truck, which was parked on the sand a few feet away. It looked sleek, and the black and white paint scheme made it seem faintly ominous.

"Twenty-six days or less," I said.

"Another victory for man and machine against time and the elements."

"And it'll be fun."

"Fun," Garry said, and he began telling me about a pamphlet he once saw as a teenager: something titled *Dating Dos and Don'ts*.

"The Do guy," Garry said, "borrows Dad's car, which was, I remember, a '56 Buick. He pulls up at his date's house and introduces himself to the parents. He has a wonderful time at the dance, takes the girl out for a soda afterwards, then drives her right home. We fade out with them standing on the doorstep.

"The Don't guy borrows Dad's car, pulls up at his date's house, and sits there, honking the horn. He's driving a '56 Buick convertible. After the dance, we see him in the car, with the top down. There are people in the backseat and the guy's driving so fast that his hair is streaming out behind him in the wind. He's not even looking at the road. He's completely turned around, talking to people in the backseat, and they're going about a hundred miles an hour.

" 'Good clear night,' " he says. " 'Let's see what this baby'll do.' "

We both glanced out at the truck.

"It's a ritual with me," Garry said, "the way I like to start these record attempts."

"What?"

"With those words: 'Let's see what this baby'll do.' "

"But, I mean, the way you described it, the guy saying that is a guy about to die."

"And then when we get to Alaska in twenty-five days, we say, with great dignity and a small degree of modesty, the words that will catapult us into history."

" 'Where's the nearest bar'?"

"No, no, no."

" 'We need many women now'?"

"No. We say: 'Another victory for man and machine against time and the elements.' "

JOHN FORD
WITH FOLIAGE

September 19–20, 1987 • Montana to Manaus, Brazil

WHEN I AM CONFINED to my home in Montana, there are high winds driving fierce ground blizzards, and the cattle lie dead in the fields, frozen stiff, with their hooves in the air. Or so it seems. Most anytime I leave home, however, the weather turns spitefully glorious. I become convinced I live in splendor and feel compelled to wonder, in a state of pitiful and romantic melancholy, why the hell I would ever want to leave.

At eighty miles an hour, the closest airport is half an hour away, over the Bozeman Pass, where Indians once attacked miners attracted to the Montana gold fields. And the miners, of course, sought to kill those Indians. One of the least obvious ways they did that was to slaughter the buffalo, to destroy, as General Sheridan put it, "the Indian's commissary."

It was quite early in the morning the day I left for the end of the earth. The sun had just risen, so that the east was on fire and the snow on the Bridger Range to the west was watermelon pink. The air tasted crisp and clean, and the cottonwoods along the creek bottoms were just beginning their autumn blush. Pastel streaks colored the monumental dome of sky above, and a slanting shaft of sun illuminated a stand of aspen set in a pocketed groin of the mountain, so that the trees seemed translucent as they shivered in a slight breeze.

Leave this to get on an airplane? An airplane!

In Chicago, some months earlier, I had purchased a Banana Republic khaki shirt at Water Tower Place and wore it out of the store. Across the hall, there was a cutlery shop. I examined several survival knives which might be used to Zorro assailants. I needed one with a sheath that would fit inside my pants, a knife that felt comfortable in my hand, one that was double-bladed and sharp. Perhaps the clerk was impressed with me: a guy who needs a close-quarters weapon and knows what he is looking for; a mild-mannered 007 kind of a guy with nice taste in shirts.

The Tekna diving knife seemed a good choice. It was flashy enough, a shining silver thing, and the sheath had a series of round holes in it so that it was very light. I felt the heft of the blade, did a modest Zorro, tested the edge by shaving a thin layer of nail off my thumb, then deftly slipped the knife back into the sheath and sliced off a small portion of my left index finger, which was stuck inside one of the holes in the sheath.

The clerk, to his credit, did not immediately burst into convulsive squeals of uncontrolled laughter. He impassively handed me a Kleenex from a box he kept under the counter for just such minor amputations.

"Maybe," he said, handing me a knife in a solid sheath, "you'd prefer this model."

I had blood on my Banana Republic expedition shirt and felt as if the remainder of my life would continue apace and not be filled with satisfaction or spiritual enlightenment. Someone once described this feeling of unease and perceived mortality as the sound of rat claws scrabbling at the edge of the universe.

That perception, a sickly syrup of regret, returned under the impossible deep-water blue of the Montana sky as I drove.

So, OF COURSE, it was raining a sad, dirty rain in New York. Everything seemed dingy and polluted, though I've traveled enough to understand that my interior landscape colors the exterior.

Garry Sowerby was staying at the JFK Hilton with his wife. They were sitting on a made-up bed in their room watching the Miss America pageant on TV and Garry was making snide comments about the intellectual attainments of the contestants. He was more caustic than seemed absolutely necessary.

I sensed that he had also heard the scrabbling of those cosmic rat claws. We were unprepared. Someone was going to get hurt. South American perpetrators would laugh in the face of our four-inch knives. Bad guys would rip us open with Uzis. They'd use our own knives to carve rude messages into various portions of our anatomies. Nothing would go right. We would encounter unpleasant circumstances. My only reading material for the better part of two months would consist of a single ungrammatical sentence:

OBJECTS IN MIRROR ARE CLOSER
THAN THEY APPEAR

Remorse before the fact is a common preadventure sensation. There is an overwhelming sense that you left the water running in the bathroom. You have, in fact, neglected something so simple and self-evident that people didn't see any reason to tell you about it: the Wall of Flames in Chile, for instance, or the Big Hole in the Earth that Swallows Trucks just south of Río Gallegos, the River of Acid, the meteorite Firing Range, the Living Dinosaurs . . .

Garry called his mother, who was taking care of Lucy and Natalie. He was about to travel to the end of the earth. Soon he might find himself in a situation where it would be necessary to Zorro gasoline bandits. That jittery thought, along with the pervading sense of regret, rendered him suddenly sentimental.

I imagine he saw, in his mind's eye, an idyllic vision of New Brunswick: his parents' home at Hopewell Cape, a house surrounded by flowers and set high on a green hillside above the Bay of Fundy. It is an airy place, where sunlight falls through large windows onto polished wood floors. One room is dominated by an old-style divan upon which there are dozen of antique dolls in their starched white dresses. It is in this sunny room, among the dolls, that Garry envisioned Lucy, dressed in lace and crinoline, waiting breathlessly for a call from daddy.

Lucy, in point of fact, was sitting in front of the television watching *Zig Zag,* a *Sesame Street*–type program. It was her favorite show and she was used to having her father call from all over the world.

"Dad," she scolded, "*Zig Zag*'s on."

"It broke my heart," Garry said.

Garry told me that he had finally arranged for insurance which would be worth the carnet value of the truck in case of a complete loss. It had cost him $6,000 for sixty days, with a $5,000 deductible. The terms did not seem a vote of confidence in our planning, skill, or Latin America in general.

After Kellye Cash was crowned Miss America in a great spectacle of emotion and perfect teeth, Garry and I took the truck to the Flying Tigers cargo terminal at JFK International. It was a hardworking place, not clean, functionally inelegant, and the computers at every desk carried greasy finger smudges on the keyboards. We arranged to have the truck put on the plane. It would cost $13,000 to ship it to Buenos Aires. From there, we would drive to the end of the world, take a deep breath, turn around, and begin the long drive north.

When Garry started negotiating with Tigers, he was told it would cost $18,000 to airfreight the truck to Buenos Aires. He checked Lufthansa. It was less, but we had to go via Frankfurt. He went back to Tigers. With this sort of Ping-Pong negotiation, he got the price down to $13,000 for the truck and for us.

We still had a place for a logo on the truck—a prize position on the crash bar (and I wanted the growling Tigers logo for ram-and-drive-through ambush situations)—but none of the freight companies were interested in sponsoring us in return for such excellent placement.

Garry had decided that the crash-bar position that he had been saving as a negotiations ploy should go to Stanadyne.

"How come?" I asked.

"Joe Boissonneault has been real helpful. And he gave me a bulletproof vest."

"I got one from a literary agent," I said.

"Why would a literary agent need a bulletproof vest?" Garry asked. He didn't understand the publishing business. Not even a little bit.

We went back to the Hilton, slept for a few hours, taxied back to the airport, paid our freight bill, and loaded the truck onto the plane. It was a 747 and there were metal rollers all over what had once been the passenger compartment of the plane. Between the rollers were thick rubber wheels. Cargo is loaded onto pallets, then forklifted onto another pallet that hoists the freight up a sloping escalator to the cargo compartment, where men roll the loaded pallets neatly into the plane. The truck was put on with no difficulty. It was surrounded, on all sides, by great columns of fifty-five-gallon drums containing insecticide.

Garry and I had first-class seats in the upstairs bubble. There was no door between the cockpit and the cabin. Passengers on the flight, aside from Sowerby and myself, included an on-board mechanic and a pricing agent for Tigers who said they take a lot of horses to Argentina. He was used to horses and their handlers. We described ourselves as international rally drivers.

Cargo planes are generally scheduled to take off and land at slack times, especially at major airports. We took off at four in the morning.

The inside of the cockpit was not shiny clean. There was a pencil sharpener on a shelf and it was grimy, in the way that a pencil sharpener in a factory foreman's office might be grimy. No need for shiny-clean planes. You wanted something that would fly and you didn't need to convince passengers it would fly because it was clean. The plane, according to the pilot, had 60,000 hours in the air. (Let's see, divide by 24 in a day for, uh, 2,500 days, divide by 365 days in a year to get, holy shit, damn near 7 years in the air. Seven years 30,000 feet above the surface of the earth. No wonder the pencil sharpener looked tired.)

We took on more freight at Miami where a cargo agent from Flying Tigers said that the plane was also making an intermediate stop in Manaus, Brazil, and that it was his impression that we would need visas. Mine was expired. He clicked his tongue.

"But we're only there for an hour or two," I said.

"This is a cargo flight," he replied. He was a black man with a slight Caribbean tinkle to his speech. "Let me put it this way, mon: do you drive your car without a spare tire?"

So it was a nervous flight over the Amazon jungle to Manaus. How could I have forgotten to renew my visa for Brazil? I would be deported, flummoxed before we even got to the starting line.

A MAN WHO IMAGINES he has visa troubles will find the carpet of jungle flowing below a plane ominous. Natch. The trees—Garry said it, but everyone does when they see the jungle from the air—the trees looked like giant stalks of broccoli, closely spaced, oddly placed. It was very colorful in a green sort of way, which is to say, while everything was green and seemed to stretch out beyond imagination, there were a lot of different shades of green. There were small ponds and lakes and shiny-black forest rivers that generated their own small pockets of clouds so that the whole of the jungle seemed to be steaming.

There were roads down there, roads I'd driven in the rainy season which, the locals say, lasts four hundred days a year. Blue-black clouds, the color of a bad bruise, congregate in the sky and conspire for several minutes. Lightning, striking internally, gives these clouds a garish neon aspect. They are bullying, operatic, Wagnerian clouds, all low, ominous rumbles and thundering crescendos.

The rain starts with surprisingly large drops, with fat globules of water the size of a quarter, an apple, a cantaloupe. Soon enough, water simply falls in sheets, and the sound is that of a big river at high water. Even at midday, a rumbling twilight descends on the forest. Streams form and cross the road, or flow down the right-of-way, or puddle up in large lakes anywhere the land sinks. It is a strange, dark-green, sub-aqueous world.

The road I drove was a red clay strip scraped out of the forest. There were pockets of greasy gumbo mud and holes full of sick tomato soup, all of it half underwater so that the brakes—slick with gumbo—refused to operate in the conventional sense. The surface of the road was a sort of muddy red quicksand, and it seemed wise to drive fast, to surf the red glop. There was a sense that stopping could be fatal, that the vehicle would simply sink beneath the surface of the earth. The perceived necessity to drive fast and the complete lack of brakes combined to produce a provocative sense of impending doom. I had never before worried about being buried alive while driving thirty miles an hour. Usually, in a car, there are other things to worry about.

On the road I had driven there were frontier settlements: one place in southern Venezuela is called Kilómetro 85 simply because it is 85 kilometers from another place with a name. The bar and general store there had a dirty floor, and the price of a beer seemed floridly excessive. There was a scale set dead center in the bar, and men paid for their purchases in gold nuggets, in diamonds.

In the 747, as we passed over the approximate location of Kilómetro 85, it occurred to me that I had been traveling for thirty hours and had slipped back 125 years into the history of the United States. The scales at Kilómetro 85 were precisely like those used to weigh gold dust in the bars and brothels of the mining camp at Virginia City, Montana, during the 1860s. The stories I heard at the bar in Kilómetro 85 read like the history of the Montana gold strike. Claim-jumping was common. A man might bring gold or diamonds into town, an Indian might be hired to track him back to his dig. Men would come with guns. There were firefights over holes in the ground. Screams and blood in the jungle night. Sometimes men were robbed on the roads. Sometimes miners gathered together, tracked down the road agents, and killed them just as George Ives and Henry Plummer were killed by vigilantes in Montana in 1863 and 1864.

I had once hiked through the forest just north of Venezuela's border with Brazil to a small mining operation. There was a trail that led along a river which fell from a high flat-topped mountain. Presently I could hear the sound of a gasoline-driven generator. It seemed wise to hail the camp from a distance. A white man whose thin face was all cheekbones and sloping planes motioned me to the dig. There were three other men, two Brazilians and a black man from Guyana. They had dug a hole perhaps twenty feet deep in the soft red earth next to the river. The black man stood ankle-deep in the mud at the bottom of the hole. He was spraying the sides of the pit with a high-powered hose. When the red sludge at the bottom got knee-deep, the hose was somehow reconnected so that it pulled water and soil up out of the pit to a kind of mechanical panning device called a *lavador*.

The men lived in small shoddily built lean-tos with dirt floors. There was a hammock in one shack, an uncomfortable-looking canvas cot in another. All these men did in camp, it seemed, was work and sleep. When such men finally came to town—so said the bartender at Kiló- metro 85—they generally consumed numerous alcoholic beverages, stood the house to drinks several times, staked miners down on their luck, and ended the evening with a congenial fight.

The white man, who spoke English with a central-European accent, said that there was gold in the old riverbed. He thought there were diamonds atop the strange, flat-topped mountains that surrounded the camp. These mountains—the Indians call them *tepuis*—caught much of the rain, and that rain formed rivers, and these rivers swept the diamonds from the earth so that when the water fell from high cliff faces, it contained the wealth of dreams. Showers of diamonds.

We talked for a while about the theory of plate tectonics: how the earth's continents once fit together like a jigsaw puzzle, how these pieces were drifting apart, how the hump of northern South America fit against the westward protrusion of northern Africa. And there were diamonds in both places. Fewer in South America, but they were there.

Had they found many diamonds? Could I see some?

"We have found nothing."

How long had they been working the claim?

"Four months."

"Why would anyone work a dry hole for four months?"

I noticed that one of the other men had come up behind me and that both of the miners wore holsters and handguns. A third strolled over to join a discussion in which nothing was being said. He was strapping on a holster. Asking about what they had found seemed to have been bad form. Maybe these gentlemen thought some claim-jumping gang was using dumb guys with notepads to gather intelligence.

"I'm sorry about your bad luck here," I said.

No one replied.

"No gold," I said, "no diamonds here."

I found myself walking backward and the smile on my face felt ghastly.

"Well, thanks again," I said. Glancing behind me I could see the tree line another ten paces away. The three armed men stared at me with hard eyes. I waved what I hoped looked like a friendly good-bye. As soon as I hit the trees I would run. There came a brief vision of a character in an old western movie: the moronic dude reporter who asks the wrong question of the wrong man; the guy who gets to tap-dance with bullets zinging around his feet. Sometimes, in some westerns, the guy dies, shot dead so fast he doesn't even have time to be surprised.

The Amazon, I thought later, is John Ford with foliage. It's high-plains history replayed in the tropics. Certain sad commonalities exist. In the jungles of Brazil, there had been genocidal tragedies: Amazonian Indians given blankets infested with measles, sugar laced with arsenic. The perpetrators of these astoundingly brutal and cowardly murders— they were enforcers for various development corporations—might have devised their strategy from reading the history of the United States.

And it's true, small groups of miners or missionaries were sometimes attacked by aboriginal people defending their land from the interlopers. Massacres on both sides. Mostly, these days, the "Indian problem" is considered to be under control. There are occasional reports of violence, but any North American driving the new roads through the Amazon will see the beginning of a forlorn and familiar pattern. Indian people, wearing the ragged clothes of their conquerors, beg alongside the road, engage in sex with truck drivers for money, or simply stumble about in an alcoholic daze.

The people are driven from the forest by mining operations, by giant ill-conceived cattle-ranching schemes, by enormous agricultural projects. They stand alongside the roads where the forest once stood. Destitute and demoralized, they are the roadside symbols of progress.

Progress requires that the jungle be cleared. The nearly three million square miles of rain forest in the Amazon basin, it is said, are the "lungs of the planet." Wholesale deforestation, environmentalists warn, would sharply reduce the world's supply of oxygen, increase carbon dioxide, and add to the greenhouse effect, raising temperatures around the world to such a degree that U.S. farmers, for instance, could expect devastating dust bowl–type droughts.

In addition, clearing the forest has seldom proved profitable. The soil itself—battered by heat and constant rain—is poorer than many deserts. Rain rinses the soil of organic materials so that only the first few inches are fertile. In the Amazon, plants recycle up to 75 percent of their nutrient requirements: dead foliage dropping to the ground rots and is reabsorbed rapidly.

The astounding variety of plant life is, ironically, an indication of the poverty of the soil. Each plant has slightly different nutritional needs, and there may be a hundred different types of trees in a single acre. A single type of tree, grown in a plantation, will quickly deplete the soil of needed nutrients. The trees will die.

Traditional slash-and-burn agriculture will produce good crops for a couple of years, then the thin sandy desert that is the floor of the

Amazon basin will assert itself. These failed farms, the failed cattle ranches, do not regenerate. They leave a baking red-dust desert.

And still the forest is cut and burned.

"People need jobs," a   U.S.-educated Brazilian businessman once told me. We were seatmates on a flight that took us across three thousand miles of jungle. "Look," he said and glanced down into the limitless sea of foliage. "How could we even begin to affect that, cutting down a few trees?"

"That's what we said in the United States. We said it about the buffalo. About the passenger pigeon."

"What's a passenger pigeon?"

"It's a bird. Flights of them used to darken the sky at noon. There was no way you could kill them all. Anyone could see that."

"I never heard of them."

"They're extinct."

"So you don't have any buffalo, and you don't . . ."

"There's some buffalo."

"But none of those pigeons?"

"Not a one."

"But you have progress. You have prosperity."

"We lost something of our soul, don't you think?" This is always a telling argument in South America, where a gringo is forever hearing about the great soul of Peru or Brazil or Ecuador in contrast to the supposedly spiritually barren life of the typical North American. "The great soul of Brazil," I said, "encompasses the forest. And the forest encompasses the soul of Brazil."

The man glanced down at the jungle. "Personally," he said, "I love the forest. But if it's a matter of pigeons or prosperity . . ."

THERE WAS PROSPERITY in the Amazon once, specifically in the city of Manaus, the capital of Amazonas, the largest state in Brazil. This river port on the Río Negro, about seven miles from its influx into the Amazon River, is the trading capital of a vast area. The rivers are the trade routes and there are one thousand known tributaries of the Amazon, seven of which are more than a thousand miles long. The Amazon basin encompasses the greater part of Brazil, as well as parts of Colombia, Ecuador, Peru, and Bolivia.

Manaus is about nine hundred miles from the Atlantic coast, one thousand miles if you sail up the Amazon. In 1902 the town built floating wharves to allow for the fifty-foot rise and fall of the river.

The Spanish explorer Francisco de Orellana, a conquistador with Pizarro during the conquest of Peru (1535), passed near the site of present-day Manaus in 1541 during a crazed voyage down the Amazon, a desperate descent of this world's largest river forced on him after he failed to find a city of gold in the Andean highlands. Lost, ill, out of provisions, de Orellana and his men fashioned a raft. They were two hundred miles from the Pacific Ocean, but they had to fight their way back up jungled foothills, back up over the Andes, and this eastward running river would surely take them somewhere. It would be easier than going back the way they came.

De Orellana rode the river four thousand miles—he saw monkeys, bats, rodents, toucans, parrots, cayman (a kind of South American alligator), anacondas, strange endemic beetles, butterflies, wasps, and mosquitoes—to its mouth in the Atlantic, where the river is 150 miles wide.

The history Europeans and North Americans have written for themselves suggests that it was de Orellana who first realized the riches and extent of the Amazon basin. The Andes Mountains, a series of high plateaus surrounded by higher peaks (Aconcagua in Argentina rises to 22,834 feet, the highest peak in the Western Hemisphere), stretch 5,500 miles from the tip of South America to to the continent's northernmost coast on the Caribbean. The mountains run generally north and south. For most of its length, the Andean chain of mountains is visible from the Pacific Ocean. In some places, the continental divide is no more than fifty miles from the Pacific coast. The great rivers of South America, then, run east, almost all of them. It is estimated that 20 percent of all the water that runs off the earth's surface is carried by the Amazon. One hundred seventy billion gallons of water are discharged into the Atlantic every hour, about ten times the amount carried by the Mississippi.

De Orellana, perhaps crazed by hardship and the constant death of his men, still managed to sail to Trinidad and finally returned to Spain, where he spun tales of gold and spices and fierce tribes led by women who reminded him of the Amazons of Greek mythology. De Orellana was granted the right to explore and exploit the basin of this river of Amazons. He returned to South America in 1546 and, near the mouth of the great river, his ship sank and de Orellana drowned. The great mass of water in the Amazon turns seawater brackish to one hundred miles. De Orellana's last breath was filled with the brackish water of the river he named.

*   *   *

OUTSIDE MANAUS, there are great trees 125 feet high, huge trees with smooth white bark and silvery leaves, "trees that weep." At about the same time gold was discovered in Montana, *borracha,* a kind of foul-smelling gum derived from the "tears" of the trees, became the "black gold" of Manaus. For centuries Indians had decorated their ears or lips with tubes and disks made from *cachucho,* the wood which wept.

Columbus had described this substance on his second voyage to the New World. In 1495 he watched Indians in Haiti play with balls made from the gum of a tree. Some of the stuff eventually got back to Europe. The English found that it could be rubbed over paper to eradicate pen and pencil marks. Such a device was called a rubber. The name caught on: the substance itself became known as rubber.

Amazonian Indians also brushed the gum on their clothes as protection from the rain. The waterproofing was effective. The clothes, however, were also sticky, brittle, and odorous. In 1820, a Scottish chemist named Charles Macintosh placed a solution of rubber and naphtha between two fabrics to create rainwear that did not stick, smell, or crack. British people, to this day, describe any double-textured waterproof coat as a mackintosh.

It was, however, the American inventor Charles Goodyear's work which created the boggling phenomenon that was Manaus in the 1890s. Rubber tends to harden in the cold, soften in the heat. In 1839, Goodyear invented a curing process that came to be called vulcanization. This new form of rubber could be used in machines, especially as drive belts. Previously, these belts had been made from cured buffalo hide, but by 1890 there were virtually no buffalo left in Montana or the rest of the United States. At the same time, the rise of steam and electric power brought a huge demand for proper belt material: rubber. And in 1888 John Dunlop—Goodyear and Dunlop: old tired names—patented a pneumatic tire for bicycles and tricycles.

What these events meant to Manaus was money. The rubber boom of 1890 to 1920 made Manaus arguably the richest city in the world.

The rubber was collected by men who lived alone in the jungle, *seringueiros.* They worked as many as two hundred trees separated by swamp and twisted foliage, for trees in the Amazon cannot grow in groves. The men walked over trails that needed clearing every few days. Gashes were made in the trees, the sap was collected in ceramic pots, then cooked over an open fire in a copper pot. Stirred with a wooden spoon, the pots would, after days, yield up a hard, black, foul-smelling ball weighing perhaps forty pounds: *borracha.* When the *seringueiro* had thirty such balls—they might take months to accumulate—he carried them to the river, loaded them into a boat, and paddled them to Manaus, where they were purchased by a "patron."

The French writer Lucien Bodard described the riches of the rubber barons, the madness of Manaus, circa 1895:

> Manaus, the metropolis, was the Babylon, the Sodom, and Paris of the borracha, all in one. . . . A throbbing distracted city of inequable wealth, of extraordinary luxury in the splendors of its vulgarity. Manaus flung its rubber out onto the world and received in return countless billions and all the treasures of bad taste. Steamships from Anvers, from London, and Le Havre made fast mid-river in the Río Negro to floating docks. . . . Diamonds twinkling on every finger. . . . Brothels everywhere. Mean brothels, splendid brothels, the most beautiful brothels in the world with the girls from the rue Saint-Denis at a premium.
>
> It was symbolic; the jungle was not far away, but what people saw was a temple of glazed tile, bushes pruned like wedding cakes in the flowerbeds. . . . There were almost as many palaces as brothels: brand-new palaces in all the ancient styles—Gothic à la Versailles, Venetian, Buckingham Palace. . . . There was a whole population of flunkies and ladies' maids who knew how to flatter their mistresses, most of whom were former shrill-voiced whores. Men sent their shirts to London to be ironed.

A new cathedral was built. A court of law. Men competed to construct finer, more baroque or rococo castles in the land of the weeping trees.

When the opera house, the Teatro Amazonas, opened in 1896, Enrico Caruso sang for the assembled rubber barons. The greatest actors and singers and dancers in the world sailed a thousand miles upriver to perform under the four white Italian marble balconies. Sarah Bernhardt. Pavlova.

And then, in 1920, the boom was over. Rubber trees grew in the Amazon and nowhere else, though there seemed to be no reason why the great trees could not be cultivated anywhere ten degrees north or south of the equator, provided the climate was warm and humid with heavy spring rains. The billionaires of Manaus, the men who simply made their living in the forest, the brothel owners, law-enforcement officials, everyone agreed: the seeds of the rubber trees must remain in Brazil. Seed smugglers were executed. Foreigners were followed, everywhere.

Nevertheless, in 1877, an Englishman named Henry A. Wickham, an explorer and hunter who was trekking the jungle supposedly in search of certain rare orchids, managed to smuggle 2,400 seeds out of the jungle. In the springtime flood, when the river rose fifty feet and inundated the land, when the Brazilians agreed that a man in the jungle would die, Wickham collected his seeds and—"taken by surprise on the plain by the rapidity of the flood"—walked and swam "desperately towards high land that I saw on the horizon."

He was rescued by an English trawler carrying scrap iron. To this day, Brazilians find the "rescue" so highly providential as to be planned. The seeds were hidden at the bottom of cargo boxes, and the trawler made its way down the river to the final port of Belém, where—it is said—certain hands were greased.

The seeds eventually ended up in the richer soil of Malaysia, and the trees were grown in groves, row upon row of them, so that the latex was easier and more efficient to harvest. It took thirty years before the trees were ready, but when they were, rubber bought out of Singapore was cheaper than rubber from the Amazon.

The grand palaces fell into disrepair, the opera house became a town meeting hall. It would be tempting to report that today the opera house stands abandoned and that monkeys swing from the white marble balconies. In fact, during the Second World War, when Japan conquered much of Malaysia, rubber from Brazil again became valuable. There was a minor boom.

Today, Manaus is now a major inland port, a collecting and distribution center for the upper Amazon. Principal exports are rubber, Brazil nuts, rosewood oil, and jute, the material used to make coffee sacks. Industries include brewing and oil refining (the oil is from Peru and barged downriver). This town of 1.2 million in the heart of the Amazon jungle makes electronic equipment, motorcycles, plywood sheets, and—this is not entirely a surprise—refrigerators. Tourism is a growing industry and there are botanic and zoological gardens, and a natural jungle park on the outskirts. It is the headquarters of the National Institute for Amazon Research and has both a university and a leprosarium.

It is also a town where smuggling is not unheard of; where officials, remembering the lessons of 1877, are likely to look unfavorably upon foreigners with little good reason to be in the country. Even comparatively innocent persons, such as myself, have reason to be apprehensive if they have no visa.

*   *   *

As WE TAXIED into the cargo terminal, I saw a ruined 707 off to the side of the runway. The on-board mechanic told me that the plane had come down on an incorrect runway, and sheared off part of a wing by plowing into a semi-truck. The Brazilians had simply towed the plane off the tarmac. It would never be airworthy again. There was a scaffold that was little more than a series of stepladders erected against the plane. The insides had been stripped. It was a metal shell slowly going to rust in the humid heat of the Amazon. It sat against a red mud bank, and over the years this shell of a plane would become the color of the Amazon mud. "I don't think that's real good for their tourist trade," the pilot said.

I went down into the cargo hold and looked at the truck. Workers were moving some gear. Two of them simply pushed the truck on its rollered pallet to a different position using mechanized rubber wheels. Moving the nine-thousand-pound truck seemed to cost them almost no effort at all. With the cargo in the hold and the cabin unpartitioned by compartments as passenger flights are, the interior of the plane looked huge. The pilot, a sandy-haired fellow who had come down to look at the truck, said, "Sorta like the Holland Tunnel in here, isn't it?"

I got into the truck and crouched down in the passenger seat. The pilot leaned into the window and stared at me.

"What are you doing?"

"I'm afraid someone is going to ask me for my visa."

"You don't have one?"

"Not for Brazil."

"I don't think you'll have a problem."

"But I could have one, right?"

"It's possible."

"I'll stay here."

"And hide?"

"Yes."

"Then maybe it isn't such a good idea for me to stand here talking to you. If you're hiding."

"Right."

"It's going to be hot."

A team of men moved the insecticide out of the plane. It would be used in those areas where the trees, the lungs of the planet, had been cleared. Slash, burn, then pour a 747 full of insecticide on that land so that the poisons can be washed down the river and flow out into the ocean, along with twenty percent of the freshwater on the face of the earth.

After the drums of insecticide were off-loaded, electronic equipment manufactured in Manaus was stacked on pallets around the truck. Parts made in the United States or Japan were assembled here in the Amazon jungle and sold in Argentina.

We, Garry and I, had decided against coming up through the Amazon. The road past Kilómetro 85 was now paved, but the rising cost of petroleum, a major component of asphalt, had defeated plans for paving many of the roads that crossed Brazil's lowland jungles. Instead, we would drive that narrow strip of desert between the Andes and the Pacific. The Pan-American Highway.

It was sweltering inside the plane, hotter still inside the truck, and the special racing seats were not made for slouching with the head below window level. I went through the papers in our document case to pass the time. There was a six-page letter Garry wrote to GMC entitled "Progress Report #5, Pan-American Challenge." The letter was a report on our recces and conclusions, and formed the basis of our master plan. In essence, what the letter said was that we had decided to go all out, do the drive in under twenty-six days, forgo press conferences along the way, and change the look of the truck. The road through Brazil—the most scenic and difficult route—would be abandoned.

> Since my meeting with various associations in northern South America, [Garry wrote] I have been receiving warnings and signals to forget the transit of the Amazon area. Apparently, when the dry season is north of the Amazon, the wet season is in the southern area and vice versa. We have reports of one road of about 1,000 kms that takes up to ten days in the dry season. North of Manaus the road is not much better, so aside from the delays involved in taking the Brazil route, there would be very difficult terrain for the truck, coupled with virtually no service support for thousands of miles. In a nutshell, we are going to forget the Amazon route and stick to our original mandate of obtaining the best possible time for the record by heading up the west coast of South America.

As for security, especially in regard to Central America, Garry wrote that

> we have heard of a number of cases where people have safely transited this area in recent months. However, I am concerned with the conse-

quences of the many . . . guerrilla groups, etc., knowing our route. For this reason, and the very real threat of kidnapping or attack, I think we should consider a press blackout until we have at least reached Mexico City. There are other advantages in that if, for some reason, problems with the vehicle interfere with the success of the project, then GMC will not be out on a limb with a lot of advance publicity. Also, we will not be hampered with making a number of untimely stops for press conferences while en route through South and Central America. Essentially I feel we would be able to make the best possible time through the areas where there are few advantages and many disadvantages in gaining exposure.

Garry wrote that we had learned of an unpublicized, self-financed drive from Prudhoe Bay to Tierra del Fuego in twenty-six days. "Although the forty-day time period had been discussed, this was in the event we took the Amazon basin route." We would be shooting for twenty-five days or less. "With this approach to the project, there are a few changes to the project vehicle which would alter the image of the truck somewhat from an expedition vehicle to a very serious road machine."

Those recommendations were:

Take [spare] tires from the roof and install inside box on each side behind wheel wells.

Remove roof rack.

Install one-hundred-gallon fuel cell which will increase range from about five hundred miles to over two thousand miles. Removal of the gear from the roof will also decrease fuel consumption.

Place one bunk only in the pickup box running down the center as low as possible.

Keep the truck as aerodynamic as possible.

The results of this treatment, Garry wrote, "will considerably cut down on fuel stops, lower the center of gravity to substantially increase stability and handling, and produce a vehicle more in line with the 'it's not just a truck anymore' slogan."

And then Garry went right ahead and told them what it was. "It's an aerodynamic, one-ton, long-range, high-tech, head-turning, fuel-efficient, record-breaking, one hell of a road machine."

The public-relations plan was proceeding apace.

I finalized an arrangement with *Popular Mechanics* magazine to do a feature story on the project. They will do their cover photography in

Tierra del Fuego prior to departure and have a writer traveling with us for a few days.

Tim Cahill has finalized a deal with Random House to publish the book on the project.

Considering the proposed new strategy for the press, I feel we should be set to go with an on-the-fly press announcement when we hit Mexico City or Texas. I think we could possibly do press in Las Vegas or Los Angeles, then Calgary, Fairbanks, and possibly at the finish in Prudhoe Bay. We could also consider airfreighting the truck immediately from Fairbanks to either L.A. or Detroit for a final wrap-up.

I think this new strategy is safer for the drive team and GMC, provides a more honest approach to our mission, and could be quite a bit more cost-effective to GMC. This new plan allows us to operate stripped of ancillary commitments until we reach the prime area for marketing the Sierra, all of which results in a more impressive, safer, tougher-to-beat world record.

The paper was sticking to my fingers, which were damp with sweat. I had been slouching in that seat for more than two hours. It was very quiet in the cargo hold. The workers seemed to be gone. I glanced up into the side mirror and saw, in the distance, a man wearing a short-sleeved uniform shirt and carrying a clipboard. He was walking toward the truck. His face was bronze and he wore a thin black mustache: just the sort of man who might ask a stowaway for a visa. I slipped lower in my seat. All this thought poured into the project and here I was, hiding in what amounted to a Dutch oven. When I checked the side mirror again, all I could see were an enormous pair of sunglasses above a bunch of white letters that read:

OBJECTS IN MIRROR ARE CLOSER
THAN THEY APPEAR

THE CITY OF FALCONS

September 21–26, 1987

"**W**HAT DID HE SAY?" the pilot asked. We were airborne, flying south over the jungle, toward Buenos Aires.

"I don't understand Portuguese," I said, embarrassed.

"He didn't speak English?"

I had to admit that he did.

"So?"

"He asked me if it wasn't hot in the truck."

"That's all?"

"I told him it was real hot in the truck."

"Ah."

Irregular regulations: it's a pattern of frustration familiar to people who travel in South America. Someone who ought to know, someone like a cargo agent for Flying Tigers, tells you something—like you need a visa for a cargo stopover in Manaus—and the information turns out to be entirely incorrect. In Latin America, it is best to ask several different people familiar with important regulations what will be required. In general, you will get as many interpretations of the rules as you have informants. These conflicting bits of information are collated and considered until you arrive at a reasonable matrix of expectation. Formalities in South America are rather like IRS regulations in the United States: no one can know all the intricacies or keep up with all the changes, so that everyone is at risk. This puts the government in the catbird seat.

Catbird regulations would be our biggest problem on the drive. We had done our best to butter the borders in thirteen different countries. It was possible that somewhere, at some blistering desert border point, our information would be wrong, incomplete, or simply out-of-date. It was daunting to think that, in such a situation, we would have to depend on charm.

I THANKED THE PILOT, unhooked the military-style six-point harness, and went into the passenger cabin, where I put a frozen chicken entrée into the microwave oven. Later, I went to bed in the back of the first-class cabin. It was a three-layered-bunk affair. Soon enough—seventeen hours after leaving New York—we were in Buenos Aires.

It was 12:30 A.M. Buenos Aires time, and the airport tarmac seemed virtually empty. We deplaned and watched the workers unload our truck. It was rolled to the cargo door on its pallet and loaded onto a device that looked a little bit like a construction crane. The truck swung out and swayed just in front of the growling Flying Tigers logo on the side of the 747. There were glaring lights and men shouting in Spanish.

They wouldn't let us stay with the truck. We insisted and were rebuffed. The Tigers people felt that the airport was safe enough. For Christ's sake, just go clear immigration and customs. Get the truck out later.

We were directed to an old red Ford Falcon. A man drove us to the main airport. Two men in blue work shirts were mopping a large empty expanse of floor. There were no commercial flights scheduled that night. The Falcon man took us to a door and indicated that we should knock. The Buenos Aires airport is bright, modern, efficient, but we had arrived at an off-peak time. The immigration official had been asleep. Nevertheless, he stamped our passports with good grace.

We went to customs. No one was there except for a man of about sixty, who appeared to be of Italian origin. He was wearing a miracle-fiber suit that was shiny with wear, and when he saw our cameras he shook his head sadly. "Electronics are prohibited," he said. We couldn't go through.

We found it difficult to believe that a country like Argentina, which has a large tourism industry, would ban cameras, and we mentioned this to the agent, offered it as an observation. The man noted that different countries have different laws. Yes, we said, that was certainly a fact that no one could deny and we absolutely had to agree with him there. It was strange, however, that when we had been to Argentina only a few months ago and had flown into this very airport, there had been no such prohibitions.

We showed the man our letters of introduction from the Canadian government, from various officials in Argentina. We gave him a thick paper handout that described our trip. We showed him our passports. All were in order and very impressive, but it was his bitterly sad duty to inform us that we could not enter his beloved country with specifically prohibited electronic cameras. We were alone with the guy. There was no one around. Over the public-address system, very bad American-style Muzak—symphonic versions of Beatles songs, and at that particular moment, "My Love Is Blue"—were playing, loudly. It occurred to us that this guy might accept a bribe.

The gentleman simply stood there, smiling with theatrical helplessness and shaking his head sadly. He was relatively short, about five five, round, and gray. He had a great W. C. Fields honker of a beak wondrously corrugated by hundreds of tiny flesh-colored wartlike protuberances and striated by branching rivers of veins. I gathered the gentleman enjoyed an alcoholic beverage now and again.

We pretended not to understand. Garry dug out a Canadian-flag lapel pin. We had purchased several hundred of these for just this sort of situation. The high-quality pins—we also had a bag of pins that were exact replicas of our truck—could be used as gifts. We liked the idea of gifts rather than bribes: pin money.

Garry had used the system on previous trips and was of the opinion that every single human being on earth wants a lapel pin.

The man examined the metal maple leaf for some time, then asked if it was something that he could wear in the lapel of his suit. We assured him that it was. This seemed to delight the fellow and he asked if we had any more. Garry gave him about thirty. The customs official said that he really sympathized with our plight, that he wished us the best of luck on our Pan-American endeavor, and that—here he put his finger to his lips—if we did not tell anyone, he would let us pass.

The transaction had taken just over an hour. I had a vision of this gentleman in a Buenos Aires café, sitting there with his shiny suit and glowing nose, proudly wearing his maple-leaf lapel pin as if to say, "Look at me, I'm a real dickweed."

And so we emerged into the main terminal of the Buenos Aires Ezeiza airport which was, at two-thirty in the morning, completely empty except for one sleepy soldier. We had been told to wait in the "international hold" and had no idea where that might be. The soldier said we couldn't go back and look for the truck. We stood there for some time, with our bags, wondering what to do. I asked the soldier for some information, explained the project, and told him that I was an international rally driver, which seemed to impress him. He took me to his commanding officer, who was in an office not far away.

We found out that the truck could not be picked up until the next morning at eight. We had reservations at the Sheraton and decided to go there. Somehow.

Outside it was forty-five degrees and dark. There were perhaps twenty cars parked in the large lot in front of the international terminal. I found a Falcon parked along the curb and saw a man sleeping in the backseat with an overcoat over him. I knocked on the window. "Taxi?" Yeah, he said, I'm a taxi. He'd take us to the Sheraton. And so we left the beautiful Buenos Aires International Airport via the wide and well-lit freeway. The freeway, in fact, is so well lit that thrifty Argentines often drive it with their lights off.

We checked into the Sheraton and Garry said he wondered if we were going to have problems getting the truck out of customs. In New York, he had told Flying Tigers that the truck was worth $50,000. It was a self-declared amount, for the purposes of the flight airbill. The problem was that the carnet stated the truck was worth $25,000. Would we have trouble tomorrow with that discrepancy? The worst-case scenario was that we might have to post a $25,000 bond. Garry was worried.

We had not completed all the work on our visas as well. I needed extensions on Panama, Guatemala, and Honduras, and a visa for Costa Rica. We also needed to check on our "drive-in" status in Ecuador and Nicaragua.

Tomorrow, I would work on the visas and permits. Garry would attempt to get the truck out of customs.

AT NINE-THIRTY the next morning Garry called GM Argentina. Duilio DiBella, the executive who was to be our contact, a man we had talked with for some time on our last trip, was not in. Garry was referred to Raul O. Capuano, who was, in fact, the former director-general of the company until his retirement. Sr. Capuano was a gentleman in his sixties, wearing a tastefully muted glen-plaid suit. DiBella, who was out of town, had asked Raul to help us and he accompanied Garry to the airport to get the truck.

They walked into a long hallway, which was about the length of a football field and which was filled with agitated men dressed in a kind of unofficial uniform of black slacks and leather jackets. The customs agents all carried briefcases and they gathered at tiny open portholes in the wall. Behind the portholes, there were men sitting at desks— perhaps one hundred men and fifty desks—and in that room all was pandemonium: the New York stock exchange conducted in panic Spanish. The customs agents shouted through the portholes at the men milling around on the other side. Behind the desks were goods that had come in by air, and the men were in the process of claiming them.

This appeared as if it would be an exercise in frustration, since just getting the attention of someone behind the wall looked to be a several-hour proposition. Raul Capuano, however, saw someone he knew in the hallway. The man had worked for him at GM before GM pulled its operation out of Argentina. Many of the GM people had gone to work at customs. This man was an expediter assigned the task of helping people with complex customs problems. It was best if the persons with complex customs problems also had money in their pockets.

The expediter opened a door, and Garry and Raul were inside looking out at the faces of the men looking in.

The truck, it seems, had come in late and had not been "put in the system." It would have to be done "by hand." This took five minutes. There was a storage charge of 1 percent based on the stated worth of the truck ($25,000), or $250, for which Garry got a receipt. As for the problem of the stated worth on the airbill ($50,000) as opposed to the $25,000 on the carnet, well, the expediter had to agree with Garry that the airbill was the stated worth for insurance purposes, while, in fact, it was perfectly obvious that the worth was as stated in the carnet. "Flying Tigers," he said, "made a mistake." Still, it would take two or three days to work this all out.

Unless . . .

It was a pretty straightforward deal. Fifty dollars to the expediter and two hundred australs to be distributed to the other workers. Garry cleared customs in two and a half hours.

In all, it was $250 for storage and about $100 for unreceipted services. This was all accomplished with much smiling and a great number of handshakes all around. Garry gave a copy of the trip description—a heavy paper handout with our pictures, an explanation of the run in Spanish, and a map on the back—to one of the customs officials, who promptly pinned it to a bulletin board.

Garry was convinced that it was a good deal. In the normal course of events, it would have taken three or four days to get the truck out of customs, and we surely would have paid well over $100 to stay in Buenos Aires for that amount of time. (Indeed, because of the stated airbill value of $50,000 as opposed to the carnet value, Garry might have been a week or more sorting out problems.) The overworked customs agents made a few dollars. This was not, we were given to understand, bribery of any sort. We had simply paid some individuals to "find" our work on their desks.

Garry had a drink with Sr. Capuano. About a decade ago, GM had pulled out of Argentina. It was a time of extraordinary turmoil. In 1946, Juan Perón had come to power, supported by the military and the labor unions. Perón's wife, Eva, was particularly loved for her devotion to the poor, the "shirtless ones." The government practiced Robin Hood economics: the living conditions of the workers improved but the economy was left in shambles. In 1955 a military coup unseated Perón. A succession of five governments—three military and two constitutional—followed. Perón again took power but died in 1974. His vice president and widow, Eva Perón, "Evita" of rock-opera fame, assumed the presidency. The shirtless ones gathered at her office every morning, but Robin Hood economics left the country in chaos. Radicals—unionists, students, intellectuals—mounted an armed insurgency and there was guerrilla warfare in the streets. Murder and kidnapping.

GM executives were often targets of the radicals. They were men whose parents had immigrated from Italy as peasants and had risen to high positions in the country. They would get telephone calls—"there is a bomb in your house"—and a man would have to decide whether to evacuate his family. Were killers waiting for the family out behind the hedge with guns? Or was there really a bomb in the house?

It was the kind of decision executives were making in the mid-seventies.

The military deposed Señora Perón and set about suppressing dissidents with extraordinary brutality. In the "dirty war" that followed—it was called "the process" or "the trial"—the military crushed the insurgency. Some radicals were killed without a trial.

With the insurgency in tatters, virtually destroyed, the military continued its campaign. "We have," one highly placed Argentine official told me, "a German-trained military."

Intellectuals were rounded up. Members of unions. People who had once been members of unions. People who once knew someone who had once said something critical of the government. The terror was now sanctioned, official, and torture was its instrument. People named names and those they named disappeared, nine thousand of them in all.

The official terror did nothing to improve economic conditions. Still, the one thing the military was supposed to be able to do was fight wars, and after Argentina lost the Falklands conflict to Great Britain in 1982, pressure for a return to constitutional government was irresistible. A civilian candidate won the elections of 1983. In 1985 two of the former ruling generals were sentenced to long jail terms for their part in "the trial."

But in the mid-seventies, with terror in the streets and a failing economy, GM had a decision to make. They realized that in order to be competitive, they would have to introduce a new car. That involved tremendous expense. GM simply decided to cut its losses.

In 1987, Argentines were making an old GMC pickup, importing parts for a truck that was partially built at the Sevel plant, in accordance with Argentine law. Sevel, a consortium of Fiat and Peugeot, was authorized to market the truck under the Chevrolet name and GM had a skeleton staff installed there.

Raul Capuano had been called out of retirement to help with the project at Sevel. He was delighted because it got him out of the house and out from under his wife's feet. We were looking for an electric heating coil for the truck—something to heat up water for our freeze-dried food—and Sr. Capuano called several places, then said he'd look for one for us tomorrow. Garry said, "But you must be busy." Sr. Capuano said he'd love to do it and his wife would thank us as well. It seemed strange to have a former director-general of GM working as a gopher for us.

MEANWHILE, I was burning up the phones at the Sheraton. It seemed wise to hire a translator in my quest for visas. My Spanish was rusty and, in any case, I speak it one painful word at a time, all in the present tense, like Tarzan: we eat much food now; I have many women now.

I finally contacted a translator named Andreas Polacek who spoke good English, seemed enthused about the project, and said he would call the various embassies for me.

At two, Garry returned with the truck, introduced me to the very pleasant Sr. Capuano, and went off to lock the truck in a secure compound at Sevel. The consortium was having a convention for dealers and wanted to display the truck, take some pictures of us. Garry was happy we didn't have to park the truck in some city lot where one of us would have to sit with it twenty-four hours a day.

Polacek called back and agreed to accompany me to the various embassies the next day. He said he would be at the hotel at 8:00 A.M. but that it could take a couple of days to secure the necessary visas.

We went to dinner at La Cabaña, a snazzy steak house featuring enormous slabs of meat. To get into the place, you walk by two stuffed

Herefords in the lobby. It was all dark-paneled wood and waiters in tuxedos. A gran baby beef at La Cabaña weighs enough to seriously injure people who might try to eat it. If dropped from a moderate height, a gran baby beef could squash a small animal, say a cat. The Argentine wine—an '83 pinot noir—was as smooth and complex as all but the most aristocratic of French or California wines. It took a couple of bottles to wash down the beef, which was exceedingly tasty although not nearly as marbled in fat as the best U.S. cuts. It was the finest steak I've ever eaten.

A cabdriver in one of the yellow-over-black Falcons offered to take us to a nightclub where there was "a striptease." He gave us a card for the club with his name scrawled on it. The last time we had been in Buenos Aires, only a few months ago, a cabdriver had taken us to just such a place. Two lovely young women sat on our laps and told us that, as soon as we had walked in, their hearts had begun to burn for us, bearded gringo adventurers that we were. The women were *cuparas,* cup bearers, B-girls, and a waiter in a tuxedo put an opened bottle of champagne on the bar along with a check for what amounted to $190. This seemed extravagant for the vintage and when I said as much, the young women lost their desire for us. More men in tuxedos appeared. There were negotiations that involved a bit of pushing, a few curses in English and Spanish. It seemed that the lovely young women, standing a safe distance away, were doing most of the cursing now. They were, I thought, somewhat fickle.

Garry and I, shouting and shoving, made our way to the door, and I believe that I gave someone a ten-dollar bill. The ten, it appeared, was not enough. More shoving. Garry found a five. Still not enough. By this time we had pushed our way close enough to the door that a quick head fake, a little juke, and a brisk stiff arm took us out into the Buenos Aires night. Our new friends stood in front of the cabaret and shouted merry good-byes. It seemed they believed we were homosexuals.

"I think," I told Garry in the cab, "the place the guy wants to take us? That's the same place."

Since our experience with Argentine striptease had, to date, been neither uplifting nor satisfying in any way, we chose a path of wisdom rather than valor and went back to the hotel.

THE NEXT DAY, Garry telexed the Canadian embassy in Costa Rica concerning the problems involved in bringing a truck into Nicaragua. (The Canadian embassy in Costa Rica handles Nicaragua.) We had been getting conflicting reports. On the one hand, we had been told we would need no visa; on the other, the U.S. State Department's background notes on Nicaragua say that U.S. citizens arriving by land or sea (not air) need visas.

Meanwhile, I met with Andreas Polacek and set off to secure those visas we still might require. Andreas was twenty-two, a slender, handsome young fellow who wore a neatly trimmed beard; he was dressed in a blue blazer and gray slacks, carried a backpack that doubled as a book bag, and might have been a North American student, right on down to his ambitions for the future. He was studying marketing and publicity.

We took cabs to the various embassies, all of which seemed to be in venerable buildings with heavy wooden doors equipped with peephole-intercom security systems.

Panama was easy.

Honduras was a piece of cake.

Ecuador was *simpático*.

More cabs. Because inflation runs at rapid and unintelligible rates, metered cabs in Buenos Aires simply cough up a number every few blocks and that number is a code. The driver hands you a sheet of paper that translates the code into money. It is easier to print a new sheet of paper every month than to recalibrate the meter.

Guatemala was simplicity itself.

Central Buenos Aires might be Manhattan in some places, with garment workers bustling to off-load double-parked trucks and fashionable women in furs walking past glittering shop windows. There are wide boulevards—the widest in the world, the Argentines say—and with the early-morning temperature standing at fifty degrees, it seemed anomalous to see well-dressed businessmen in overcoats hurrying to some meeting while the palms trees were being whipped about by a brisk wind.

Buenos Aires is certainly the most European city in the Americas, a sophisticated metropolis of restaurants and shops. There are great plazas, wooded parks, lakes, sports stadia, and horse tracks, all interspersed with crenelated buildings that call up the architectural wonders of Europe. The National Congress building, for instance, carries all the options for political buildings: a dome, pillars, battlements, and cupolas.

Buenos Aires, except for the central area, has been almost completely rebuilt since the turn of the century. It is a city of functional skyscrapers and buildings that are more experimental in nature. Novelty buildings. Certain experiments are carried too far, however. Art nouveau bathrooms may be momentarily amusing, but square toilet seats are neither charming nor particularly utilitarian.

We passed the Casa Rosada, the office of the president, an imposing pink building which is the same color as the National Museum of Fine Arts. Grand hotels flank the boulevards, and a few hardy patrons were drinking strong coffee at the sidewalk cafés.

People in Buenos Aires are nothing if not urbane. Forty percent of the population of Argentina lives in the greater Buenos Aires area, and the people are almost exclusively of European ancestry.

They call themselves *porteños,* but it wasn't much of a port, not until the 1870s. In 1852, the population of Argentina was just over one million. In the next few decades, during the Industrial Revolution, with Europe booming and the population there rising exponentially, a great demand developed for inexpensive food, for wheat and cattle products. The first refrigerated cargo ships intensified the demand. In the flat, fertile grasslands south of Buenos Aires, called the pampas, cattle were bred and wheat was grown. Argentina never looked to the north, to Canada or the U.S. In point of fact, the three countries were in the business of exporting the same products. And the same process, beginning with subjugation of native peoples, took place. The cattle ranchers came next. Cowboys were called gauchos and a romance as persuasive as that of the American West grew up around them.

The pampas were perfect for sheep. Agriculture.

The riches of Argentina brought immigrants, mostly Italians and Spaniards, with a smattering of Germans and Jews. A significant number of the Jewish immigrants became gauchos. Between 1857 and 1930, over six million people immigrated to the country.

Argentina still stays afloat on the returns from export agriculture. There is little trade with the north. The United States does not need wheat or beef. Argentina looks to Europe for trade and for its considerable style. Europe, in turn, borrows from Argentina.

In the 1880s, a disreputable dance called the tango swept through the teeming lower-class districts of Buenos Aires. By 1915, the dance was a European craze. These days, the tango is a kind of mustache cup of a dance, a quaint anachronism, performed for tourists in immense clubs full of Japanese aficionados.

To a North American, the lyrics of the tango seem familiar: it's country and western gone urban. Take any American C&W song that hints of danger—something like "(Don't Let the Sun Set on You in) Tulsa," a bit of musical advice to a man who has treated another man's woman with a certain lack of respect—take this song, dress it up in a tight suit, slick back its hair, put patent-leather shoes on its feet, paste a thin black mustache on its lip, and you have the lyrics of a proper tango. Put a razor in its pocket for good measure: my wife ran away with the milkman and now someone bleeds. It's arrogant and stylish, dangerous and sometimes sappily melancholy.

The form, it is said, is moribund. Yet the tango, in its sensuality and arrogance, its ardent self-pity and provocative romanticism, somehow informs the character of Argentina.

In the cab with Andreas Polacek, I found myself noticing all the Falcons. The vehicle you most often see on the streets of Buenos Aires is the Ford Falcon. It is generally gussied up with elaborate chrome bumpers, with different arrangements for headlights or taillights, but the car is a Ford Falcon with the dowdy twenty-five-year-old side panels: instantly identifiable.

I told Andreas that I was beginning to think of Buenos Aires as the city of Falcons. Andreas didn't much care for the vehicle himself: it wasn't that hot a car. The new car young and sporty folk wanted was the Ford Sierra, like the Mercur sold in the U.S. The Falcon, Andreas thought, was "for conservative people."

Indeed, during the dirty war, the unmarked black Ford Falcon inspired a kind of mind-numbing fear. Men in leather jackets came into your home in the middle of the night and took your sons away and you never saw them again. They took them away in Ford Falcons, in frumpy little cars designed thirty years ago. It was the banality of evil writ large: terror as a black Ford Falcon.

Falcons, as far as Andreas was concerned, were politically crummy cars. As for the dirty war, he believed that the generals had given the orders, certainly, but that lesser officers had carried out these plans with a brutality that extended even beyond the generals' orders.

There were others in Argentina who felt that the generals had been punished, were being punished, and that expanding inquiries down into the ranks of lieutenants, for instance, constituted a witch hunt of sorts. The lower ranks were only following orders. It was time to sweep the dirty war into the dustbin of history, time for Argentina to look to the future rather than the past. So some people thought.

Crowds gathered in the street to support both points of view. Andreas believed that the dirty war was a shameful episode in his nation's history. Still, something of the sort goes on at a much lesser level in the United States, yes?

I told him that no, I knew of no systematic program of torture, murder, and disposal of corpses directed at any group in the United

States. Andreas shrugged. He was under the impression that all governments do pretty much the same thing. He was a young man of liberal opinions and his comments were vaguely frightening. In a country where kidnapping, torture, and "disappearance" have been rampant for years, terror becomes as mundane and ordinary as an old Ford Falcon.

After securing the necessary documentation for Colombia, Andreas and I met Garry for lunch at the Sheraton. We had only Costa Rica and Nicaragua to go. It would be a piece of cake. We could leave tomorrow for Tierra del Fuego.

THE NEXT DAY, Garry called Jacques Crete, our contact at the Canadian embassy in Buenos Aires. Crete said they would call the Nicaraguan embassy for us. All we would have to do was appear. They'd have our documentation ready for us.

Andreas and I left to do some shopping. We walked down Calle Florida, a shopping street full of expensive shops, newsstands, and good bookstores. The street is reserved for pedestrians. We visited five bookstores before we found a Spanish copy of the *Guinness Book of World Records,* which we felt might be useful in demonstrating to border guards and others what the project was about. There was Garry's around-the-world record, right there on page 120.

"You are a writer?" Andreas asked. "You will write a book about this trip?"

"Yes."

"And will you write about the politics in each country?"

"No. I'd rather write about sewage."

"Oh." Andreas took some time digesting this. How could you go somewhere and not write about politics? It was as if I had told him that I was going to build a house out of peanut butter. He didn't get it.

"What does Garry do?" Andreas wanted to know.

"You mean how does he make a living?"

"Yes."

"He drives."

"Who pays him?"

"People who make milk shakes that last nine months without refrigeration."

"I see," Andreas said, though I don't think he did.

Spring had been a long time coming to Buenos Aires this year. The deciduous trees, the elms in particular, were still bare, but it was a brilliant, sunny day and the temperature had risen to the mid-sixties. Yesterday had been Student's Day—Andreas said Argentina has a day for everything: Mother's Day, Father's Day, Children's Day, Grandmother's Day, Grandfather's Day, Student's Day—and that all were rather unfortunately commercialized. School is out on Student's Day and there is usually a minor riot. Yesterday had been so drear, with a cold wind whipping, that the riot had been something of a disappointment.

We stopped at a camping-goods store, where I found a twelve-volt heating element and a teapot Garry and I could use to heat water in the truck for our freeze-dried food. Garry had looked all over Moncton for just such a coil. To find one in South America, and at the last minute, was something of a coup. We could eat on the record run. It had, up to this point, been a very good day.

WE WENT to the Costa Rican embassy for the second-to-last visa. It was located on the sixth floor of an older building on fashionable Calle Esmeralda. The door, with its security peephole and buzzer, was open. There was a man in a pinstriped suit sitting at one of two desks in the lobby, and he told us to knock on a door with the Costa Rican seal on it. We knocked lightly and waited for ten minutes. We asked the pinstriped man if we should knock a second time. Why not? We knocked and waited five more minutes. Finally the door opened, revealing a short man in a tweedy jacket with neatly combed white hair. He seemed annoyed. Why wouldn't people leave him alone to do his work, his expression seemed to say.

He said he was the acting consul and that his name was Dr. Arnaja. It would only be another short moment he said. Ten minutes later he ushered a woman from the room, a Costa Rican in her late sixties. She wore sensible black shoes, a neat, prim, dark dress, and looked like anyone's favorite grandmother. She had a small sad smile as of someone who had seen a number of tragedies in her life. She took a chair in the lobby across from Andreas and me.

Andreas told me that he had some trouble with the people who lived in central Buenos Aires. In the outskirts and residential sections people were more easygoing, but in the central section they were aggressive, loud. There were merchants "who would sell you a door and call it a house." There were self-important bureaucrats who would delay important documents just to demonstrate their power. There was a name for this sort of insufferable person: *chanta*.

The woman sitting in the chair opposite said that the word wasn't exclusive to Argentina. There were *chantas* from many different countries. She nodded slightly toward the closed door.

There was a frosted-glass window beside the door and some teacups so close to the inside sill that you could make out their colors. We heard a teapot whistle and then saw a hand remove one of the cups. There was the clicking sound of spoon against cup. We waited another half hour.

Presently, the door opened and the good doctor handed the woman her passport with the air of a king bestowing a gift on a simple peasant. He did not invite us into his office but sat in a chair in the lobby and asked what it was that we wanted. I tried to explain the project, which seemed to bore him immeasurably.

I couldn't get a visa, he said, because I was entering Costa Rica by auto and the only way I could get a visa would be if I had, in my possession, a piece of paper from the Costa Rican embassy stating that the truck was in transit. I showed him the map and pointed out that the point of the entire project was to be in transit. Could he himself fill out such a form? Of course, but—and this he explained in the tones of a man explaining something exceedingly simple to a pair of very young children—very few people drove their cars directly from Argentina into Costa Rica. He didn't have the form. Without the form he couldn't give me a visa. This thing we wanted, it wasn't his job.

Abruptly, the acting consul cut the interview short. He disappeared behind the door. We considered the alternatives, Andreas and I. Finally we knocked again. Dr. Arnaja appeared, now very annoyed. Since I did not own the truck, I suggested that the doctor issue me a visa as a passenger. My partner would take care of the paperwork regarding the truck because he owned it.

Such a thing, the doctor said, was unheard of. The very idea seemed to insult him.

We left defeated, and I was depressed. There is no way to drive from Argentina to Alaska without passing through Costa Rica. And there was, apparently, no way I was going to get a visa. The whole project, it seemed to me, hung on one visa and one very disagreeable man. Garry was much more calm about this than I was. "It's a paper war," he said. "Every day a new obstacle. I think we can get them to come around."

Garry had fought paper wars before. It was why we had come to Argentina two months ago: to make connections, to locate the strings we might need to pull in just this sort of situation.

The Canadian embassy wanted us to meet with a man named Roberto Raffo, an Argentine who was planning to ride horses from Argentina to Alaska. We had drinks in a bar that was all dark-paneled wood and hanging ferns. There were pictures of rugby players on the wall. Raffo's projected trip would take two years, and he wanted to make a film of the long ride. Garry suggested that Raffo strike his major deal with a company that could supply film, which would be his major expense. Raffo should not give it all away: he should not sell the project to a single sponsor. The closer he got to the United States, the more people would see that his project was a winner. It would be easier to pick up big corporate sponsors and the expedition should have something to sell them by then.

Raffo asked Garry if there was anything he could do for us. He was wealthy and well connected in Buenos Aires. What he could do for us, Garry said, was figure out how we could put some pressure on the Costa Rican embassy. Raffo said he'd think about it. It might take only a single call from the right official.

We called Raul Capuano of GM who said he'd try to have someone call the embassy in the morning.

Garry had some papers coming from the Costa Rican embassy in Ottawa to his office in Moncton. They hadn't arrived before he left. He wasn't sure what they were. Perhaps they included the "in-transit" form. If not, he could get his visa service in Ottawa to go to the Costa Rican embassy early and see if they had the form. They could fax it to us and we could take it to the disagreeable Dr. Arnaja.

Back at the hotel, Garry called Jane in Moncton. He asked her to check the mail to see if there was a letter from the Costa Rican embassy in Canada, which had been very helpful. Maybe they could call Dr. Arnaja.

It seemed to me that the Costa Rican snafu was critical, but Garry was calmly taking care of other business. Jane should call a photographer named Rich Cox in California. Cox would be shooting us for *Popular Mechanics* magazine and would meet us in Tierra del Fuego at the start of the trip. "Tell him to bring some malaria pills down to us." Occasionally, we had heard, Nicaraguan borders are closed to those who can't prove they are taking the pills. Also, we had not heard from the Nicaraguan ministry of tourism. They had promised us a letter when we visited Managua, something to flash at the border.

It was an hour-long business call. Garry hung up and said that he hated the telephone. "I'm used to Jane," he said. "And she's used to being called from anywhere, used to the work, used to me being frantic. But Lucy grabbed the phone. She said, 'Dad, I miss you.' "

"You should have told her to go watch *Zig Zag*," I said.

Garry would not be jollied out of his sudden funk.

"Little voice from the top of the world," he said. "It broke my heart." Which, as I recalled, was just what Garry had said when Lucy hadn't wanted to talk to him in New York. The little girl could break his heart with a word.

THE NEXT DAY we were up early, waiting for Jane's call. For want of anything useful to do, I tried to see if I could get the American embassy to help me out with Costa Rica. I was shuttled from one voice to another and finally fobbed off on a man who said he really didn't know what he could do for me at all.

For contrast, and by way of making a point, Garry called Jacques Crete at the Canadian embassy. Not only had we met with Crete on our last trip, but Garry had written him frequently with progress reports. Garry explained the Costa Rican problem. Crete said he'd see what he could do.

Ten minutes later Crete called back to say he'd talked to Dr. Arnaja at the Costa Rican embassy. The man was not very helpful, he said, but he had agreed to meet with us again.

"Which is why," Garry explained, "you need to make your contacts months ahead of time. This is why there is such a thing as reconnaissance."

I called Andreas and had him make an appointment with Dr. Arnaja at one. Andreas called back to confirm the appointment. He said the doctor sounded pretty sour on the phone.

Jane called at noon. The Costa Rican ambassador in Ottawa did not know anything at all about a specific in-transit form. It seemed to have been something the acting counsel had made up out of whole cloth for reasons that weren't at all obvious.

The Canadian ambassador to Costa Rica had, however, written a letter to the minister of transportation in Costa Rica requesting his cooperation and assistance in this project. The minister had replied immediately and with grace. Costa Rica, his letter said, saw our trip as a way to promote tourism and inter-American friendship. Jane had a copy and would fax it down to the hotel immediately.

At twelve-thirty, letter in hand, we took a cab to the Costa Rican embassy. Andreas met us there.

We knocked on the acting consul's door. He opened it about twelve inches, muttered something about not being able to get any work done because of all the telephone calls that morning—here he shot us an accusing look—and asked for our passports and the carnet. We slipped the letter from Canada in along with the other documents.

We sat in the lobby, which was the size of a walk-in closet. It was paneled with very dark brown wood, and one wall was a smoky mirror that you didn't want to look into because it distorted your features. Ten minutes later the consul opened the door and handed out Garry's passport along with the carnet and letter. He still had my passport but he seemed to be growing smaller inside his office.

About twenty minutes later the door opened a few inches. There was a tiny gibbering gnome inside and he handed out my passport with a grunt. We examined it. Sure enough, there was a Costa Rican visa there on the page, along with two stamps and an official signature. It said that I could pass into Costa Rica by land provided I had documentation to leave. It was valid for thirty days, and there was a space for a date, but there was no date on it.

"This could mean trouble at the border," Garry said. We looked at each other. "What's he going to do," Garry asked, "revoke it? He's committed himself. He can't revoke a visa because he forgot to date it."

Andreas knocked on the door. There was a grunt from behind the great seal of Costa Rica. Andreas knocked again, somewhat louder.

"This must be dated, could you do that, please," he said with a courtesy I found wondrously excessive.

"Argghhh," the counsel screamed. In point of actual fact, he grunted sourly again, opened the door a crack, took the passport, and disappeared for five more minutes, at which time the door opened only wide enough for an arm to reach out with the passport. Now it was dated. With a grotesque and illegible scrawl.

"What was wrong with that guy?" I wondered aloud.

"He's a *chanta*," Andreas said.

"What's a *chanta*?" Garry asked.

"A dickhead," I explained.

"Guy's got the bad attitude," Garry said. "He can't be having very much fun."

We said good-bye to Andreas, who wished us luck.

The Nicaraguan embassy occupied an entire house and was located on a pleasant, tree-lined street. There was an iron gate leading up to the door. A woman answered the door and asked us to please come back at two-thirty. Garry and I took a walk. It was almost seventy degrees, the sun was shining brightly, and we were both in a good mood. The trees were glorious. In just one day leaves had virtually erupted on the elms. "When we left New York," Garry said, "it was the beginning of fall. The temperature was about the same, but the feeling was totally different."

"I know," I said.

We went back to the Nicaraguan embassy. There was a secretary sitting at a desk in front of large wooden doors. "Canadian?" she asked.

She had been expecting us. They had spoken with the Canadian embassy and were happy to help. The American would not need a visa. Garry's passport was taken behind the wooden door. We should sit in a small room off to the side with Queen Anne chairs, a lopsided chandelier, a fireplace, and two intriguing portraits of Augusto Sandino. One was a filmy monochrome. The other was a poster that identified Sandino as "the General of the Army of Free Men and the Leader of the Anti-imperialist Revolution." I read this to Garry and he muttered, "Shit."

Garry, I knew, had a problem with Nicaragua. He had hated it when we were there and, in our travels, referred to any hot, miserable place as "a real Nicaragua." I found it strange: for all practical purposes, Garry Sowerby was apolitical. I glanced up at the portraits and noticed that, in each one, Sandino seemed to have one bad eye. I wondered if he had been cross-eyed and thought I might look it up someday.

There was a click and then the sound of classical music coming from two speakers. It was something melodically frenetic and slightly discordant, something with violins in rapid conflict that I couldn't identify, perhaps Bruckner. I wondered what it meant. Why here, under the portraits of Sandino? Presently, a voice came over the speakers and identified a Buenos Aires classical music station. An older woman who looked as if she might do a lot of mopping brought us two cups of coffee in flowered demitasse cups.

A short time later a tall dark-haired woman in a sweater that looked Scandinavian came out to smile and hand Garry his passport.

We walked a few blocks, feeling spring come in. "All our problems are solved," I told Garry. "Nothing can go wrong now."

"Don't say that," Garry said.

We walked for a while under the new leaves, for the joy of it, then took a cab back to the hotel. We passed a grassy park in which young people were studying under the suddenly magnificent trees, either that or holding each other for the rapture of spring and their own youth and beauty.

There was a sheaf of telexes and faxes for Garry at the hotel desk.

Good news and bad news. The ship from Colombia that would take us around the Darien Gap was definitely booked for October 10. The bad news was that the documentation involved in getting the truck on the ship would take a day. That meant we should probably be at the port the night of Thursday, October 8. Which meant we should probably start a day earlier than planned. Which meant our schedule was suddenly jammed up. Which meant we had to check out of the hotel—right now—and get the truck 1,800 miles south, to the start of the drive. It would be a relatively easy three- to four-day warm-up drive to the end of the earth.

We drove south through the traffic of Buenos Aires, passing middle-class neighborhoods that looked a bit like something you might see in the Sunset district of San Francisco: neat wood-frame houses and small yards with flowerbeds about to erupt into color.

The roads wound about themselves—it was almost as difficult as getting out of London—and there were occasional hard knots of poverty: a square block of brick shacks, all perhaps twelve feet by twelve feet, hastily and haphazardly constructed, set cheek by jowl on a muddy plain. Through open doors I could see dirt floors and walls decorated with illustrations torn from magazines.

Everywhere, there was graffiti spray-painted on whitewashed walls and roadside political billboards. ELECT A WORKING MAN TO WORK FOR YOU, advised one sign that featured a picture of a real bruiser in a blue work shirt with a noble look on his face. There were small signs, white letters on a blue background, informing the driver that, despite whatever he may have read in the newspaper, THE MALVINAS [Falklands] BELONG TO ARGENTINA. Some of the graffiti I found entirely opaque: ENOUGH OF PAPER, NOW WE WORK FOR OUR CHILDREN.

The traffic was brutal, even when we got onto Route Three out of the city. Though the weather was dry, the road itself was slick with the secretions of various vehicles. Trucks crept along at twenty-five and thirty miles an hour on a two-lane highway.

The industrial section, infested by these creeping trucks, extended for what seemed to be a couple of hundred miles. The sunset on this splendid spring day was intense, consisting of flashes of crimson which muted down to rose, and pink streaked with bands of gold. The whole effect was magnified tenfold by a thick haze of industrial pollutants that hung in the air and took on the colors of the setting sun, so that, for just a moment, that which is ugly by definition partook of beauty.

By eleven, five hours later, we were out of the metropolitan circle, out in the ranches of the pampas.

We were standing there, Garry and I, beside the truck on an empty highway, relieving ourselves under unfamiliar stars. The night was moonless, black, and there were frogs in the irrigation ditches setting up an eager cacophony. The velvet night was full of amphibian mating calls—"take me, take me now"—and the sound of it was odd, a note struck on a large stringed instrument, or perhaps a padded mallet on a metal bar.

"Sounds like marimbas," I said, but Garry didn't reply.

"What?" I asked, and he didn't reply. "What?"

"That telex about the boat in Colombia," Garry said.

"Yeah?"

"It said they had a container for the truck. It's a containerized ship, right?"

"Right. Everything packed in metal crates."

"Well, it said that they had reserved a twenty-foot container."

"So?"

"Truck's twenty-one feet long," Garry said.

It was probably that little uncertainty as much as anything that kept us up, moving, driving until dawn, and then until dawn the next day. It would be much colder at the end of the world and I had been in Buenos Aires long enough to absorb a bit of its style, its mad tango of self-dramatization. The way I saw it, we were running backward in time, out from under spring: we were running directly into the howling heart of winter itself.

ZIPPY'S DISEASE

September 26–28, 1987 · Ushuaia, Argentina

IT ONLY SEEMED like winter over the rugged mountains north of Ushuaia, where eighteen-wheel trucks, unsuited to the narrow earthen track, lay on their sides in the snowbanks lining the side of the road. Jackknifed semis blocked the sparse traffic which consisted, for the most part, of other semis waiting their turn to take a spin through the ice and mud and snow. The big Scania trucks were taking a gamble on a quick plunge over deadly drop-offs so they could unload vegetables, then pick up a load of Sanyo television sets and Philips stereos manufactured in the most southern tax-abatement zone on the face of the earth.

The people of Ushuaia live on a narrow strip of land between the mountains and the Beagle Channel. Ushuaians take an inexplicable pride in the fact that, while they may look up and see the Andes every day, they are not, in fact, an Andean town. "We are situated," one proud resident told me on my last visit, "at the very base of the spine of the continent." I did not say that the metaphor seemed unfortunate. I like Ushuaia very much and the anatomical feature located at the base of the spine is an inappropriate appellation for this graceful little town at the tip of South America.

The road over the last of the mountains into Ushuaia was lined with snow, but spring temperatures, during the day, rose to well above freezing, so that slush and mud made driving immoderately provocative. At twilight, our headlights shone off puddles the size of small ponds, and the ponds themselves took on the sunset color of the sky above, so that our truck threw yellow tracks across sheets of bloody pastel.

I was driving, and after we shifted into four-wheel drive to skirt another defeated truck, we found ourselves alone on the road. It felt like a good time to push the Sierra a bit, to see how it would handle in mud and slush in an environment where a mistake could be highly unpleasant. Garry seemed fairly relaxed about this.

Our rule was that backseat driving was allowed and indeed encouraged. If one of us felt that the other was taking chances, he should say so. The driver was obliged to desist. It was a promise we had made to each other.

The truck took slushy corners on track, and it was difficult to get the back end to come around in a power slide.

"Try the brakes," Garry said. "Get a feeling for performance characteristics in extreme conditions."

We were cruising down a straight, flat road in the saddle between two peaks and there were no drop-offs to consider. I slammed into a full-panic stop, and the truck stopped dead in its tracks. It felt as steady and sure as if it were on rails.

"Antilock brakes," I said.

"Don't think I'll ever buy another vehicle without them," Garry said.

"You want me to push it anymore?"

"No. Take it easy."

"I drive a lot of this kind of stuff in Montana," I said.

"You have a pretty good sense of it."

I had once owned a three-quarter-ton pickup, a Dodge Power Wagon, with full-time four-wheel drive. It got eight miles to the gallon—a real insult to the energy crisis—but it would motor right up the side of a cliff. "I know what I'm doing in a pickup," I said.

"You're pretty good with it," Garry said.

"Pretty good?"

"Yeah."

I thought about this for a time. Pretty good? In ice and snow and slush and mud in a truck? I'm *damn* good.

"In what way," I asked, "would you suggest I could improve?" I felt aggrieved.

"We don't want to get into arguments about driving," Garry said. "We haven't even started."

I drove in silence. We were passing a huge mountain lake, Lake Fagnano. It was seventy miles long and surrounded by snow-covered peaks. The last of the sun glittered across the water in a long, glittering, golden track.

"What it is," Garry said, "you're used to a three-quarter ton. This is a one ton, and we're carrying almost a thousand pounds of diesel. So it's heavier than your old truck. You have to drive further ahead than you do because with this weight, even with the brakes we got on her, she's not going to be able to stop as fast."

"There's ruts in this road," I said. "Potholes that have lakes in them."

"You're still driving too close. Look out further ahead. Believe me, you'll see the ruts and rocks and potholes. It's really tiring to drive close. Things seem to be coming at you faster. You have to make decisions faster. It wears you out."

The sun had set behind the mountains, but there was still a last glimmer of silvery light in the sky. Another lake below the road—there was a sign that thoughtfully identified it as Hidden Lake—was shiny black below the pine trees that ringed the shore. We were surfing down a slope in the mud, and there was now a skim of ice forming on the surface of the pothole lakes.

"Another thing," Garry said.

"What?"

"I'm not criticizing."

"Tell me."

"We have an extended cab, right?"

"You mean this area directly behind us where we've been sleeping? Is that what you mean?"

"The extended cab, yeah."

"I can really see what you mean now, Garry," I said. "Why hell, I should have thought of this before. We have an extended cab. Affects the performance characteristics. Any moron could see that."

"Didn't we agree about the backseat driving?"

I had to admit that we had.

"And I do this for a living, right?"

I took a deep breath. "I think . . ."

"You're sensitive about your driving."

"I think I'm pretty good."

"You are. That's why we got into this in the beginning. When we drove that ALCAN 5000, I could sleep when you were driving. You were steady and didn't take chances and didn't try to push it too fast. I mean, you know what usually happens on a trip like that one? I get people from the automotive press, I let them drive, they want to impress me. They push it. They have no regard for the vehicle. And I feel like I have to watch them every minute. But I feel pretty comfortable with you driving. I think I'll be able to sleep when you're driving."

"Yeah, but you start telling me about the extended cab, like it would have something to do with performance. I almost get the feeling I'm being picked on."

"Because you're sensitive about your driving."

"I'm a pretty good driver."

"Do you know any American male who doesn't think he's a good driver?" Garry asked reasonably.

I didn't. Every American male who owns a car thinks he's hot behind the wheel.

"Any male who owns a car anywhere in the world thinks he's good," Garry said. We were coming around a fairly sharp corner. "Take it into an easy power slide up here and stop."

I came around nicely, in complete control.

"Let me show you something," Garry said. We both got out of the truck and followed our back track through the icy mud. The tire track on the inside corner was only inches away from the edge of the road, where there was a small ditch.

"You're used to a shorter truck," Garry said. "You're used to a truck without an extended cab. So what you're doing is, you're taking these turns too tight, and pretty soon you're going to drop the back end off the road. I mean, what if this ditch was a cliff?" Garry kicked at the tire track nearest the ditch. "About, what, three inches?"

It's extremely irritating to have some jerk denigrate your driving ability which, of course, means your manhood. A wise man, confident of his own virility, should scream back spittle-spewing insults at the top of his lungs. He should stop the truck and say things like:

"Okay, Mario goddamn Andretti, get out of the truck. It's go time."

Unfortunately, when the jerk in question can prove that he is entirely correct—three inches from the damn ditch—the proper response is much less satisfying. A wise and virile man is obliged to drive in silence, to fume and sulk for about half an hour.

Garry Sowerby, big-deal endurance driver. The guy, all he can do is drive. Never went out for sports in school. You ought to see him try to throw a football. Canadian beaver-brained butthead. Dink. Shit weasel.

After passing the obligatory half hour in this way, it began to occur to me that Garry had perhaps a small point. He was, after all, a professional. Maybe there were a few small things I could learn from him. The truth was: I was cutting the corners a little too close.

"You know why I feel confident about this drive?" Garry said after a time. I knew he was trying to mollify me. "I'm confident because we

get along. We aren't going to have any ego problems. I mean, you listen.
You're taking the corners wider now. And I know you can tell me
things and I'll listen. Really. The way you took a little mild criticism:
a lot of guys would have gotten mad, started yelling. Seriously. I admire
the way you listen."

"Thank you," I said, stiffly, bitterly.

WE ROLLED INTO USHUAIA on a street that parallels the Beagle Channel and pulled up in front of the Canal Beagle hotel. Most of the logos
on the truck were covered with mud, and there were clots of solidified
glop hanging out of the fender wells. It was warmer here, below the
Andes, and a cold rain was falling. We'd driven about two thousand
miles and accumulated what appeared to be several tons of frozen black
mud.

"You thought of a name for the truck yet?" Garry asked. The Volvo
he drove around the world was called Red Cloud. The Suburban that
had gotten shot up in Africa was Lucy Panzer. Garry, I knew, loved the
truck and the way it handled. I glanced at the filthy Sierra and, in an
ungenerous attempt to annoy him, said, "This truck's name is mud."

"Wait," Garry said, "the truck will take on a personality. I guaran-
tee it. We'll give it a name then."

The only logos and markings on the truck that were not covered
over with filth were the two large signs along both the side windows of
the camper shell. The signs—English on one side, Spanish on the
other—read ARGENTINA TO ALASKA IN 25 DAYS OR LESS.

We checked into the Canal Beagle hotel. In the dining room, which
was quite busy with international customers, we suffered the atten-
tions of a waiter wearing a dark pompadour that was combed straight
back from his forehead and that seemed all of a piece. Perhaps Bela
Lugosi was his hairdresser. He wrote his orders rapidly and virtually
ran between tables. He gave us a menu and stood there, tapping his pen
impatiently on his order pad. He expected a drink order and a food
order all at once, right now, hurry up for Christ's sake. Garry and I
named him Zippy.

We wanted scotch and water on ice. Okay, sure, you bet, whiz, zip,
he's back at the table. There is no ice. We were stunned, speechless. No
ice? Seven hundred sixty miles from Antarctica. C'mon, c'mon, Zippy
seemed to say. He was shifting about like a man with a bladder problem. Uh, beer, then. Fine. Zip, he's gone. Zip, he's back.

Your beers and now to eat?

Garry and I stared at our drinks. Not beers at all but scotch, without ice. Zippy moved with incredible rapidity and he got almost nothing right. We felt that if we mentioned our little problem, Zippy would be off in a blur of action that could result in something worse than scotch without ice.

A German family at the next table—a handsome and distinguished-looking gentleman just going gray in a way that flattered his looks, his younger wife, and a teenaged son taller than both of them by a head—struck up a conversation. They had seen us come in and had read the truck windows. "Twenty-five days or less," the German woman said as if the concept made her angry. "You will not see anything."

It is a comment Garry hears often about his work, and it annoys him endlessly because he must explain that one does not simply bring the family sedan to one of the most remote regions on the face of earth and begin driving, as if on vacation.

Garry and I had contacts in thirteen different countries, people we knew and trusted, people we had sought out and who were enthused about the project. We knew tourist officers, ministers of transportation, garage owners, government officials, auto-club executives, automobile executives. We knew the communications matrix in each country: where telephones worked, where telex was best. We had studied the roads, the security problems, and the political situations as they applied to each border and to our personal safety. We knew a lot about each country and about how that country worked and about the people in it.

The drive itself would be a physical challenge, but we would also have to have our papers in order, and deal with the inevitable obstacles. There would be nasty surprises, which are always a good way to learn about different cultures. The tourist brochures seldom say things like:

> Dodge gasoline bandits for fun and profit!
> Outrun drunken bus drivers on slippery mountain roads!
> Thrill to mind-numbing poverty and desperation!
> Zorro Uzi-toting terrorists in remote jungle locales!
> Enjoy the staccato sounds of exotic war zones!
> Joke with armed teenaged soldiers!
> Experience the excitement of an automatic weapon at your neck!
> Join the gay, mad festivities inside typical Peruvian jail!

"There is a song in English," the German woman said, "about how you must always stop when there are roses to smell."

"That's a real good song and a swell philosophy of life," I said earnestly.

She was right of course.

On the drive down from Buenos Aires, for instance, we had passed through a town at the edge of the pampas called Bahía Blanca at about three-thirty in the morning. The night had turned a bit chilly, and there were people bundled against the wind, pedaling bicycles all over town. What were they doing? They weren't all going in the same direction: they were scattered all over the city and some passed others going in opposite directions, so, I imagined, they weren't all going to work in one place. They weren't carrying goods to or from market. It did not seem like a middle-of-the-night joyride: people rode stolidly, as if sentenced by fate to pedal on against the night for no good reason.

The phenomenon occupied my mind for hours: the mystery of the night riders of Bahía Blanca.

"Tomorrow," the woman told us, "we will take a boat ride down the Beagle Channel." She said this as if it were the only thing that reasonable people should consider doing. She did not know, of course, that we had seen the same sights a few months ago on our visit to the end of the road. We were, she implied, philistines, boobs.

If I had been peeved with Garry earlier, this woman's comments brought us together in a small spate of seething anger. It annoyed us to have a tourist tell us our business.

Travelers without some goal, some small quest, a bit of business to accomplish, are tourists. It's not a bad way to go, but I find, as a tourist, that I tend to fall into easy patterns: the hotel, the fellow tourists from my own country, the hotel dinner, the guided tour. You see much, but suffer some restrictions. You seldom, for instance, meet local people not involved in the tourist trade.

Garry said, pleasantly enough, "I am not on vacation. This is my job. It's what I do for a living. It's better than sitting in an office, don't you think?"

The distinguished gentleman blanched. Clearly he sat in an office most of the year and did not want to consider the ramifications of a mid-life crisis in some dining room at the end of the earth. He took Garry's comment as a personal affront and grunted at his family to leave us alone.

Zippy whisked our food off the table half-eaten. We stared at our empty places in bemused silence.

"It's a disease," Garry said. "Zippy's disease."

We obediently paid our bill and stumbled off to bed.

*   *   *

AT BREAKFAST in the dining room the next morning, I lingered over my
coffee for an hour and caught up on my notes. The young German boy,
who had not said anything the night before, sat for a moment to chat.
The Pan-American project, he said, was exciting and he had thought
about it all night. How many jungles would we see? How many mountains would we cross? Would there be snow in the north? How does a
person get a job driving all over the world?

The boy's mother and father took a seat in a far corner of the
restaurant. Presently, the mother walked to my table and told her son,
in German, to leave me alone. She did not speak to me. The son gave
me one of those helpless, embarrassed teenaged looks. My parents,
man.

An Argentine lady in her middle years approached the table and
asked if she could sit with me for a while. She wore a flowered dress
and her fingernails were painted green. We spoke in Spanish. Was I a
writer? She herself was a writer as well. More or less. She lifted her
right hand in a gesture of a leaf falling to the ground. Still, she would
like me to have a copy of her book of poems, *Legitimate Creations*. She
signed it for me: "To Tim, on a chance encounter in a far region of my
country."

I glanced through the book. The poems were entitled "Equilib-
rium," "Sibology," "To My Son." My Spanish was not at all good
enough to tell if the poems were any good.

"I don't write intellectually," the woman said. Instead, she wrote
from "the heart." Here she thumped her chest urgently. It was important to make interconnections between people. Was there an English
word that describes the situation where you meet someone and understand immediately who they are? I suggested *synchronicity*. She wrote
the word into a small notebook.

She was from Buenos Aires and felt there was a synchronicity
between writers far from home, as we both were. She had heard of our
project. Everyone in the hotel was talking about it. She didn't understand why the very idea made some people angry. Others thought it
was splendidly exciting.

With my limited Spanish it took a long painful time to tell this
woman that I thought there was a "dark weight" that people feel in
their lives. We call it—and I had to look the word up in my Spanish
dictionary—responsibility.

Responsibility was good but it was not supposed to be fun. A person
who wishes to appear responsible, and therefore good, should not seem

to enjoy his job. Garry and I, however, appeared to be having fun. We were irresponsible and therefore bad. We annoyed some people.

"Ahhh," the woman said, as if she understood. There was a poem in her book I should read. It was about this very idea. She opened the thin volume to the proper page. The poem was entitled "One Hundred Thousand Miles of Promises." It was about the road of life.

"We all," she said, "make different promises to ourselves. That is good. To break those promises, that is bad." She smiled brilliantly, shook my hand firmly, and said she would leave me alone to do my work.

I drove the truck to the airport to meet a flight. Rich Cox, the photographer for *Popular Mechanics,* was coming down to take a few pictures for the story the magazine wanted to do on our trip. Cox was not on the flight.

We were leaving a day earlier than scheduled because of problems with the boat in Colombia. Which meant we had only one more day for pictures. I would have scrapped the photos altogether but the *Popular Mechanics* article was very important to Garry. It was the kind of press his sponsors expected him to generate. We were going to have to do something about photos and do it immediately.

Garry went to the nearby Albatross Hotel and telexed his office in Moncton: find out what happened to Cox. We thought maybe he was stuck in Buenos Aires, having a long conversation about prohibited electronics with a warty-nosed customs official wearing a maple-leaf lapel pin.

In the hotel, there were several large framed pictures of the land around Ushuaia: pictures of the town from the water on a clear day with the snow-capped mountains behind rising against an impossibly blue sky, pictures of golden trees in the fall, pictures of Lake Fagnano. A caption at the bottom of each shot read, "Photos by Eduardo."

We went to the desk and told the man we needed a professional photographer. Could he get us Eduardo? Surely. It was no problem. One telephone call.

Half an hour later a short young man dressed in a blue blazer and gray slacks met us in the lobby. He had a mustache, glasses, a neat short haircut, and carried a large bag containing several camera bodies and lenses.

"Ahh," I said, "Eduardo."

"Yes." He spoke fairly good English but there seemed to be some problem concerning his name. He was Eduardo, of course, and he had

taken the pictures we had seen. Yes, yes, the pictures he had taken
were the same: pictures very like the ones we had seen. They were his
pictures although not the same ones.

None of this seemed very clear to me.

As we were getting into the truck, a local fisherman stopped to chat
with our new photographer. I couldn't help but notice that he kept
calling Eduardo "Pedro."

We drove an hour to the top of the mountain and took some pictures
near Lake Fagnano. Eduardo worked like a professional. It was a
cloudy day, and occasionally the sun would break through so that a
celestial spotlight illuminated the blue-gray waters of the lake.
Eduardo thought he could get some shots of the truck sliding through
the mud with this scene out of a Catholic holy card in the background.

Farther north, men were working to pull another truck out of the
snow and back onto the road. The semi's back end had slipped and
crashed through a metal guardrail. The rear wheels were hanging in
midair over what looked like an eight-hundred-foot drop, straight
down. There were half a dozen trucks backed up behind the wreck, and
we stopped for a few pictures designed to emphasize the dangers of our
expedition.

There were, I noticed, holes in the guardrails about every mile or
so.

Eduardo said these twisted bits of metal did not necessarily indicate
a death. Mostly the big Scania tractor-trailers only went partway off
the road. A wheel might slip but very few drivers died. The last persons
to perish on the road did so two years ago, in a taxi coming over the
mountains from the northern town of Río Grande. It was a snowy night,
the windshield must have gotten covered over in snow, and the car
went over the edge. It took searchers two days to find the taxi, which
was buried in snow six hundred feet below the road.

"Nothing to worry about then," Garry said.

"Oh no," Eduardo agreed, "all very safe."

At dusk we drove Eduardo back to his house on the outskirts of
Ushuaia. The neighborhood was called "Forty Homes" because,
Eduardo explained reasonably, there were forty families living there
in forty separate homes. The houses were newly built of artfully weathered wood, like condos at Lake Tahoe, but they were closely spaced and
set along muddy roads. Eduardo asked us to stop at his photo store,
Bariloche Photo, for coffee. The shop, we discovered, was also his house.
A curtain behind the counter opened up into a pleasant living room set
under a cathedral ceiling.

Eduardo's wife, a pleasant-looking woman with freckles, was watching some sort of variety show on television. There was some commotion from above, and a six-year-old boy and a four-year-old girl bounded down the side stairs and into their father's arms.

Eduardo said that his parents were Chileans but that he had grown up in the Argentine ski resort town of Bariloche. He'd been a tourist guide there for a while and had studied English with a stern Scottish woman who said that his accent gave her "a hiddach."

"What's a hiddach?" I wondered.

Eduardo put his hands to the sides of his head and made a face that indicated he was in extreme pain.

"Headache," I said.

"Yes. That is what she say. 'You give me hiddach, Pedro,' " Eduardo said.

Garry was playing with the little girl, Lorena. He said, "How come everyone calls you Pedro, Eduardo?"

"Ah, yes. Ah. I don't know. Sometimes, I guess, they call me Pedro."

"A nickname," I suggested.

"Yes. I am Eduardo. My nickname is Pedro."

Garry and Loreena were leafing through one of her books: *My First English Dictionary*. There were colored pictures of frogs and cows with the Spanish and English names underneath. In the front of the book were pictures of flags from various English- and Spanish-speaking nations. Garry showed Loreena the Canadian flag, then gave her a dozen maple-leaf lapel pins. The little girl clapped her hands in delight.

"I have a daughter about her age," Garry told Eduardo. "I would like her to learn Spanish. You want your daughter to learn English. Maybe my daughter could write to yours. They could be pen pals."

Eduardo said he thought that would be a very good idea. He seemed suddenly very emotional, choked up about the idea.

It was time for us to leave. Eduardo walked us out to the truck. He kept clearing his throat, as if he had something difficult to say. Finally, at the last moment, during the last handshake, he mumbled, "They called me from the hotel and said some Americans needed a photographer. I am a photographer, but . . ."

Eduardo stared at the ground for a long time, as if shamed by what he had to say. "But . . ."

"But you're not Eduardo," I said.

"No."

This was not entirely a surprise.

"Don't worry about it, Pedro," Garry said.

*   *   *

THE NEXT MORNING Garry took the truck to a local garage to have the fluid levels checked and the mud scraped off. I found a line of cabs outside the hotel. Pedro was sitting in the third one back. It seemed he worked as a cabdriver every other day. I was glad to see him, and realized that I liked him, whatever his name was.

Pedro took me to the airport, where I expected to pick up Rich Cox who, once again, wasn't on the flight. Pedro said there was one more flight, at 3:30. What did I want to do until then?

We were starting the drive early the next morning. There was plenty to do. I needed to buy a few pillows for the back bench seat in the extended cab. On the drive down Garry and I had decided not to sleep in the bed under the camper shell. It was lonely, and it locked from the outside, so you felt trapped in there. At border points, customs officials searching the truck regarded persons in the camper shell as an unpleasant surprise. Guns were sometimes drawn. This complicated the formalities.

I wanted to buy a new coil to heat water for our freeze-dried food. The one I had gotten in Buenos Aires was not very good: it took over half an hour to heat enough water to hydrate the dinners and, in the space of half an hour, in South America, a driver will inevitably hit a large hole in the road, which causes moderately hot water to spill onto the chef's lap. Sometimes, when the water spilled, it was almost ready and very hot. The chef, in such circumstances, wonders about his ability to pass his genes on to future generations.

We had also decided to pick up some canned food which we could eat cold, just in case there were similar problems with the new coil. In addition, we needed garbage bags for trash. And I had two large bags full of clothes to wash.

Finally, I had to go to the tourist bureau and talk with Veronica Iglesias, the "ship" lady, who had told us that she could arrange to have police officers sign our logbook when we left. I wanted to confirm that and let her know that tomorrow was the day.

Pedro regarded this as a large list of things to do. He sped through town, from the laundry to the dry-goods store to the tourist bureau, at top speed. After he had run ten consecutive octagonal signs clearly marked ALTO, I asked Pedro what a prudent driver should do at an Argentine stop sign.

"Look both ways," Pedro said.

*   *   *

RICH COX ARRIVED on the 3:30 flight. The plane out of Los Angeles had been canceled. He had spent four days trying to get to Ushuaia and hadn't slept in twenty hours. Pedro and I piled him into the cab, and we sped down the waterfront to the garage where the Sierra was being serviced. The truck was spotless, ready for pictures, and we had less than four hours of light left in the day.

Cox wanted some shots in the strangest southern landscape we could find. That would be down the west road at the national park called Lapataia. We splashed through muddy puddles at seventy miles an hour and found ourselves in an area of meandering streams, grassy meadows, and trees that had apparently died in a flood. The dead, splintered trunks were a ghostly gray color, and dozens of hawks perched on the bare branches, surveying the lush green meadows below.

We really should have been carefully packing the truck, Garry and I, but, as Garry said, nothing's free. He quite literally owed these pictures to his sponsors.

We arrived back in town after dark. Veronica from the tourist bureau met us at Tante Elvira, the best restaurant in Ushuaia. It was a small place, with fifteen or twenty tables, and the local king crab was marvelous. Veronica said that the police would be delighted to sign our logbooks and escort us out of Ushuaia. They would be out in front of the Canal Beagle Hotel at four-thirty in the morning.

"Why do you not start at the end of the road?" she wanted to know.

Garry explained that the editor of the *Guinness Book,* a man named Alan Russell, had taken another job. The old editor, Norris McWhirter, was now in charge. McWhirter felt that the record should be set from the last settlement in the south to the last settlement in the north. Both were on the water. It was a race, McWhirter felt, from one distinct geographic point to another. The rule would eliminate arguments about where the road actually ended.

"And you double-checked this?" I asked Garry.

"I have it in writing."

It was better, Veronica said. This way the police could be on hand. The start would be a formal ceremony.

Veronica made us feel like important visitors. She was good at her job. Everyone agreed that she deserved champagne. And Rich Cox, who now hadn't slept for twenty-eight hours, had certainly earned his own bottle. Garry and I deserved a bit for ourselves, just for getting the truck to the end of the earth.

It was 11:30 before we started back to the hotel. Darío Iglesias, Veroncia's husband, was waiting for her in the lobby. The police, he told us, would appreciate it if we could leave a bit earlier. Could we start at 4:10 instead of 4:30?

No problem.

It was midnight. The truck wasn't packed, but Garry and I had been up since dawn and we were both very tired. We could pack in the morning.

"What a good idea," the champagne said.

We talked to the man at the hotel desk and told him that it was important that we get our wake-up call precisely at 3:15.

Yes, yes. No problem. Good luck on your drive.

I fell into bed at 12:30 and at 3:15, precisely, the phone rang.

I had a hiddach.

LET'S SEE WHAT THIS BABY'LL DO

September 29, 1987

A WAKE-UP CALL, in my opinion, is not a fire alarm. It is best to loll about for half an hour or so, contemplating the task ahead, which, on this morning, was a month-long drive at top speed through thirteen countries. It was 3:20 in the morning in the last hotel in the last town at the end of the earth. I was reading a small pocket Bible: reading Psalm 91 in search of inspiration.

In Montana, my next-door neighbor, an Episcopal priest named Michael Morgan, had honored me with a blessing before I left home. Father Morgan's house is close enough to mine that he is often treated to involuntary glimpses of a less-than-spiritual life-style. He is, therefore, in the habit of giving me books with titles like *Answers to Tough Questions Skeptics Ask About the Christian Faith.* We do not discuss these books, and Father Michael gives them to me, I suspect, out of a sense of duty rather than any real hope for my immortal soul. This is one of the many reasons that I respect my neighbor. You get your inspiration where it falls, and for my part, Michael Morgan's faith is inspirational.

His blessing had consisted of a brief prayer, smack to the point. Father Michael used to own a motorcycle, a great screaming hog that he liked to ride through Yellowstone Park. Ahh, the wind in his face, the odor of fertile land . . . the sound of police sirens yipping behind. He has since sold the big bike but he knows something of the high edge of the highway.

"Psalm Ninety-one," Father Michael said, "is a prayer of protection. It's a good highway prayer."

My neighbor gave me a pocket Bible to pack away with my newly purchased knife and borrowed bulletproof vest. In a pinch, he thought, when quick action was called for, a prayer might consist of simply saying, "Psalm Ninety-one, Lord."

So, at the end of the earth, by 3:25 A.M., I was in the process of pulling my way up out of two hours and forty-five minutes of sleep. The world felt thick, like fetid custard, and I tried to draw a bit of spiritual motivation from my neighbor's impressive faith.

Trust in God, the psalm says, and

> You will not fear the terror of the night,
> Or the arrow that flies by day.

There came an impatient knocking at the door: bam, bam, bam.

In Psalm 91, the devout reader is cautioned to make the Most High his or her dwelling.

> Then no harm will befall you,
> No disaster come near your tent.

Or I suppose, by extrapolation, your new GMC Sierra.

The knocking became more urgent and protracted. It was Garry, sounding alert and Canadian: a real eager beaver.

"Tim, there're about thirty people standing around outside. The police are there. Everyone's waiting. And we still have to pack the truck."

I read:

> For he will command his angels concerning you,
> To guard you in all your ways.
> They will lift you up in their hands,
> So that you will not strike your foot against a stone.

Bam, bam, bambambam. "We're late! People are waiting!" There was a silence that lasted for a minute or more: an agitated void.

The psalm read:

> You will tread upon the lion and the cobra;
> You will trample the great lion and serpent.

Bambambambam. Garry's voice had an edge to it. "Let's go."

Oh boy. Wake up groggy to a friend suffering a full-blown case of Zippy's disease. It took three trips to carry everything out of the hotel room and I was bounding up and down two flights of stairs two or three steps at a time. We threw suitcases and duffel bags in the back of the truck, under the camper shell, and there was no rhyme or reason to the process. It was all just hurry-up time. People were shouting and laughing in the darkness.

The police were there, four upright officers in comic-opera dress uniforms: all crossed white webbing and lacy cuffs. They signed our logbook at 4:15 for a 4:30 departure. Rich Cox took pictures and Pedro took pictures. Veronica and Darío Iglesias were there along with the young German boy (sans parents) and the Buenos Aires poet.

It had rained heavily the night before and the streetlights gave the scene a kind of gritty film-noir look: long sallow streaks on the dark wet streets. There was the felt presence of mountains, looming above. Strobe lights were flashing randomly in what seemed to me to be a scene of gross confusion.

At 4:43, thirteen minutes after our official ceremonial starting time, we piled into the cab of the Sierra and fired her up.

Garry had offered to let me start the trip. He wanted to finish it, and it was only fair that I start. Garry Sowerby had worked two years for this moment. It seemed to me that he should both start and finish.

"You sure?"

"Do it," I said. "We're now"—I checked my watch—"fifteen minutes behind schedule."

There was a police car in front of us, with the lights flashing. The officers had decided against using their siren in deference to the sleeping citizens of Ushuaia.

"All right." Garry tapped the horn, and the car in front of us took off slowly down the street.

"Let's see what this baby'll do," Garry said.

THE ROAD OVER THE MOUNTAINS had developed more ruts and bigger puddles over the past few days. Ten miles into our trip to the other end of the earth, snow began to fall in great wet flakes that splashed against the windscreen like the flabby kisses of fate.

We made thirty miles the first hour. High in the mountains, in the slush and snow, we were startled by the sudden flash of strobes in the darkness. Pedro had driven Rich Cox up the hill in his cab. They had found a vantage point, and both were shooting pictures of the truck as we shot by. Flash, flash, and then we were alone in the somber snow and darkness, with only a month or so of driving ahead of us.

*　　*　　*

AN HOUR AND A HALF LATER, we were down out of the mountains on
our way around the town of Río Grande. As we descended through a
series of muddy turns, the snow stopped, and the sunrise at 6:20 was
glorious: all shades of crimson and rose against a lowering sky full of
low clouds without a break. In only a few minutes the sun was above
those clouds and the sky seemed suddenly low and gray and glacial.

The land on the north side of the mountains was a plain, perfectly
flat, and it seemed to cower under the weight of the sky. In places, the
sparse grasses were tufted against the hectoring wind. A stand of sage
spread itself flat under the sky. There was an occasional bush, low,
dusty, and whipped by the wind into some grotesque gnomish parody.

There were no trees anywhere, as far as the eye could see, and it
seemed as if the wind owned the land. A man on horseback, bundled
in a coat and multiple scarves against the wind, drove a pack of horses
across a field the color of suede.

The road was dirt and gravel. For a time we ran parallel to the sea
and the Bay of San Sebastián. The ocean was cobalt blue, bold against
the muted palette of the land. A ruffle of penguins on a rocky beach
near the road regarded the truck with mild curiosity. Guidebooks say
there are no penguins on Tierra del Fuego, but there they were, rock-
hopper penguins, all in a row on the low rocky headland. They dove into
the sea in a line, one after the other, like bathing beauties in a Busby
Berkeley musical.

Farther north on the island, the tufted grass turned a deeper dusty-
golden color. Rivers wove through the country in sinuous curves. Geese
by the dozen flocked near one large stream, which, in the glacial early-
morning light, seemed the color of dirty silver. A large gray Fuegan fox
crept catlike through the sitting geese. A black-and-white goose rose
against the fox, its wings spread in warning.

Much of the land was fenced and, in some pastures, robust sheep
grazed placidly. There were a few small lakes and ponds, widely separated, and occasionally the land humped up on itself and formed small
hillocks. When we passed over one of these higher points, I could see
the road to the north, winding on forever through the tufted grass and
low sage.

In places, the road branched and there were choices to be made. We
saw no signs at the crossroads, but we generally chose the path more
traveled. When that was impossible—when there was no discernible
difference between branches—we drove for a time, checking our best
maps against the compass mounted on our dash. I had always thought
a compass on the dashboard was a moronic affectation. On the flat plain

with strange roads stretching out in all directions, it was a necessity. Happily, we made no wrong turns and it usually took only fifteen or twenty miles to confirm our decision.

A rancher's house—the first we had seen—was set just below a knoll and out of the prevailing wind. It was the kind of place photographers win prizes shooting in the Plains States of the U.S.: a broken-down abandoned cabin low in the composition, with the sky and land rolling away in indifferent majesty so that it seems as if the land itself defeated the homesteaders. This rancher's house, however, looked newly built and was freshly painted. It was like a child's drawing of a house: a box with a door and one window on either side. It was dark blue with bright yellow trim—a child's cheerful colors—and it stood out against the leathery-looking fields like an act of bravery.

Where did the rancher get the wood for his house? Had the material come down from the north in one of those big semis? Did one of the big orange Scania trucks simply stop on the road and dump out a load of wood?

Other houses—we could count those we saw on one hand—were similarly painted, but three out of the five were constructed of corrugated metal. The colors on the wooden homes and the corrugated homes were all fever bright: magenta, purple, fire-engine red. They seemed the colors of courage and cheer.

The northwestern part of Tierra del Fuego is owned by Chile, and to catch the ferry we had to pass into that country. There were a series of weather-beaten wooden-frame customs buildings on both the Argentine and Chilean sides. We went from one building to the next, getting our passports stamped, our visitor's cards validated. We filled out forms that asked about our marital status, and our mother's maiden name. An officer on the Chilean side came out to search our truck. We had described ourselves as international rally drivers, and I suppose the Sierra looked enough like a vehicle that might be used in an international rally that the officer simply waved us through. We asked him if he wanted to come with us to Alaska. The comment struck him as a very good joke. Fellow officers encouraged him to go, as if they were tired of having him around, and the officer himself pretended to seriously consider our proposal, as if fed up with his colleagues.

"Let's remember that one," Garry said later.

"What?"

"Asking them to come with us. Seems to soften them up."

As Garry explained it, it was wise to develop an act for policemen, customs officers, and other officials. The idea was to treat them with great respect initially, give them every paper they asked for without much comment, and then, once it was clear that our papers were in order, start barraging them with a blizzard of other papers, good fellowship, and bad jokes.

"We give them," Garry said, "all the required papers, then we start with the handout describing the trip, the *Guinness Book* in Spanish; we show them letters requesting assistance written by bigwigs in their own government. And we do it lightly. We don't want them to think we consider ourselves big-deal guys. Don't want to alienate them or challenge their authority in any way. The best thing, I think, is to start joking when we bring out our heaviest letters of introduction."

So we left the friendly Argentine officials laughing and wearing new maple-leaf lapel pins in their uniforms.

On the Chilean side, we refined the act a bit, then went back into one of the offices where a man sitting behind an old manual typewriter stamped the documents we'd need to enter Chile.

Garry said that I would come to love that sound: the solid thud, thud, thud of the last few stamps on the last few documents.

The road to the north was little more than a cruel joke. It was a dry scar scraped across a monotonous plain and sometime, perhaps years ago, gravel had been dumped into the scar and spread. Now that gravel was compacted and hard as concrete. Large tooth-rattling ruts ran across the road itself, at right angles to our direction of travel. This truck route from the mainland was even more punishing, if less dangerous, than the road over the mountains.

We seldom saw any cars, and the semi-trucks we did see came in small convoys of three and four, fresh off the ferry across the Strait of Magellan. They came barreling down the road, this most important artery of commerce on the island, and showers of gravel accompanied them. In Tierra del Fuego, wise drivers protect their windscreens with chicken wire stretched across a frame that can be raised or lowered depending on the condition of the road.

Garry was checking the rearview mirrors. It seemed that the camper shell on the back of the truck was undulating to the rhythm of the ruts.

"We're going to lose that cap," he said. "It's going to start cracking. We can't take much more of this."

It had always seemed to me that Garry was the star of this trip, the man who could drive any eventuality, and my job, as I saw it, was to keep his spirits high. Consequently, I said something about this being the worst and roughest road on the entire two-continent trip. The concept, as I presented it, was that if we could make it off Tierra del Fuego in one piece, everything else would fall into line.

That was to be our goal for the next few hours: get off Tierra del Fuego in one piece. Garry grunted, preoccupied.

A llamalike animal, a guanaco, stood in the road at the crest of a small hill with the dim sun behind him. The animal was pale-brown with a white belly. Unlike the llama and alpaca, guanaco are not domesticated. The animal's head was silver-gray. It stood sideways to our oncoming truck, then easily leapt a five-foot-high barbed-wire fence.

This route into and out of Tierra del Fuego was the fastest and most direct route from the mainland. The ferry from Punta Arenas, Chile, costs twice as much, takes five times as long, and runs only once a day. If there had been trouble in the mountains, we could have missed the ferry to Punta Arenas and lost a day. Research, I thought, reconnaissance, smart thinking.

WE ARRIVED at a place called Bahía Azul, Blue Bay, on the Strait of Magellan, at eleven-thirty in the morning. The bay, however, was not blue, like the Atlantic near San Sebastián. It was a chill roiled gray carrying high whitecaps. The road to the strait simply ended in a muddy path that ran down to the water at a shallow angle. The wind was fierce.

The ferry was just pulling out when we arrived. Garry and I watched it leave with something less than good cheer. A schedule nailed to a wooden post said that the ferry would be back from the mainland in two hours. As we waited, several of the big Scania trucks rolled up behind us.

We got out in the mud and chill to examine the truck. Garry said that the camper shell, hammered badly on the rough Fuegan roads, was pulling away from the bolts that held it to the bed of the truck. He didn't know if the shell would last and was talking about our options.

GM officials in Santiago, Chile, had our schedule. They expected us at noon on October 1. We knew there was a GM plant in Santiago, and Garry thought they might be able to repair or replace the camper shell very quickly if we gave them a day or two's notice. There was, we knew, a telex at a hotel just north of us in Río Gallegos. If the shell got any worse, we'd stop and contact GM Chile.

"Every time," Garry muttered bitterly, "and I mean *every* time I modify a vehicle, the after-market stuff craps out on me."

I looked at the camper shell. There were some small cracks around the bolts that held it to the cab. That was all. Garry was lying in the mud, under the truck, checking for fluid leaks. It didn't seem like that big a deal to me.

We hadn't had any breakfast—nothing to eat for eight hours—but I couldn't find the camp stove we had bought in Ushuaia. It was buried under the gear we had thrown into the truck so haphazardly. I finally decided to try the new heating coil. It took forty minutes to heat enough water to make lukewarm macaroni and cheese. There was simply no way we would be able to use the coil to heat food on our trip.

It occurred to me that we were embarking upon what was likely to be a long, involuntary diet. The food had been my responsibility, and I had failed. I dug through the mess in the camper shell and brought out several bottles of water, a box of beef jerky, and another box of milk shakes. I wondered if we could exist on dried beef and warm milk shakes. Probably not: we would starve to death long before we reached the first drive through McDonald's. Everything, in all directions, was dismal and gray.

In 1520, FERDINAND MAGELLAN sailed through the strait that bears his name, and everywhere, as far as he could see, there were fires burning. Local Indians, who paddled the sea in canoelike vessels, no doubt watched the alien vessel in the kind of alarmed awe Japanese actors reserve for Godzilla. The fires were signals to others: "It's Godzilla."

Off to my east, not far away, an oil-fire flare was burning in a pit in the ground. The fire looked feeble against the brown land and cloudy water. There were oil facilities on the other side as well and we could see another flare burning on the mainland. No pure-blooded Indians survive on Tierra del Fuego, and these oil flares were the only fires we ever saw on the island Magellan called the land of fire.

Two HOURS LATER, the ferry coughed and spluttered up to shore. It was a small roll-on roll-off barge, which is to say, one end of the boat dropped down to form a ramp, like an amphibious landing device. It could take four large semi-trucks and several cars as well as a pickup or two. The ferry worked the narrowest section of the Strait of Magellan, called, locally, the First Narrows. Twenty minutes after departure, we landed on the mainland and drove off the ferry into Patagonia.

THE AREA around the mainland oil patch was littered with garbage. Fifteen miles later, we were back into the dull brown-under-gray color scheme of northern Tierra del Fuego. Off to my left, in a plain of sage, there were four rhea, large flightless birds, like ostriches. The birds measured about four feet high, and they were standing with four grazing guanaco. As we drove past, the guanaco ran off and the birds waddled along with them, keeping pace.

I told Garry that in Africa, ostriches sometimes run in herds with zebras. He said something about getting rid of the camper shell and maybe using a canvas cover over a stock rack.

Not far into the mainland we passed from Chile back into Argentina and worked on our act at customs. Respect, papers, passports, carnet, forms, jokes, lapel pins. We were delayed by a bus that had just gotten in ahead of us. I found myself behind a tall thin American fellow wearing jeans and a professorial white beard. He was a scientist, he said, and he had been studying a big hole in the atmosphere's ozone layer that seemed to be centered over Antarctica. I asked him if the hole was very big. "It's huge," he said. The man seemed genuinely alarmed and described the situation as a potential global disaster. I decided not to tell him that we had a problem with our camper shell and that the heating coil I just bought two days before didn't work very well at all.

The road on the mainland was not much better than the one on the island. Garry fretted continually and without surcease about the camper shell. "We can," he said, "jettison the shell. Figure a different way to pack the spare tires, and put a plywood board over the bed of the truck."

It had rained heavily the night before and the storm had softened the road a bit. After about fifty miles of somewhat less-punishing driving, Garry began talking about how long the shell might last. "We could get lucky, get it all the way to America," he said.

Just outside the town of Río Gallegos, I changed our first flat, while Garry tightened up the shock absorbers that had taken a bad beating over Tierra del Fuego. I don't know: maybe you don't tighten shock absorbers. All I know is that Garry went around the truck and fiddled with gadgets that I'm positive were shocks. Both of us were lying in the cold mud, working together.

North of Río Gallegos, we knew, the road was paved, straight and very fast. Garry checked the camper shell. It was his momentary opinion that the thing might hold if we could hit the pavement without much more damage.

Río Gallegos is a deep-water port, famous for its nearby colony of penguins and the fact that, in 1911, two famous outlaws on the lam from police in the United States successfully robbed the local bank. As we drove into town I wondered about that robbery. This part of Patagonia is infinitely, immensely, and criminally flat. You could see a man on horseback for about twenty miles. How did Butch Cassidy and the Sundance Kid ever make their escape?

The night's rain in Río Gallegos had been torrential. Wood-frame houses lined streets that ran with muddy water. Some citizens had dug earthen levees to protect their homes, and they had gotten the dirt from the streets, so there were little lakes in the residential section, along with ten-foot-high piles of dirt to skirt. We passed lines of snarled traffic, cars stranded in puddles three feet deep, and helpful civilian volunteers at every corner pointing in every direction and gesturing urgently.

People stared at us oddly as we passed, and it occurred to me that both of us were filthy from working under the truck in the mud. Garry had caked dirt in his hair.

Out of Río Gallegos, we hit the paved two-lane highway, which was straight as an arrow. The compass was pegged on north, due north. I was driving and Garry was doing some calculating. We had come 330 miles from Ushuaia to Río Gallegos and had averaged twenty-nine miles an hour. That included two borders, four separate sets of formalities, a two-hour wait for the ferry, and thirteen lost minutes at the start. It seemed to me we were doing pretty well, but Garry was obsessed.

"If we lose the camper shell," he said, "and spend a day getting it fixed in Santiago, we'll miss the boat in Colombia. So . . ."

We had decided, after listening to enough horror stories, not to drive at night in Colombia. But if we lost a day in Santiago, we could make it up in a couple of Colombian night drives, which, I suspected, would be genuine nail biters. This was not a happy prospect and I wondered where in the back of the truck our bulletproof vests were. I had already lost my combat knife. It was probably lying in the mud where I had changed the tire outside of Río Gallegos.

Psalm 91, Lord.

GEOLOGISTS ARGUE about where Patagonia begins and ends. People on Tierra del Fuego, for instance, do not care to be called Patagonians. They are Fuegans. But there are some scientists who would include the monotonous plain of the northern part of the island in their definition of the great Patagonian desert. Geographers agree that the southern portion of Argentina, below the fertile pampas, is the largest desert in the Americas, with an area, by some definitions, of 260,000 square miles.

The aboriginal inhabitants of the region were thought by Europeans to be surprisingly tall and well muscled. They wore their hair in long bushy mats, clothed themselves in fur against the wet and wind, and painted their faces in a way that terrified Europeans. Magellan named them Patagones, after Patagon, a dog-headed monster in a sixteenth-century Spanish romance.

For a time, English pirates found hideaways in the coves off Patagonia. The Spanish attempted to found colonies to clear the coasts of the English pestilence. None of the settlements lasted for more than a few years. Some would-be settlers were driven off by the fierce Patagones who were, themselves, virtually wiped out by the newly independent Argentines in the wars of 1879 to 1883. The defeat of the Patagones opened up the pampas of the north to stock growing and agriculture. English, Welsh, and Scottish immigrants were attracted to Patagonia.

Today the desert remains rural, and, except for oil works at the town of Comodoro Rivadavia, Patagonia lives on woolly profits derived from sheep. The *porteños* of Buenos Aires like to joke that the sheep of Patagonia are a special breed, clawed animals who grip the spare sandy soil so the howling winds won't send them spinning out into the Atlantic.

The people of Patagonia live a hardscrabble life and seem, for the most part, to be boundlessly exuberant. These descendants of Welsh and English agriculturalists exhibit a kind of brash, likably unsophisticated frontier spirit generally associated with the American West.

The government, in an effort to develop the overwhelmingly rural vastness of Patagonia, subsidizes flights to the various towns of the desert. A flight from Buenos Aires, two thousand miles south to Ushuaia, costs the equivalent of $150, round-trip. These flights are full of large men wearing cowboy boots and hats. They speak a slow, drawling kind of John Wayne Spanish, and smoke constantly during the flight, which makes five stops. At each airport, during the twenty-minute deplaning and boarding process, Argentine stewardesses attempt, without success, to stop the big men from leaving the plane.

"No can do, little missy," they say, or Spanish words to that effect. There are footraces to be run on the tarmac. None of this jogging nonsense: these big men, some of them in their forties, run fifty-yard wind sprints in cowboy boots. The race ends with much shouting, a mock wrestling match, and a new challenge.

*   *   *

THE HIGHWAY THROUGH THE SAGE FLATS was a pleasure, and it was
no trouble to hold at seventy-five miles an hour. The houses we saw,
separated one from the other by 150 or 200 miles, were small, well
tended, and brightly painted, like the ones on Tierra del Fuego. Occasionally we'd pass the failure of some grand scheme: a large two-story
Victorian home with gables, abandoned, beaten dead-gray by the wind
and the weather. The grasses of the desert are so sparse that a year or
two of overgrazing results in pastures of sand. Small family farms, in
contrast, survive.

The small settlements we passed—Santa Cruz, for instance—announced themselves dozens of miles away with bits of cloth and paper
impaled on the branches of the sandy sage. These wind-driven perime-
ters hinted at certain elemental hardships. Living in a place like Santa
Cruz, I imagined, must be like working in space. Anything vulnerable
to the wind would simply float away, never to be seen again.

I thought about this for twenty or thirty miles and decided that I
was wrong. You might see things again. You'd probably see them for
years. The wind blows in Patagonia, but it does not always blow in the
same direction. You could lose something, say a scarf, and have it go
skittering out into the immensity of the surrounding desert. It might
catch on the sage half a dozen miles away. Then, one day, just the right
storm might lift it into the sky and it'd come screaming back through
town at about forty miles an hour.

"Wasn't that your old scarf, honey?"

We crossed the Santa Cruz River, a large, wild, rushing body of
water, running through a wide shallow valley filled with real trees. The
water was a pale aquamarine, and though the valley looked fertile,
there was no development anywhere, only flocks of geese as far as the
eye could see.

Garry was sitting next to me, studying the master plan and trying
to calculate various times of arrival against our progress so far.

I felt like talking. "You know these signs that say *vado,* and the
ones that say *baches?*"

"Means potholes," Garry said.

"There's a difference, I think. It seems to me that when the sign says
vado, there's a little roller-coaster dip in the road. *Baches* are potholes.
Usually with water in 'em."

"We could knock this thing out of alignment, break an axle in some
of the *baches.* "

"You don't see them but every hundred miles or so."

"Watch out for the *baches,*" Garry said.

"That's why I'm not using cruise control," I said, full of virtue. It could be done, but it would be wrong.

"You ever see that movie, *The Treasure of the Sierra Madre?*" I asked.

"Humphrey Bogart, John Huston?"

"We don't need no steenking baches."

"Steenking baches," Garry echoed.

And then, because we had had less than three hours of sleep the night before; because we had survived 330 miles of exceptionally bad road; because we had worried about camper shells and shocks; because we had had one bad freeze-dried meal in the sixteen hours we had been driving; because the road was paved and fast; because the compass was pegged on due north; for all these reasons, we laughed and giggled like schoolgirls. Steenking baches. Ha.

The sun was setting in the north, and we were driving directly into it. In the long slanting light, the expanse of flat brushy land took on a muted aureate radiance, like a golden sigh. The sky was still gray, covered over in cloud, but the northern sun broke through in places, so that long bright streaks, orangish red, spread over the horizon ahead. This far southern sunset took an extraordinarily long time to purple down into darkness.

Every half hour or so we encountered a car or truck running south. Argentine drivers do not waste headlights on the dusk. I was driving with the lights on, just the way American gym coaches teach you to do in Drivers Ed. For reasons that remain opaque, this seemed to annoy drivers in the oncoming vehicles. The road was so flat and straight that you could see vehicles coming at you for miles. The drivers would flash their lights on and off, once. I'd flash mine—dim, bright, dim. A minute, or several, might pass before the other driver flashed again. And then, invariably, these drivers would wait until they were directly in front of our truck and then hit us with their bright lights, full on. A blinding flash in the dark of night as two vehicles roared by each other at about 150 miles an hour.

In full dark, some drivers favored parking lights. There was no coherent local custom. No matter what I did, what courtesy I tried to employ—dims, parking lights, anything at all but complete darkness—the Argentine drivers fired their brights at about twenty feet.

Garry read the master plan under a specially installed passenger-side map light on a flexible gooseneck. I asked him what he thought I should do about the Battle of the Brights.

"Drive safe," he said.

"There's nothing I can do. They give me the brights every time."

"So?"

"I'm going to nail the next guy."

"Good," Garry said reasonably. "Blind the sucker. He'll lose control, crash right into us, and you'll win. Lie here bleeding in the sand thinking about how macho you are. Real good thinking."

"You're right," I said.

"Remember at the embassy in Buenos Aires," Garry said. "Who was it that said that Juan Fangio was the worst thing that ever happened to the Argentine road system?" Fangio, who was born in Buenos Aires, dominated automobile competition in the 1950s, winning sixteen world championship Grand Prixes. We had been told that every male Argentine driver believes he is Juan Fangio.

"Just ignore the Fangios," Garry said.

I told him that I would attempt to err on the side of safety at all times.

"Remember that waiter at the Canal Beagle?" Garry asked. I understood that he wanted to take my mind off the continuing Battle of the Brights before I became entirely obsessed.

"Zippy?"

"Yeah. I thought we had a bad case of Zippy's disease this morning. Did everything real fast. Got it all wrong."

There was a pause. "When I was a kid," Garry said, "I had this teddy bear named Zippy. Larry, my twin brother, had the same bear, but my older brother, Bruce, threw a pillow at it or something. Took the head right off of Larry's bear. So his teddy bear was named Headless."

We discussed our route for a bit—damn! another driver, another flash of the brights—and Garry asked me how I felt. I told him I thought I was good for several more hours. He excused himself, crawled back onto the bench seat in the extended cab, arranged the pillow under his head, and said that he was going to try to get a bit of sleep.

"What's the rule about sleep?" he asked.

"The rule is," I said, "if you think you're tired, you are."

"So wake me if you feel tired."

"Absolutely."

Some Juan Fangio, pushing ninety in a Peugeot, gave me a taste of his brights.

I covered another fifty miles before Garry said, "Headless and Zippy." I realized that he was thinking about his own children.

"Did I ever tell you about this thing Lucy does?" he asked. He yawned hugely and his voice sounded foggy. "She comes galloping into my office, she's got a mop for a horse, and she's wearing a little cowboy hat. Little scraped knees, and she's making the mop rear up like the Lone Ranger." Garry yawned again. "She's done this about four times," he said, "and it breaks me up every time."

There was a brief silence and when I glanced back, Garry was dead asleep.

We had a bank of driving lights mounted on the front of the truck—one-hundred-watt high beams, Halogen foglights—and they were controlled by a series of toggle switches on a console below the radio. We had bright lights on either side of the truck for security and for night work. There were high beams on the back of the truck as well, for the same reasons. All were controlled by separate toggles. I practiced with them for a while on the empty highway, flicking the index, middle, ring, and little finger in sequence—boom, boom, boomboomboom—so that the night exploded in all directions.

An hour later, when I saw a pair of parking lights hurtling toward me, I was ready. I checked the extended cab. Garry was snoring lightly. The car was less than half a mile away. My fingers tingled at the toggles.

We closed to twenty feet and drew simultaneously.

Die, Fangio.

I had him outgunned. Boom, boom: high beams and Halogens, both at once. I could see two dark heads in the passing car. The night blazed with painful brilliance. They were beaten, fried, and I imagined I could see both their skulls behind the skin, as if in an X ray.

No mercy: as they passed, I hit the sidelights, and then nailed them in the rear high beams.

In the side mirror I saw the car weave across the center line, then right itself. I heard, in my mind's ear, the driver ask his passenger, "What was that?"

And the imaginary reply, uttered softly, in humble terror: "It must have been an angel of the Lord."

I felt I was beginning to master the local customs.

BEYOND THE HOUSE
OF PORK

September 30–October 2, 1987

G ARRY WOKE UP about midnight. He made himself a cup of instant coffee using the heating coil and bottled water. The coil was made for boiling eight ounces of water at a time and it did that quite nicely, but gave up entirely when confronted by quarts. We would, out of relentless necessity, live on coffee, beef jerky, and milk shakes.

Garry needed two cups of coffee and twenty minutes to wake up. He took the wheel, and I sat up for a while in the passenger seat. It was my duty, before I retired, to note driving conditions on a yellow pad. I was also to mark our route on the current map with a dark marking pencil. This information went on the clipboard that was stuck low on the driver's side windshield with a suction cup. I thought of this device as the suckerboard.

I wrote that there had been intermittent drizzles, nothing serious, and that if he found himself in the town of Comodoro Rivadavia, he had missed the westward turn to Sarmiento. If he felt good at Sarmiento, the road we wanted continued on to a place called Esquel.

I ate a hardy dinner of beef jerky washed down with two nourishing chocolate milk shakes, and crawled into the back to sleep. The extended cab was not wide enough to stretch out in, but not so narrow that sleeping required an entirely fetal contortion.

It seemed to me, in drowsy repose, that I had been oversensitive about my driving. There was, I realized, more arrogance in my technique than competence. What was that all about? Sociologists, I supposed, would natter on about motor vehicles and male appendages. Was it that simple?

I knew people who would say so. As a young reporter, I had been assigned to cover a number of women's meetings in Berkeley, California, during the early seventies. The women who chaired the meetings called themselves feminists, but it seemed that, stripped of rhetoric, the female persons in question just purely hated men. The meetings were so disagreeable that one of those angry women immediately took up figurative residence in a cobwebbed, contrary corner of my psyche. In certain bad moments, when I am consumed by self-doubt, I get to hear her merciless and hateful rasping. "Little boy thought he could drive, got his feelings hurt, and now he has to worry about his little thingy."

The truth was that Garry was a professional driver and that he was better behind the wheel than I was. It stood to reason and had nothing at all to do with the size of my thingy.

In the ALCAN race, for instance, after five thousand miles, Garry Sowerby had placed eighth in a field of twenty-nine. He was driving a nine-thousand-pound Suburban with a diesel engine. Most of the other vehicles were sports cars costing in excess of $40,000. A lot of Audi Quattro drivers finished behind Garry Sowerby in that event.

And when we'd rented cars in South America, Garry always drove in the teeming cities and handled the scittering confusion with perfect aplomb. He had the techniques of Third World driving down after his around-the-world project. In contrast, I was always flustered trying to horse the big truck through the choked arteries and alleyways of places like Lima or Bogotá.

But that would come. By the end of the trip I'd have it knocked. No problem.

I had a happy vision of the finish line in Alaska: all snow under a blinding sun. "Another victory for man and machine against time and the elements." We'd say it in tandem, get out in the snow at Prudhoe Bay, and shake hands. Garry would then say something about my driving. He'd probably exaggerate how badly I took the mountains to Ushuaia. "You were hopeless at the beginning," he would say, "but by the time we hit the States, you had it. You're as good as anyone I've ever driven with. The best."

We were a team, and each of us had different talents. My job, I thought, was not hot, fast driving. I was there to talk our way past police and customs officials and to take up the slack when Garry was tired. We knew we would go through terrific mood swings: euphoria and depression generated out of fatigue and tension. So: though I couldn't drive as well as Garry, I could contribute by providing the needed emotional balance. I could tell jokes, laugh, and ride my own emotional roller coaster entirely behind my eyes. Let Garry be the hero: I would be the comical sidekick. It was the way to win.

Garry was driving the road about ten miles an hour faster than I
would have. The rule about speed was simple: if you think you're
driving too fast, you are. The idea was to drive just under the limit of
one's abilities. It was safer, and less tiring. You could put in more hours
behind the wheel that way.

The corollary of the speed rule was: if your partner thinks you're
driving too fast, you are. Garry hadn't said anything about my driving
on the long, empty, paved roads of Patagonia where I averaged seventy-
five. Maybe I was starting to get it.

I felt as if I had worked out my sensitivity problem and a wave of
confidence washed over me: we were going to make Alaska in less than
twenty-five days. And, at the end, Garry would say, "Tim, man, I never
saw anyone improve as fast as you." Something like that. I fell asleep
composing a number of accolades Garry would feel compelled to fling
my way at Prudhoe Bay.

ABOUT FOUR-THIRTY, Garry woke me and said he was beginning to
fade. That was the last rule: if you think you're tired, you are.

I made myself some instant coffee, drank it, made another cup,
drank it, and told Garry I was ready. It had rained during Garry's stint
at the wheel, but now, as we rose out of the desert up into the dry
steppes that led to the Andes, the weather had cleared, and brilliant
stars trembled in the southern sky.

Garry's instruction on the suckerboard said that I was heading for
a town called Esquel, then El Bolsón, then Bariloche in the Andes. The
road he had driven had been paved but it took a sharp corner now and
again. There were a few fairly awesome *baches*.

I took the wheel. Garry crawled into the back and fell asleep immediately, without a word. Two hours later I found myself in the town of
Esquel. A long road, lined with poplar trees, led to a dead end and not
to El Bolsón at all. This seemed to be the major road, but there was
nowhere to go, which meant that I had just gotten us lost.

I stopped, compared the map to the compass, and decided I must
have missed a turn somewhere out of town. A bus with a sign on the
front reading PATAGONIA was parked by a station, and several well-
dressed people were sitting on benches under the poplars outside of a
closed café. The driver of the bus said that, yes, I had missed the turn.
It was about fifteen miles out of town, back the way I had come.

When I got back into the truck, Garry was awake.

"Wrong turn?"

I had hoped that I could get us back on the right road while Garry slept. "About fifteen miles back," I said.

Garry stayed awake until we hit the crossroad. He wanted me to go back down toward the desert for a mile, then come up on the crossroad again, very slowly. It was incredibly dark—darker than any road I had ever driven in the United States—and, at the crossroad, the major highway curved around off to the south. There were no signs.

Garry saw what I'd done immediately. The larger, better road went into Esquel. That made sense. It was the largest city for one hundred miles in any direction. The road to El Bolsón looked like a side road.

"How many crossroads did you see in the last hundred miles?" Garry asked.

"This was the first one," I said.

"We can't just blow by an unmarked intersection," Garry said. "All right. Slow down here. Just creep by."

There it was, nailed to one of the poplars. The road sign was a weathered board the size of a carton of cigarettes. It said ESQUEL, with an arrow pointing left, and EL BOLSÓN, with an arrow pointing right. "Which," Garry said mildly, "is why we want to slow down and think every time we hit a crossroad."

"We lost half an hour," I said. I heard an internal warning siren, and a large mental neon light blinked on and off: MOOD SWING . . . MOOD SWING . . . MOOD SWING. I felt like a dope. Garry, I realized now, would never tell me what a terrific driver I was. I cut corners too sharply in the mountains and now I had gotten us lost. "I'm sorry," I said. Intellectually, I realized that this half-hour error wasn't critical, and that I was shooting fast down the first big drop on my emotional roller coaster. It was time to play gutsball but I was a soiled pile of soggy tissue.

"It happens," Garry said brightly. He had caught the tone in my voice and was going to stay awake until he could jolly me out of my sudden funk. I thought: first I get lost and now Garry has to do my job. There was nothing in the world I could do right.

"Last night," Garry said, "in the rain, I guessed on a road at an unmarked crossing. It took fifty miles of staring at the compass and the map before I was sure I made the right decision. That was an hour's worth of navi nightmare."

Navigational nightmare was draining and could cost time. In each of his record runs, Garry had suffered some degree of full-blown navi nightmare—that is, he had gotten lost for a time—and he wanted me to know that this little misadventure wasn't serious.

"You're doing fine," he said. I began to feel better and Garry, sensitive to the moment, dropped off the edge into unconsciousness.

The road turned to gravel and at about six that morning, in the
ghostly light of false dawn, I saw the Andes to the west, straight ahead,
rising up out of an enormous valley. We were crossing a high plateau,
looking down into the valley, and the world seemed to open up all
around in the silvery light.

The mountains were capped with snow and dominated the western
horizon. They seemed to glow, as from within, and the snow had the odd
color of white things seen under a black light. This light felt vaguely
lunar.

As the sun began to rise, the distant snow took on the colors of the
eastern sky, and there was a long period in which the entire world
blushed, pale pink. The valley was set in the rainshadow of the mountains, but it was fertile, alive with rushing rivers. The sage was green,
and the rivers I saw below took on the pale watermelon color of mountains and sky.

It was mid-spring in the valley, and there were trees that looked like
aspens and some that looked like cottonwoods along the creeks. There
were simple ranch houses in the valley with sleek horses running in
the fields. I felt at home in the valley—it could have been Montana—
and thought that this was the most beautiful sunrise I had ever seen.
My eyes began to tear and there was a vaguely pleasant choking sensation in my throat.

Mood swing . . .

In the full light of day, the road turned to dirt and followed the
meandering course of a river running gray with snowmelt. Just before
El Bolsón, we hit pavement. I was careful about the crossing roads, and
was doing seventy when I felt the truck wobble through a turn. It didn't
feel right at all and I woke Garry. I thought one of the shocks that had
taken such a pounding in Tierra del Fuego had failed.

We stopped and it turned out that one of the rear tires was very low
on air. The sides of the tire were blistered and it was virtually useless.
We had one spare left.

"About forty miles back I hit a board in the road," I told Garry. "It
might have had a nail in it."

Garry was silent, sulking, hardly awake, and in contrast to his
tolerance in Esquel, he seemed to be in a very dark frame of mind. I
had just come through a sunrise that brought tears to my eyes and
couldn't help it: I felt good. Garry didn't talk as I changed the tire. He

spent the time working under the hood, muttering something about the fuel filter.

"What?" I asked him.

And in a voice that conveyed monumental despair, he said: "We've got one spare tire, the cap is disintegrating, and I think we got some bad diesel in Patagonia. The fuel filter is beginning to clog up. I just changed it." These were major disasters, his tone suggested, comparable to learning that a loved one has been given a month to live. He poured some of the Stanadyne diesel mixture into the tank while I fixed him a cup of coffee.

"Didn't you notice that the truck was handling differently?" he asked.

"It just started to feel a little slushy around the corners about fifteen miles back. I thought it was one of the shocks."

"Anything changes," Garry said curtly, "anything at all, you stop. You pay attention to every little noise, every ping. And when you're driving at night, you don't go zipping by a sign near your turnoff."

"I'll be more careful," I said, not at all sensitive and full of humble virtue.

Garry took the wheel and began driving in a fierce, monomaniacal manner. The truck had not started at the first turn of the key. "Goddamn Patagonian diesel," Garry muttered. "Clog up our filter and now we have to go over the Andes . . ."

"There's this pirate," Garry Sowerby's comical sidekick said. "He's sitting in a bar, he's got a wooden leg, and this guy with a pig under his arm comes up . . ."

GLACIERS ROLLED OUT of the Andes two and a half million years ago. They advanced on the desert to the east, pushing rock and dirt ahead of them. These eastern moraines formed levees as the glaciers retreated, and the levees held the meltwater. To the west, water was trapped up against the forested slopes of the Andes themselves.

The Lake District of Argentina and Chile is dazzling. There are still glaciers on the high peaks, seven thousand square miles of ice up there, glittering in the sun above blue lakes and fjords surrounded by forests and granite cliffs.

Both Argentina and Chile see this area as a prime tourist destination for summer hiking and winter skiing. On the Argentine side, a new road from the east is being built to the resort town of Bariloche.

I was driving that road, cursing through continuous curves. That, in fact, is what a yellow diamond-shaped warning sign read: CONTINU-OUS CURVES AHEAD. The road was one lane wide, gravel, and it wormed its way along the side of the mountain so that first Garry was looking into a two-thousand-foot drop and then I was. The slopes I was driving were sparsely forested and free of snow, but a thousand feet above, glaciers groaned in the sun.

The continuous curves were closely spaced, and the road was so steep that I had to take it in first and second gear. Garry, who had been sleeping off his last stint at the wheel, was up, watching me drive.

"You got it," he said, apparently comfortable with the way I was driving. He had liked the story about the pirate and the pig.

In certain places, the single-lane road made 90- and 180-degree loops, so that it was impossible to see ahead. Trucks, coming the other way, plunging down the Andes fully loaded, couldn't stop, so that it was sometimes necessary for me to stop and back up, quick, with a big Mercedes semi looming over us, its brakes moaning in protest. Garry helped me find wider spots in the road. We'd back the truck up toward the side of the mountain and let the semi roll by, its far wheels sending little showers of gravel into the drop-offs below. Sometimes the drivers would flash us a V-for-victory sign.

The route over the Andes was, in fact, a major artery, and there were trucks coming at us every five minutes or so. The semis hit their air horns at every turn, and this made enough sense that I began hitting our big air horn on each blind curve. It was an annoying, nerve-racking drive through some of the grandest scenery on the face of the earth. Garry calculated, after taking a half-hour average, that I was shifting every fifteen seconds.

Shift, count ten, honk, count five, shift: it was tedious and dangerous both at the same time. Argentine road crews were working the wider spots with dozens of Cats and backhoes. They looked efficient and experienced.

In one of these areas, we were stopped by a flagman, then allowed to proceed. The crew was digging its way into the mountain side, widening the lane, and there were rocks and boulders scattered willy-nilly across the right-of-way. I was driving a five-mile-an-hour slalom course through them but lost my concentration for a minute and hit a volleyball-sized rock with the right front wheel.

"Jesus," Garry growled, suddenly angry.

I was about to snap back, to say that nobody could drive this stretch of road without hitting a rock (Garry could), and anyway, what damage could I do to a heavy-duty four-wheel-drive vehicle by climbing over a small rock at five miles an hour (break an axle, knock the front end out of alignment)?

"Sorry," I said, too tense to be anyone's sidekick, comical or not.

The road past the construction took a sudden vertical jump and the truck handled it with power and grace.

"I think that fuel stuff is working," I said.

"It's working," Garry said. And then: "Hey, I didn't mean to bark at you back there. This is tough and you're doing good."

Shift, honk, shift. In three bad hours we made forty-five miles. At the paved road just outside Bariloche, I felt that I could honorably let Garry take the wheel.

"I think I'm tired," I said.

I had been driving for eight hours and we were thirty-one hours into the trip.

BARILOCHE IS A PRETTY RESORT TOWN on the southern shore of the 210-square-mile Lake Nahuel Huapí, which is the largest body of water in the Lake District, and the most spectacular. The area was declared a national park in 1934.

It was a calm day, not much wind, and the glaciered peaks surrounding the lake were reflected in its surface: white on blue.

Bariloche is set in the humped glacial rubble below a mountain called Cerro Otto. There were outdoor cafés along the cobblestone streets, and wood-frame chalets perched on low ridges above the town. It felt more like Switzerland than South America.

We stopped to fill a thermos with good strong Argentine coffee, then headed west to the crest of the Andes and Chile.

Above and to the west, dark clouds obscured the mountains. A brisk wind had sprung up on the lake and battered the reflected peaks with whitecaps until the entire surface of the Nahuel Huapí was a white froth. Our route took us along the lake shore, over an ungraded dirt road with sheer cliff faces dropping down to the water.

Garry and I talked a bit about Enrique Gutiérrez, a representative of the Chilean Auto Club. When we had interviewed him several months ago, he had said that the road we were taking into Chile was "very bad."

Why was that?

"It is only an earthen road." While Sr. Gutiérrez was studying a map, Garry caught my eye and made a brief masturbatory gesture. "Earthen road?" In Colombia, when they tell you a stretch of road is bad, they mean that it is frequently the scene of ambushes.

The tourist brochures and auto clubs fail to mention one of the more attractive features of the Lake District, namely that terrorists in Argentina and Chile, where they exist, work the cities. There are no bandits, no drug barons, and no hostage-takers in these mountains.

The earthen road left the lakeshore and shot straight through a forest of sixty-foot-high cypress trees. These cypresses, unlike the North American variety, were tall and straight with heavy trunks and looked a little like small redwood trees. Sunlight fell through the trees in shafts, as light falls in a cathedral.

Presently, the clouds to the west drifted over the road, and the forest seemed suddenly sepulchral and gloomy. There was the brooding threat of a storm. I felt as if I had walked out of Notre Dame Cathedral and into an Edgar Allan Poe poem.

THE BORDER between Argentina and Chile is the crest of the Andes Mountains. Puyehue Pass, at about four thousand feet, is a fairly easy drive, at least in comparison to the fifteen-thousand-foot passes common in Peru or Bolivia. Argentine and Chilean customs stations are both situated well below the divide on their respective sides. We cleared Argentine customs, and started up over Puyehue Pass with Garry driving.

A cold rain fell, and as the road rose, the vegetation changed. Great leafy ferns, six and eight feet high, stretched out to caress the truck. What trees we saw were lower, stunted by the altitude, and their trunks were covered over on every side by moss. The scene felt vaguely prehistoric.

The rain became snow, and some of it settled, unmelted, on the black volcanic mud of the road. A strange forest of low leafless trees was hung with great drapes of moss that looked impossibly green through the falling snow.

At the crest of the Andes, the snow lay three feet deep, and Garry drove for five minutes through what amounted to a heavy blizzard. As we descended into Chile, the snow turned to rain.

A yellow warning sign featured a picture of a car pointed about ninety degrees downhill with a small diamond-shaped hunk of land under it. I liked the sign because the wheels of the car didn't touch the ground. It was going like a bat out of hell, this boxy little car on the sign.

The temperature rose at least thirty degrees, and the rain hissed and steamed on the black mud track ahead of us. Trees erupted out of the earth at this altitude and they were not the straight-trunked variety of the Argentine side. These were trees with slender trunks; trees that twisted this way and that to steal the sun from myriad competitors. They leafed out only at the very top and looked a bit like the broccoli-shaped trees of the jungle.

The road, on this wet western side of the continental divide, became a great green colonnade of trees interspersed by the occasional mountain meadow. At one point, we drove through a cloud of small yellow butterflies, and Garry slowed it down to about twenty-five to avoid splattering this sudden beauty against the windshield.

"Wouldn't hurt a fly," I said.

"No need to."

"Norman Bates wouldn't hurt a fly."

"Who?"

"The guy in *Psycho*. The psychotic killer."

Garry thought about this for a time, then laughed in a manner that he imagined sounded maniacal.

The Chilean checkpoint was located in a forest. Like the Argentine customs officers, the Chilenos wore clean uniforms and were pleasant and efficient. We had passed through four customs points and three Argentine police points on our way through Patagonia, but this was our first search. One of the Chilean officers looked in the cab and another wanted to see what we had under the disintegrating camper shell. It was a mess back there, and the officer simply pointed to boxes at random and asked us to open them for him. Of the five boxes he wanted to see, four contained milk shakes. He seemed bitterly confused about this.

We showed the officer how to take the plastic straw off the milkshake box and insert it into the container. He drank a bit and shrugged as if to say, "not bad." Another half-dozen officers came out to look at the truck and we gave them all milk shakes and lapel pins.

One of the officers signed our logbook. We asked him to note our mileage, the time, and the date. He added his stamp for good measure. When we left, there were seven bemused officers standing in the middle of the road, watching us. They were wearing maple-leaf lapel pins, sucking on milk shakes, and waving.

"The guy who was looking in the back," Garry said, "he didn't get it about the milk shakes."

"Probably thought we were big-time milk-shake smugglers."

"*Mission Impossible*," Garry said. "Men, your mission, should you decide to accept it, is to take these milk shakes to the tip of South America . . ."

"Drive them to Alaska."

"The milk shakes that conquered the Pan-American Highway!"

As GARRY DROVE, I took all our documents for Argentina and filed them away.

"What's happening in Chile?" Garry asked.

I got out a three-ring binder that contained news clips I had compiled over the past six months. The human-rights group of the Catholic church had accused the government's National Information Center (CNI) of using torture. The CNI is an internal intelligence agency whose top official was directly appointed by General Augusto Pinochet, Chile's seventy-one-year-old ruler. Human-rights lawyers were alleging not just brutality on the part of the government, but murder as well, and these murders were committed under the country's embracing antiterrorist laws. There were student protests, a bus strike, and—most painful for Pinochet—growing dissent within the armed forces. Powerful military leaders were telling the foreign press that the next president should "be a vigorous man perhaps fifty-one or fifty-two years old, and he should be a civilian."

On the other hand, everyone we'd talked to said that Chile was a relatively safe place for a foreigner who was not involved in the country's politics. You could drive at night, for instance, and the police, the *carabineros,* would not only not accept bribes, they might actually arrest a person who offered one.

A diplomat we'd talked to was the first to point out what I began to see as a bitter irony. Right-wing countries, known for abusing human rights, were generally the safest. People disappeared from their homes, the press was censored, but you could drive at night.

"So these are nice places to visit," I had said. "But . . ."

"Exactly," the diplomat had replied.

CHILE, as any U.S. grade-school teacher can tell you, is "the string-bean country." It is 2,700 miles long and averages only 110 miles in width. "Chile," Henry Kissinger is supposed to have said in assessing the country's strategic significance, "is a dagger pointed at the heart of Antarctica."

In the south, near Antarctica, the country is damp and cool, not much good for agriculture, but it possesses a kind of soaring beauty absolutely foreign to the rest of the world. In the south, tidewater glaciers formed on the coastal mountains flow down to the sea through dense rain forests. Seals share the beach with hummingbirds.

Seventy percent of the population of Chile lives in the center of the country, around the capital of Santiago, where the climate is Mediterranean, rather like Southern California. The northern part of Chile is arid, and the Atacama Desert there is the driest desert on the face of the earth.

The country's physical diversity and beauty remain abiding mysteries above the Rio Grande. A story is told of a competition among *New York Times* correspondents: write the world's most boring headline. The winning entry read, SMALL EARTHQUAKE IN CHILE; NOT MANY DEAD.

It's a reasonably good bet that not one in a hundred readers would find themselves reading that story. On the other hand, I was fascinated by a piece in my clip file: "Quake in Northern Chile Kills 6, Triggers Slides." The quake in question had happened thirty-five days earlier. "A landslide and rock slides on the Pan-American Highway," the piece in *The Miami Herald* read, "cut off Chile's main north-south road."

Our road.

AT OSORNO, we stopped at a clean gas station that might have been a truck stop in the United States. Garry phoned Santiago to tell them we'd be there at nine the next morning. The truck needed to be serviced, and Garry would require the use of the telex. I filled the fuel tanks, suffering a little pit-stop case of Zippy's disease—get this done before Garry gets off the phone!—and managed to drench my left arm with diesel.

The road ahead, Highway 5, was paved, in good condition, and the compass was pegged, once again, on north. I was driving, and Garry was working on the problems ahead. What were we going to do about the twenty-foot shipping container and our twenty-one-foot truck; where did we have any slack for emergencies; was it possible to get someone in Colombia to do the paperwork for the boat; did we really need to replace the camper shell; was it possible to get to Dallas on time for a press conference GMC wanted to schedule?

Garry was thinking out loud: "So if we get out of Panama on Sunday night . . . let's say we don't get out until Monday morning. Okay. We're in Costa Rica Tuesday, Managua Wednesday, Thursday Guatemala. We hit Texas on Sunday, and, oh shit, no one goes to press conferences on Sunday and GMC is going to have a fit. But, all right, let's say we drive at night in Mexico . . ."

The land was summer green, and large rivers, rushing down from the nearby Andes, screamed "trout." Occasionally, we'd pass a man on horseback wearing a poncho made of a blanket. Men and women rode bicycles past fields where fat dairy cows grazed. There were people traveling the shoulder of the road in horse-drawn carriages. Chilean drivers were generally courteous. The sky was blue and clear.

After sunset, large lumbering trucks seemed to own the Pan-American Highway. The fastest trucks were doing forty, the slowest twenty, and a man felt obliged to pass them. The trucks traveled in packs, like hungry wolves, and every time I'd manage to pass four or five in a row, I'd find myself behind another grouping. Our Sierra, with its weight and its diesel engine, was not particularly fast, and there was plenty of oncoming traffic, so that passing was an unpleasantly tense experience. Estimating our speed relative to the other vehicles was maddeningly difficult: a set of taillights ahead could be good lights half a mile in the distance, or very dim lights only four hundred feet ahead. Pulling out to pass in the face of oncoming lights was a gamble: to conclude that the dim lights meant distance could be deadly. It was one life-or-death judgment call after another.

There was never a time to relax, to glory in having spent some anxiety and skill passing the last line of diesel belchers. It was seven straight hours of driving that consisted of nothing at all but passing trucks.

I felt like Sisyphus, the mythological king who was punished in Hades by repeatedly having to roll a huge stone up a hill only to have it roll back down again. Sometimes, when I found myself out in the oncoming lane with headlights barreling out of the night at me, I felt I had pushed the tolerance a little. At those times, I had to edge back into my lane a little faster than I would have liked. Either that or die. Sisyphus, as I recalled, was punished for cheating Death.

Every truck, without exception, featured a large sign on the back that said, FRENOS DE AIRE, air brakes, but I couldn't help reading the first word as an English cognate: friends. Friends of the air? All of these trucks belched out diesel fumes in great choking clouds that were blacker than the night itself.

"These trucks," I told Garry, "are no friends of the air."

"Why?"

"Can't you smell the diesel? The whole highway stinks like diesel."

"That," Garry said reasonably, "is because your left arm is soaking in it."

"Oh."

"How did that happen?" Garry asked.

"Case of Zippy's at the gas station."

*   *   *

WE STOPPED THAT NIGHT at a motel on the highway about 130 miles south of Santiago. After forty mostly sleepless hours, I fell into bed, fully clothed, while Garry took a shower. My dreams smelled like diesel. Five hours later—and those five hours felt like a luxury—we were both up and I took a shower. The bed I had slept in was filthy with dirt and smelled like petroleum products. It looked like a pack of filthy rabid animals had gotten into a big dog pile and had sex on the sheets.

The road to Santiago was not nearly as infested with trucks as it had been the night before. There was a low fog swirling across the highway, and the trees in the river bottoms, when we could see them, were in full leaf. There were houses two deep lining the road, and fields in the back. A man on horseback, wearing a sport coat and tie, rode along the black shoulder of the road.

On the outskirts of Santiago, we stopped a taxi. I gave the driver the address of the GM facility and rode with him as Garry followed, so we never missed a turn and arrived at nine in the morning, exactly as we had said.

Al Buchanan, GM's executive vice president for overseas sales, happened to be in the office. Buchanan had arranged all the GM contacts on the reconnaissance trips, and the last time Garry had seen him was in his office in Detroit. Al seemed to feel as if he had a stake in our success and was exceedingly helpful. A quick call confirmed that the road in the north had been cleared of earthquake debris. There was a GM factory in Arica, Chile, twelve hundred miles north, up near the border with Peru, where there were some ingenious mechanics who could put in a superstructure under the camper shell.

Garry called the Canadian embassy in Santiago and was told that packages had been hand-delivered to the tourism ministers in Honduras, Panama, and Nicaragua, but there had been no reply from any of them as yet. He asked the embassy to send a telex to Joe Skorupa, of *Popular Mechanics,* who would ride with us from Lima to Colombia. Skorupa was supposed to be at the Gran Hotel Bolívar in Lima. We would pick him up at four in the morning, on Sunday, October 4.

The truck was serviced, but we asked them not to wash it. A filthy truck was less attractive to potential gasoline bandits. We stocked up on tires so that we had three spares on rims and a fourth not on a rim.

Daniel Buteler, an Argentine executive, called GM Colombia to see if they could have someone at the border to ease us through customs there. Buteler said that not only would they have a customs expediter, they'd also provide a chase vehicle to, as Garry put it, "baby-sit us straight through."

We had lunch at a place that advertised itself as the House of Pork. Al Buchanan said that GM executives all over South America were feeling particularly good this week. The company had just broken all existing sales records, and a project like ours was something executives had time to think about. Something to add to the resounding glory of GM and all that.

Al Buchanan had just come from Colombia. He liked the country and thought it generally got a bum rap in the international press, though night driving there was still not a good idea. There had a been a large mud slide just the other day in Medellín, but the road would probably be cleared by the time we got there. Thieves were another problem: they tended to hijack fully loaded trucks, though bandits seldom went after vehicles as small as ours. The biggest danger, Al Buchanan thought, would be ambush and kidnapping. The United States had just extradited drug lord Carlos Lehder. It was possible the drug traffickers might want to take revenge on United States citizens.

We talked for a time about the courteous drivers of Chile as opposed to the Fangios of Argentina. Buchanan said that he had a special affection for Chilenos: they were less aggressive than Argentines, but honest in their business dealings. There was a kindness about Chilenos that moved him.

"You know how they have days for everybody down here?" Buchanan asked.

"Student's Day," I said, "Grandmother's Day . . . "

"Chilenos have a day of the *rotos.*"

Rota is the Spanish word for "broken," but the masculine form, *roto,* was a new one on me. I asked what the word meant.

We were walking out of the restaurant, full of pork, which, for me, was a welcome change from jerky and shakes, when Al Buchanan pointed out a man lying in a street corner cradling a bottle. *"Roto,"* he said.

"You mean," I said, "they have a take-a-wino-to-lunch day?"

"You have to love Chilenos," Al Buchanan said.

THE CENTRAL ROADWAY out of Santiago felt a little like Santa Monica Boulevard in L.A. There were a lot more church steeples, but the haze that shrouded the snow-capped Andes in the distance was depressing and familiar.

Outside of the city, the traffic was bearable and the scenery splendid: we saw vineyards, orchards, small wooden houses, green pastures, and horses behind newly painted white fences. There was a sense of Mediterranean ease that lasted for over a hundred miles.

It got drier and the trees began to disappear. The hillsides, though still green, supported small stands of cactus. Farmland was being worked in stone irrigation terraces. Occasionally, we passed a small town of weathered adobe huts with dirt floors and corrugated tin roofs.

Late that afternoon, we drove through an area of sand dunes and saw the Pacific, glittering under a cloudless blue sky. The road turned back inland, and the desert began to close in on us.

"We are," I announced portentously, "even now rolling into the dreaded Atacama Desert."

We passed a man and his wife in a turbo Peugeot, and when they read the logos on the camper-shell window—ARGENTINA TO ALASKA IN 25 DAYS OR LESS—they sped up to keep pace with us. Garry was driving.

"Fools," he said. "We have two thousand miles worth of diesel. Try to keep up, Peugeot. You'll exhaust your fuel and die in the desert."

Near the town of La Serena, just at sunset, we switched drivers, and the tourists in the Peugeot blew by us. I noticed that, for the first time on our trip, the sun was setting to the south of us. I had a piece of jerky for dinner and pushed the Sierra to ninety, running fast down a big hill toward La Serena, where I could see the festive lights on a Ferris wheel slowly turning in the purple desert twilight.

La Serena, a town of about a hundred thousand, is a growing tourist destination. There are colonial homes, pretty gardens, and a forest of steeples. I caught up to the fools in the Peugeot at a traffic circle on the way out of town. The Peugeot seemed to know where he was going and veered off onto one of the side streets. I watched him, sure now that he wasn't going to go on through the desert, and disappointed that I wouldn't have someone to race through the desolation.

But where was my turn? It occurred to me that I had come into the circle much too fast.

Another car entered from a side street at normal speed. I nearly sideswiped him, and both of us turned away from each other, he to the outside of the circle, me to the inside. From behind, a driver I had cut off hit a long angry blast on his horn.

"You want that turnoff," Garry said, pointing the way.

The street was lined with trees and clearly led out of town, but Garry wanted me to stop. He cleared his throat, tried manfully to speak in a calm voice, gave it up, and began shouting at the top of his lungs.

What the hell was I doing? he wanted to know. "You were doing ninety down the hill into town!" he screamed. *"Ninety!"*

It didn't seem like a good time to tell Garry that I was trying to catch the Peugeot so I'd have someone to race through the Atacama Desert.

"You're doing ninety and you're eating and we've got a thousand pounds of diesel in the back. Tim, goddamn it, you can't drive like me. You don't know the truck. You're screwing up. You get lost, you drive over boards with nails in them, you drive over rocks in the road. You drove fifty miles on a flat tire."

Garry was brutally, almost hysterically angry.

"If I fail on this project, my family doesn't eat!" he shouted. "What the hell's wrong with you?"

I looked over at Garry and his face was lit from underneath by the dashboard lights. People in a fit of rage can look terrifyingly ugly. My own face felt as if it were on fire.

I thought: Nobody talks to me in that tone of voice. I thought: I am going to punch the shit out of Garry Sowerby. Just get right out of the truck and do it right here, on the streets of La Serena. I thought about that for a while as Garry told me that I was driving like a drunken teenager.

There was a little grass boulevard where we could duke it out. Garry said, "For Christ's sake, Tim, you don't even know how to back up."

I wondered, very seriously, how long it would take me to put Garry down. Did I want to do it with a couple of punches, or maybe just wrestle him down, not hurt him too much? Or ... and this thought came as a sudden shock: what if he fought back? What if he fought back and won? I saw myself on my back, humiliated, in front of the cheering throngs of La Serena. No.

My hands were shaking on the wheel, and I considered letting go with a swift, savage, backhanded slap. A warning.

And then if he wanted to fight?

Hell, I'd stomp him like a rat in the cheese box.

But the explosion was over. Garry was still yelling a little, but no longer entirely enraged. "We are," he said, "in a metal eggshell. You have to have respect for the vehicle and for your abilities. I wouldn't try to write like you; don't try to drive like me. You can't do it."

Of course, if we fought out here on the street, someone might get hurt. The record run would be over. And it would be my fault because I screwed up and Garry got mad, and I let that madness fuel my own. Some comical sidekick.

"Tim," Garry said, "promise me you'll take it safe."

I decided, in what seemed an enormous emotional sacrifice at the time, not to punch the hell out of Garry Sowerby on the spot. What I would do was wait until we hit Prudhoe Bay. We'd be standing in the snow at the edge of the Beaufort Sea talking about men and machines, time and the elements, and I'd just haul off and pop him a good one. Bam! That's for La Serena, you shitball.

"Tim, I want you to promise me."

He'd be lying there, bleeding in the snow in front of any reporters that might be on hand.

"Tim?"

I'd tell the reporters that sure, we got mad at each other during the trip and the only difference between us was that I was able to control my temper until the end. They'd take pictures of Garry on the ground, bleeding into the snow. WORLD RECORD HOLDER SMASHED AT FINISH LINE. The image amused me in a bloodthirsty and unworthy way.

"Tim," Garry said, "I seriously want you to promise me that you'll take it safe. Say those words."

"Garry," I said in an earnest voice, "I am going to take it safe."

"You promise?"

"I promise." Oh, buddy, you have no idea what I promise for you.

"Thank you," Garry Sowerby said, and I saw him in an imaginary AP Wirephoto with a broken nose.

"Let's go on," Garry said. "You drive."

I thought: another three weeks and you get yours, pal.

ROTO

- - - - - - -

October 2–4, 1987

GARRY DROVE over a series of low passes that dropped into bare stony valleys dominated by dry riverbeds. The night was dark, and, at the summit of the passes, there was thick fog.

Some people, I thought as I was lying in the cramped extended cab, might not think this is fun. That realization was either a sudden burst of clarity or a rush of self-pity, I wasn't sure which. It was like being quietly insane. Sleep was the best idea.

Sometime around midnight, I felt the truck stop and heard Garry talking with police. Another official checkpoint: show 'em the international driving license, the carnet, the *Guinness Book,* ask if they want to come to Alaska, hand out milk shakes and lapel pins. We had suffered through five such military checkpoints in Argentina, and this was our second in Chile. Garry's checkpoint Spanish was improving.

"Where have you been?"

"Argentina," Garry said, "and we go to Alaska."

There was some confusion then, a burst of Spanish that defeated Garry. I couldn't hear well enough to make out the words, but the officers' voices did not sound angry.

"Tim," Garry called, "maybe you better talk with these guys for a while."

Why not? I'd slept for almost two hours. Why not jump out of my nest in the extended cab and chat with five or six men carrying guns on a foggy mountaintop on an empty road in the middle of nowhere? Negotiate with them in my illiterate Spanish. Perfectly reasonable.

The officers, it seemed, were worried about our personal safety. The pass dropped off into the Atacama Desert. There were gas stations along the way, but they were widely spaced and, in any event, were not open at night. If we continued on, we would run out of fuel and find ourselves stranded in the desert.

It seemed best to show the officers our auxiliary fuel tank. I opened the camper shell and pointed out dozens of quart bottles of water. I climbed up over the mess of duffel bags and knelt on a box of milk shakes that hemorrhaged a thick, gloppy, pinkish-strawberry gruel all over the narrow single bed where our clothes were piled.

Clearing away some of the mess, I showed the officers the extra fuel tank. It was a long metal box set against the front edge of the truck bed, and there were two short boxy legs that ran down the side of the bed. The tank was baffled, that is, designed so that fuel wouldn't shift when we took the Sierra through sharp turns. The auxiliary tank held ninety gallons and fed directly into the factory-installed tank that carried thirty-five gallons.

Five or six policemen stood outside the shell, shining their flashlights inside. We were carrying, I said, over two thousand miles' worth of fuel, which was more than enough to get us through the worst of the desert. I could hear muffled conversation behind the lights that blinded me, and I dug out several of the strawberry milk shakes that had not been crushed. Garry had already handed out lapel pins and was insisting that the man who seemed to be in command come with us to Alaska.

The officers said we could pass. Just as we were about to leave, Garry had an idea. We gave them the pot we had thought we could use to cook food. It was just rolling around in the front of the cab and had become a complete nuisance.

The officers thanked us. One of them, friendly and serious at the same time, warned us that the Atacama Desert was no place for a breakdown.

Garry drove in silence, but the atmosphere in the cab had warmed considerably. Confrontations with police always charged us up, brought us together. We had to work on the act, smile, read our audience, and, together, convince these men with guns to drink milk shakes and advertise Canada on their uniforms.

"Yow!" Garry shouted.

"Yes indeed," I said.

It had been four or five hours since our blowup, and I was already refining my plans for the finish. I wouldn't actually punch Garry Sowerby. I'd slap him, once, moderately hard: that's for La Serena.

"I couldn't," Garry said, "get those guys to understand. You got up and we were out of there in ten minutes."

"Thank you," I said, formally.

We were running down a long steep slope, in the fog, directly into the Atacama Desert.

*   *   *

THE GREAT SOUTH AMERICAN DESERT is a long narrow strip of land
stretching from the Pacific Ocean inland a hundred miles or so to the
snow-capped Andes Mountains. The desert begins a bit north of Santiago and pushes up along the coast of the Pacific all the way through
Peru and into Ecuador. The driest, the most hostile land is the Atacama
proper. It is located in northern Chile, approximately between Copiapó
and Arica. There are regions in the six or seven hundred miles of
Atacama Desert that average a mere inch of rainfall a century.

About six in the morning, Garry, who had discerned, over the past
few days, that I was a passionate fan of sunrises and sunsets, woke me
in the false dawn. We were absolutely alone on the road, driving
through a flat land of dirty gray gravel, and there was a strange, thin
fog on the road ahead. It caught the color of the rising sun, all pinkish
pastels that became a feverish red, and the two-lane blacktop desert
road ahead disappeared into what looked, for a moment, like a slowly
rolling bank of blood.

I was drinking my coffee—we were putting four and five spoonfuls
of instant into a single cup lately—and Garry started telling me a
wake-up story.

"I went to this big party in southern Austria once," he said. "It was
a joint publicity stunt to promote the *Guinness Book,* the Austrian
tourist organization, and Lufthansa airlines. Anyway, they invited
about sixty *Guinness Book* record holders and sixty members of the
press.

"I got an invitation. Turned out I was in Scandinavia, promoting
Motorola, the company that provided mobile phones for us on the
Africa-to-Norway run. I was driving the Volvo, Red Cloud, that Kenny
and I took around the world. So I thought I'd motor down to Austria
for a free party.

"Well, southern Austria is beautiful, and the party went from one
resort to another: breakfast here, lunch there, dinner another place.
One or two of the record holders would do whatever it was they did at
each place: the lowest limbo dancer, that kind of thing. Everyone was
carted around in buses, but I had a car, so I ferried a lot of the press
and the *Guinness* people.

"There was one guy from one of the English tabloids who always
came along. Then we developed an inner circle. It included a French
guy who had eaten an entire airplane. It took him two years, but he ate
the whole thing. I asked him, 'What's the worst part of a plane to eat?'
and he said, 'The tires are terrible.'

"Then, let's see, who else was there? Oh, the smartest man in the world. And a guy from East Germany who rode the world's smallest bicycle. He carried it in a briefcase and was always trying to ride it whenever anybody from the press was around. Guy had a goatee, one of those little pervert beards that East Germans always have. Oh, and there was a woman fire-eater who could apparently eat fifty flames in one sitting. When she did it for us, she was wearing a real bad wig. I figured it was asbestos.

"And the giant was there. Can't forget the giant, the tallest man in the world."

I was warming up to the story. "How big is the tallest man in the world?" I asked.

"Well," Garry said, "he wasn't the tallest man in the world. He was the tallest man in the British Commonwealth."

"How tall is the tallest man in the British Commonwealth?"

"I don't know," Garry said. Five eight, five nine.

We were into the red fog then, but it was curiously dry and left no moisture on the glass of the windshield.

"Actually," Garry said, "the giant was somewhere well into the seven-foot range. Near to eight feet. And I remember I was in the rest room standing next to the guy from the tabloids who was complaining that they didn't invite the sexiest woman in the world, because he wasn't getting laid at all. Then we heard this huge crash, and it's the drunken giant. He came up to the urinal, put his forehead on the tile, moaned a little, and Tim, this guy let one fly you couldn't believe.

"So the giant stumbles back out to the bar, and I turned to the reporter and said, 'Don't feel bad: you got to hear a giant fart.'

"That was the last night, and everyone was getting drunk, at least the inner circle that traveled in Red Cloud. I was driving, careful about drinking, but when we got back to our hotel, the manager opened the bar for us. You have to imagine the scene: me, the guy who eats airplanes, a drunken, staggering giant, all led by the smartest man in the world."

"Did the smartest man in the world seem particularly bright?"

"Oh yeah," Garry said, "he didn't drink." There was a pause. "But he did hang around with us, so that made me suspect him."

"Anyway," I said, "you're in a bar in southern Austria after-hours, drinking with giants and tire-eaters."

"Right. There were bottles of schnapps, a lot of toasts, and I tried to keep up with the giant, which was a bad mistake. I stumbled up to bed, called Jane in Canada, and, I don't know, I fell asleep on the phone. Woke up and the phone was lying there beside me, off the hook.

"So that morning, I didn't feel good at all, and the last thing we had to do, we had to ride this bobsled gadget on rails. Everyone said, 'C'mon, you're the big driver, go faster.' So, of course, I flipped the thing over and broke my finger. When I got back to the hotel, they gave me a phone bill for four hundred dollars."

The story brightened my morning considerably. I thought: how could you slap a guy who hangs around with drunken giants? Who pays $400 so his wife can listen to him snore for several hours?

It was my turn to drive the good straight road.

The Atacama—the whole of the coastal desert—seemed at first a baked mud flat: cracked, dry land, totally devoid of vegetation. The wind sent forty-foot-high dust devils spinning into the distance. Sometimes I saw five or six of them dancing their dizzy fandango over the desert floor.

There were occasional low, rocky ridges separating the larger valleys and plains. Each sterile expanse of flatland was different. There were a few areas of shifting dunes, but most of the valley floors were cracked, flat, black mud plains or fields of dark gravel. One of the more fascinating valleys consisted of nothing but tufts of dried mud. The tufts looked like something that would happen if you put Vaseline in your hair, twisted it around, coated the whole affair with mud, and carefully blow-dried the resultant mess for a couple of decades. All we could see, off to the horizon in every direction, were these strange, twisted, dusty tufts.

The mud—mud that forms those strange tufts—is created during the spring runoff, when streams plunging down the western slope of the Andes pour onto the Atacama plain. Some of the water runs underground, and every few hundred miles there is an oasis. Much of the water comes down in thin, flat sheets. Most of it evaporates rapidly.

The Atacama is a high desert. The bulk of its arid plains stand somewhere near 2,500 feet, so it is not particularly hot. It is, in fact, the coolest place in the world at the latitude. The average summer temperature in the Atacama Desert is sixty-five degrees.

During most of the year, and especially during the warmer months, a cold, dirty fog hangs over the sand and gravel. The mist, called the *garúa,* rises up over the coastal headlands from the Pacific Ocean, where a cold Antarctic current—the Humboldt Current—sweeps northward along the rugged coastline. It is the interaction of warm air and frigid water that conspires to blot out the sun and cool the land.

The fog passes over the desert and rises into the foothills of the Andes, where it settles in hollows or on ridges. In these perpetually fog-shrouded areas, small stands of trees, called *lomas,* literally drink the curiously dry and sandy-colored fog from the air.

Occasionally, the spring runoff may uproot entire *lomas* and deposit them below in an arid salt pan, where the fallen trees are covered in mud, then buried under several feet of wind-blown grit and sand. People dig up these trees for firewood. The Atacama is the only place on earth where people mine wood.

WE PASSED THROUGH the mining town of Antofagasta in the dry fog that was now a sandy gray color. A beachfront road ran along the Pacific headlands, and I could see the working of a large port below. There was a small park where the city had attempted to grow bushes and trees with some small success. We passed a large soccer stadium and a twenty-story-high office building. On the way out of town, the houses began to look like U.S. tract developments, circa 1951: ranch-style buildings with sliding glass doors. One of the doors was festooned with decals: colorful pictures of Snoopy, the dog in the Peanuts cartoon.

On the rise leading to the outskirts of the town, we passed an area where the houses were nothing more than tumble-down metal sheds.

"The arse," Garry muttered, "has dropped out of the living accommodations." His voice was hoarse from lack of sleep and he seemed depressed.

Men in threadbare jackets, dozens of them, walked down the hill toward some common job. They walked with their heads down and didn't speak with one another.

Back in the desert, we saw a house made from blocks of earth that seemed to have been cut right from the ground. When you build your house out of dirt, you are not expecting rain, ever.

In the distance, atop the highest hill that flanked the road, I saw my first hallucination. But no: it was real; I was sure it was real. Twenty miles out of Antofagasta, in the Atacama Desert, atop a high, rocky brown hill that rose above the arid, pebbled plain was something that looked as familiar as a recurring dream.

"Garry, you see that?"

"Yeah."

"What is it?"

"A billboard."

"What does it say?"

"Can't you read it?"

"I wonder if I'm hallucinating."

"It says, PEPSI COLA."

"That's what I thought."

I wondered if this was the driest place in the driest desert on earth. The billboard—it was the only roadside billboard in the whole Atacama—was new and it stood out against the ocher landscape and gray fog. It was the most effective piece of advertising I had ever seen in my life.

"I want a Pepsi," I heard myself whine and realized, in that moment, why all billboards should be banned.

Garry said, "Well, we have our choice of water or milk shakes." He was definitely feeling low, and it occurred to me—after reviewing our various ups and downs to date—that Garry's spirits tended to sink just after sunrise. I hit the low point on my roller coaster a couple of hours before the sun set.

At 7:12 that morning the fog let up and we passed over the Tropic of Capricorn. I stopped to get breakfast—beef jerky and milk shakes— out of the camper shell. Garry came out and we sat on the tailgate: a sit-down breakfast. There was a fetid sour-milk smell inside the camper shell.

I made an attempt to haul Garry out of his morning funk by asking about his family.

"Ahhh," he muttered. Then: "I feel a little guilty talking about Lucy all the time. I have another daughter. And, oh man, after she was born, I just felt so down and bitter and guilty and dirty . . . "

We sat in silence, chewing the beef jerky that was making both of our jaws ache.

"I never told anyone this," Garry said. "Not even Jane."

He looked stricken.

"I knew, when Natalie came home," he said, "that I would never love her as much as I love Lucy."

The land all around was flat and sandy gray.

"I think every father feels that way about his second child," I said. "It's natural. I don't care what parents say, an infant doesn't have much in the way of a personality."

"No lights on," Garry said, "no one home."

"And everyone feels guilty and no one says anything, so you end up feeling that there's something wrong with you. When there isn't."

"I guess," Garry said. He was sounding a little brighter. "And Natalie is almost six months old now. Just before I left for this trip, it really started to happen. I began to see who she is, to get to know her. A couple of times, Jane and I would be in bed, and I would hear her fussing in her room. Jane's exhausted, and it's my turn anyway, so I go check on Nat. But she's not fussing at all. I can see her in the night-light. She's smiling and laughing and looking at her feet, her hands. This wonderful little baby, my daughter, lost in infant ecstasy."

I glanced over and caught Garry smiling.

"Let's play some music," I said.

We had two audiotapes. Each of us had thought the other was to bring tapes, so all we had was a tango that I had bought in Argentina, mainly because I wanted to study the lyrics. Garry, I knew, was pretty sick of that one. The other tape was something Garry had put in the cassette in Canada and forgotten about. I thought we should dine alfresco, to music, and put Garry's tape on at full volume. George Jones and Merle Haggard were singing a mournful duet about lost love and loneliness: "She's out there somewhere, looking for me . . . "

We drank our milk shakes and stared out into the lifeless world of the Atacama Desert.

THE NEXT TOWN was Iquique. In 1835 Charles Darwin visited the port city of Iquique and traveled briefly inland, into the Atacama. Darwin, as always, took copious notes, and wrote that he was getting pretty damn tired of the adjectives *barren* and *sterile*.

Ironically, it is the ocean that has left the land so dry and lifeless. The same icy current that sends its dirty fog rolling over the sand also creates an impenetrable high-pressure dome over the land. Pacific storms, moving in from the west, bump up against the dome and skitter off to the north or south. The strongest of the storms slide up over the dome, like a skier over a mogul, and dump their moisture on the slopes of the Andes. It is this perpetual high-pressure ridge that has parched the Atacama over the centuries. Indeed, there are small areas in the desert where it has never been known to rain, where nothing grows and nothing lives. Nothing.

The Atacama makes Death Valley look like a zoo set in a botanical garden. During a Death Valley summer, there will be coyote tracks in the central valley, and burros beyond counting feeding on the sage of the higher hillsides. Compare this to the observations of Clement W. Meighan, an archaeologist who has done fieldwork in the Atacama. During a month at one site, a list was compiled of animals seen. The list consisted of one bird and one butterfly, both transients on their way from one oasis to another. The one permanent resident of the camp was a spider. There were also "a few flies."

When you get down to counting flies, there's not much life around. What there is, is death.

The first of the mummies discovered in the Atacama Desert were thought to be a thousand years old. They were found several decades ago by an iron-willed renaissance Jesuit, Father Le Paige, who often took payment for marriages and baptisms in archaeological artifacts. Father Le Paige has passed on to his just reward, but his collection can be found in the museum at San Pedro de Atacama, an oasis in the heart of the desert.

Deserts are attractive places for archaeologists because of the excellent preservation of the sites and artifacts. Even bodies.

Recently, anthropologists from the University of Tarapacá in Chile discovered ninety-six mummies near the town of Arica, on the border between Chile and Peru. Some of the remains were eight thousand years old, three thousand years older than the mummies of Egypt.

The oasis-dwelling people of the ancient Atacama—Atacamanos— apparently used pelican beaks to strip the corpses of flesh. The abdominal cavities were emptied, filled with feathers, and the long bones of the arms and legs were reinforced with sticks. It is thought that the bodies may have been placed upright in the village in a macabre ritual. For burial, the corpses were wrapped in layers of cloth, the finest closest to the body, the coarsest grade on the outside. The dry desert air preserves fatality, and autopsies performed on rehydrated mummies have pinpointed the causes of deaths that occurred at the dawn of civilization. The autopsies have also revealed some puzzling stuff. What to make of this knowledge: 25 percent of the ancient desert people, it seemed, suffered from chronic ear infections.

The Atacamanos knew well that their climate preserves death. So do modern men. A few hundred miles north of Arica, there are other burial sites. Several travelers—notably Michael Andrews, a British filmmaker—have stumbled through that perpetual ocher fog and found themselves standing in the midst of fields of bleached bones: they have seen human skulls, scattered like soccer balls, grinning up from the sand.

Grave robbers are interested primarily in the textiles used to wrap the bodies. Those once made in Paracas, Peru, for instance, are noted for their elegance: perfectly perserved tapestries woven by unknown artists two thousand years ago. The textiles bring a pretty price, and grave robbers, Michael Andrews noted, are "none too discriminating: some of the staring skulls wear collars and ties."

*   *   *

THERE WAS, along this fast desert highway, a scene of past horror from the more recent past every fifty or sixty miles. You could see them glittering alongside the road in a bullying sun that had finally burnt away the fog. Automobiles that collide in the Atacama are salvaged. The broken glass is not. It is swept to the side of the road into a heap, and every time I saw such a pile flashing in the distance, I thought of bodies bleeding in the sand, on the burning asphalt, here, in this lonely, hostile desert.

GARRY SLEPT WELL and took the wheel about one that afternoon. We stopped to check the truck, and Garry thought he found a leak by the radiator.

We were rising out of the Atacama, pushing over passes through high rounded hills covered over in grainy black sand. When I looked ahead or to the side, I could see faint hints of green or red in the land. The green was, what, copper; the red, iron. A man wouldn't have to be much of a geologist to locate mineral deposits here.

We were careening over the hills, and Garry took the corners at a speed that made our tires scream against the blacktop. I thought he was pushing too hard and said so.

"We need to push it," Garry said. "Gotta see if the radiator will hold. We've got fifty miles into Arica, where they have the GM factory. If the radiator has a hole in it, I'm going to blow it out, and we'll get it fixed."

But the radiator wasn't leaking and we both knew it. We always had leaks under the truck after it was serviced. Mechanics, who were given to understand by their bosses that our mission was important, tended to overfill anything that required fluid. There was no room left for heat expansion, and things leaked for a day or so after every service.

We took a hillside on what felt like two wheels. I looked below and saw the line of a boulder that had rolled down the black sand. It looked like the track of a snowball rolling down a powder slope. I had a vision of the Sierra jumping the road and rolling, end over end, down the hill, leaving a curious hop-and-skip track.

"This," Garry said, concentrating fiercely, "is the classic situation for a gauge to be just about ten feet high on the dash."

"What?"

"The temperature gauge is the gauge of the day. Did you ever see a horror film called *Videodrome*? TVs and things start swelling up to abnormal size."

It occurred to me that Garry needed a daily crisis to keep him going,

and if we didn't have a crisis, he'd invent one. It was late afternoon and
I was at the low end of my cycle, feeling sorry for myself, stuck, as I
was, in a speeding truck driven by a madman through a land of horror,
where glittering glass on the side of the road meant death and dismem-
berment. . . .

"What's going on?" Garry asked.

"Depressed again," I said.

"What do you need?"

"Silence in which to brood."

WE PULLED INTO ARICA, near the border with Peru, at three-thirty
that afternoon, found the GM plant with no difficulty, and met with the
plant manager, Oscar Nuenschwander, who was expecting us. There
was a message for Garry from Daniel Buteler, of GM Chile. Call him.

So for half an hour, Garry talked to a man in Santiago, Chile,
concerning a telex that Buteler had gotten from Jane, in Canada,
which was about a call she had received from a publicity firm in L.A.
The firm was setting up a press conference for us in the United States.
People wanted to know the exact time we would be arriving in Dallas.
These people in L.A. had never heard of gasoline bandits: it seemed a
surreal phone call.

Garry had decided against reinforcing the camper shell. It had not
gotten any worse since Tierra del Fuego. While he supervised the
mechanics—the radiator was fine; any leaks were the result of overfill-
ing—Mr. Nuenschwander ran me down to the Chilean Auto Club in his
personal car.

We had heard that in order to enter Peru we would need some
document from the Chilean Auto Club. Then, in Peru, we needed a
corresponding document from that country's auto club. When we had
both documents, we would be issued decals to put on the windows.
Without the decals, police could turn us back.

A young man at the auto club said no such documents were necessary.

For a certainty?

An absolute certainty.

Why had auto-club people in Lima invented these documents then?

Who could say?

GARRY, IMAGINING that we had to clear the border and get to the
Peruvian Touring and Automobile Club before a five o'clock closing
time, was whipping the mechanics into a froth. There were five of them

in white lab coats, dashing back and forth, waving their arms and screaming about the fuel filter. Garry was, I saw, filthy and not completely coherent. He had a virulent case of Zippy's, which he had passed on to five competent and otherwise intelligent individuals in the space of one hour, Zippy's being somewhat contagious.

Garry was happy to hear that we wouldn't have to race through customs. Given the state of our affairs, however, it seemed cruel to mention a bit of bad planning on our part that had just occurred to me. There was a curfew from midnight to 5:00 A.M. in Lima. We couldn't pick up Joe Skorupa there at 4:00 A.M. as planned. Being out after curfew could be deadly in Lima.

Garry telexed Jane in Moncton. Contact Skorupa in Lima. We wanted him standing out in front of the Gran Hotel Bolívar at five P.M. instead. He should be packed and ready to go.

While Garry sat at the telex, I went out to the truck, filed away our documents for Chile, and got out the maps and documentation we needed for Peru. I brought my clip file on Peru back to read to Garry.

"We've got," I said, "terrorists in the south. Shining Path guerrillas, Maoists. They operate mainly in the southeast. Two months ago, guerrillas, armed with machines and shotguns, intercepted several boats on the Apurimac River and, after a 'popular trial' executed nineteen men who were accused of being members of the peasant militia fighting the terrorists."

The guerrillas were thought to be operating out of the jungle area of Ayacucho, which was about 150 miles from the Pan-American Highway. Worse, the guerrillas were increasingly threatening tourists in an effort to destabilize the economy, which depends a great deal on tourism. The guerrillas had blown up the train to the old Inca city of Machu Picchu.

The interior minister said that the Shining Path had declared war on Peru.

The president, in an effort to stabilize the economy and put a lid on inflation, had nationalized all banks. There was a firestorm of criticism.

And while the guerrilla cells were located in the forested eastern slopes of the Andes, where the mountains dropped down into the vastness of the Amazon, Lima was not in any way a haven of safety. A month before, "terrorists using submachine guns and dynamite killed the president of the state trading company," reported *The Miami Herald.* In the same week, a car bomb exploded at Citibank headquarters, and another bomb damaged the Lima Sheraton hotel.

North of Lima, in the middle of the country, on the coastal desert, there was noticeably less guerrilla activity. The north was noted for highway robbery, and was home to gasoline bandits.

WATCHING A PARTY of North Americans, two couples in their twenties, I wondered how they had managed to get so deeply into South America, overland, without learning anything about ordinary self-protective border behavior. They had just come off a bus and were waiting in line at the Peruvian checkpoint just over the border from Chile.

"Check out the hats," one of the men said in English. And then there was a good deal of laughter because the uniformed soldier watching the line was wearing a hat that was somewhat more ornate than the sort a U.S. soldier would be issued.

"Where do they get those hats?" one of the women asked in a tone of amused horror, much as someone else might ask where Jimmy Swaggart gets his hair greased. The party burst out laughing again. They were having a jolly time and the soldier in question began taking an interest in them. He had a nine-millimeter pistol in the holster on his belt.

It was a busy border. Chilenos from the town of Arica were traveling into Tacna, Peru, to buy fruits and vegetables. Peruanos were passing the other way, into Arica, to buy goods—clothes primarily—manufactured there under government tax subsidies. The locals, Chilenos and Peruanos, rode in special taxis, painted blue. It was a border with an international taxi service, and the people were familiar with border etiquette, which is to say, no one, except the North Americans, was laughing.

Chance had placed us just behind this party and I thought it prudent to emphasize the fact that I was not with them. We faded to the end of the line: no great problem in South America which, on the whole, does not have a tradition of orderly queuing. People will yield if you assert your right to the position you hold. Relax for a minute and you are at the end of the line. We relaxed and put some distance between ourselves and the other North Americans.

From this vantage point I saw the soldier stroll past our line—which was for the Peruvian Investigative Police's document check—and stop at the customs window to exchange a few words with an official there. Customs was the next order of business for all of us in this line.

It's always a bad bet to suppose officials don't speak some English. Win the bet and you get a cheap laugh. Lose and you may end up enduring a body-cavity search before being denied entry into the country in question. Fines or a few days in detention are a possibility.

An official came out to search the truck. He opened the camper shell, and the smell of festering strawberry milk shakes literally knocked him back a step. He was not keen to crawl around in there. Various letters of recommendation suddenly impressed him, and he waved us through.

"We should break open a few more shakes back there," Garry said. "Get up in the tropics with milk shakes baking in the back. We'll never get searched."

The formalities were endless. We signed, by actual count, twenty-eight documents. We had taken to describing ourselves as a driver and a mechanic because officials were used to that. Garry was generally the mechanic, primarily because he found *mecánico* an easy Spanish word to say. An obliging official signed and stamped our logbook with the date and time.

We weren't, Garry thought, drivers so much as men who carried documents.

"Documenteros," I said.

WE ROLLED INTO the Peruvian border town of Tacna just after dark. It was a busy night, and the long main street was thronged with couples strolling under the stately palms that lined the street. Cruising pickup trucks carried a dozen people or more, all of them hanging from the bed and shouting to friends on the street. There was music everywhere: boom boxes, car radios, loudspeakers in front of the stores, all of which were open for business. It was a cacophony of styles: salsa, disco, high Andes flutes, and American rock 'n' roll. The Animals with Eric Burdon shouting about how "we gotta get out of this place."

We asked directions from a man wearing a moth-eaten coat that had once been mustard-yellow and was now mustard-gray. He motioned us to the proper road with his right arm, which had been amputated at the elbow.

WE WERE STOPPED by armed police outside of Tacna. Garry was driving and dining on beef jerky. For reasons that have yet to be explained, he slipped the jerky under his seat, as if to hide it from the police. An officer searched the cab in a cursory fashion. He did look under the driver's seat where Garry had stashed his guilty jerky. They let us pass.

"Why did you do that?" I asked.

"Hide the jerky?"

"Yeah."

"I don't know. I saw the police and suddenly felt guilty. I suppose it's the way I feel. Like I'm on some kind of drug."

"A jerky junkie."

"Jerky junkie and big-time milk-shake smuggler."

"We are," I suggested, "beginning to lose brain cells."

GARRY WOKE ME in the middle of the night and said he was tired. I poured my cup about a third full of instant coffee and wet it down with cold bottled water. I took the wheel and read Garry's note on the suckerboard: "Switchbacks, potholes, and fog at the top of the switchbacks. Very ignorant fog."

The road was paved but in such bad condition—so riddled with deep and dangerous potholes—that driving was a nightmare. We were slaloming along the Pacific Ocean on headlands fifteen-hundred-feet high and more. Old riverbeds ran down to the sea, and we dropped into these steep valleys through a series of tight switchbacks. The valley floors were narrow, and then it was another fifteen or twenty miles of uphill switchbacks to the high plateau above where the road ran straight for fifteen to fifty miles. Each and every one of the plateaus was shrouded in a gelatinous fog. Work the switchbacks, crawl through the fog. Garry was right: the fog was ignorant.

On the plateaus, some of the rivers held water, but the bridges were rickety, patently unsafe, and most of the big trucks turned off the road and followed the riverbed for as much as a mile, looking for a shallow crossing. At some places, I got out and waded the river, just to be sure. When I got back, one of the big semis would be waiting behind me, and the driver would follow me through. Other times, I would sit behind a semi, and when the driver came back from the river, his pants wet to mid-calf, I'd follow him through.

Often we passed a few words together, these drivers and I. The words were obscene and concerned the fog. Sometimes, rounding a corner over a fifteen-hundred-foot drop-off, the lane would narrow against a cliff face. In those places, our truck and a big semi couldn't pass. I'd stop, and the trucks would stop as well. I couldn't actually see the big trucks, only the yellow foglights shining in my eyes like a nightmare predator. One of us had to back away, let the other through, and there was no macho posturing. These narrow turns were matters of life and death. Whoever had the easiest backup took it. Often the drivers flashed me a V-for-victory sign. It occurred to me that there were very good drivers doing a very hard job. I came to respect them.

There were occasional towns, mud huts lining the narrow Pan-American Highway. We were looking at monuments to poverty so grotesque I imagined people literally starved to death in these towns. Outside one of them, I rounded the first bend of an "S" curve and saw something that squeezed at my chest like a vise. On the cliff wall ahead, written neatly in white paint where every driver had to see it, was large angry graffiti that read, WE ARE NOT ANIMALS.

It is sometimes easy to let calluses form when confronted by starve-to-death poverty, to become callous. In these towns, there would be the odor of sewage and sickness. Men moved slowly, and projects were started and abandoned.

Well-fed foreigners sometimes think of these people as sluggish, lazy, dull-witted, little more than animals. The truth is, they had been hungry all their lives. It was the constant ache of malnutrition that set such a sticky, hopeless, slow-motion pace in these poor towns along the coastal desert.

THERE WASN'T MUCH in the way of a sunrise. The land was covered over in grainy sand, the cliff faces and hills were the same color, the fog itself was sandy brown, and when we passed the ocean, it rolled up onto a dirty beach in gray sand-colored waves.

Garry was up, going through his usual case of post-sunrise blahs. Along the beach, a wind off of the Pacific had piled a series of dirty gray dunes across the highway. A man dressed in rags and two small children in the filthiest clothes imaginable shoveled at the sand, clearing a lane for traffic.

It was the custom to stop, to give them a few pennies for their work. It was also clear that they only worked when they heard the distant sound of cars or trucks. They apparently lived in a nearby hut on the beach that was built of irregular pieces of driftwood, wired and tied into the semblance of a dwelling.

Garry thought the man and his children looked "stunned," a word he reserved for that slow-moving hopelessness you see in the faces of the very poor.

"Stop," he said.

Garry got out of the truck and opened up the camper shell. He took out several boxes of the freeze-dried food we weren't eating and tried to give them to the man. The ragman backed away, afraid of some kind of a trick. I stepped out and tried to explain that this was food, that all you needed to do to eat it was add hot water. The man stared at me.

He didn't know what to make of all the foil packages we were trying to give him, and needed to puzzle it out. He looked, for a moment, like a man trying to add up a lot of long numbers in his mind.

Garry had given the children milk shakes, and they were drinking them with pleasure, smiling brightly for the first time, so that I felt, through my fatigue, as if I might begin to cry.

I DROVE while Garry drank the concoction of one part instant Nescafe to one part water that we still called coffee.

"How," I wondered aloud, "do we get so filthy driving? I mean, we both had showers in Chile, and now we look like hell. I think we scared that guy back there."

"Couple of gringos get out of the truck looking like they just walked fifteen hundred miles through the jungle and start throwing foil packages at him. We look bad."

If you've lived for several days on three substances—jerky, milk shakes, and coffee—it becomes evident that coffee, as we made it, is an extraordinarily strong drug. Garry was brightening up by the minute.

"When I was nine years old," he said, "a guy came to Moncton in a fifty-nine Mercury station wagon. It had a black bubble on the top where the guy could stand up and do exercises. Turned out the guy hadn't been out of the vehicle in two years. Or maybe it was five years. There was some sort of a bet that if he could stay in there for some impossible amount of time, he'd get a hundred thousand dollars."

"This was a vision that warped your life," I said.

"It made a big impression on me. He was locked in his car forever, like us on this trip."

"The fog," I said, "was bad last night."

Garry did a quick calculation: "We made three hundred sixty miles in twelve hours."

"Was it that hard because of the road and the fog, or is it us?"

"Couldn't be us," Garry said. "What day is this?"

"Friday."

"No. Thursday."

"Wait." I needed to figure it out on my fingers. "Tuesday we left Ushuaia after three hours of sleep. Next night we got five hours in Chile . . . "

Garry began counting himself.

We concluded that it was the fifth day of the drive and that it was Saturday.

"The days and nights run together," I said.

"What I like," Garry said, "is when I put my sunglasses on the dash at sunset, then—and it doesn't seem that much time has gone by—the sun rises and I take those glasses off the dash and put them back on."

"H. G. Wells," I said.

"What?"

"In *The Time Machine,* the guy goes into the future so fast that the days and nights seem like the flapping of a great wing. That's what it's beginning to feel like to me, night and day, the flapping of a great wing."

Garry took over the driving and I decided to stay up for a while. We both felt giddy and talkative. The coffee I made was a great pile of instant, barely wetted down enough to dissolve.

I told Garry about the graffiti I had seen the night before: we are not animals.

"We," said Garry, referring to the two of us, "are not men."

I thought briefly of Al Buchanan outside the House of Pork in Santiago, and the wino that he had pointed out to illustrate the meaning of the day of the *rotos*.

"We are not men," I said, "we are roto."

"We're filth," Garry said.

"We're dirt," I shouted, "we're slime. WE ARE ROTO!"

"And we have to pick up Joe Skorupa in Lima. Like this."

"Garry," I said, "Joe wrote me a nice letter before I left. Said he was looking forward to this, and that he thought it would be the adventure of a lifetime."

"Poor son of a bitch."

"Sit all cramped up in the cab of the truck. We haven't got anything to eat. We don't even have a pot to cook in. We gave it away in Chile."

"Wait," Garry said. "Didn't you buy some bread in Arica?"

"It's in the back. It's stale. Hard as a rock. Roto bread."

"We'll pick this guy up, shove him in the back with the sour-milk-shake smell, and give him a hunk of stale bread. EAT IT! There's water back there, too. The windows are caked with mud, he won't be able to see out, but he'll have bread and water. The adventure of a lifetime."

We were laughing and giddy and exhausted and exhilarated all at the same time.

"WE SPENT," Garry screamed, "THREE HUNDRED FIFTY THOUSAND DOLLARS TO BE LIKE THIS!"

I took the pad from the suckerboard and wrote in large letters: WE ARE NOT MEN, WE ARE ROTO.

Garry and I couldn't stop saying the word.

"Roto coffee. You eat it with a spoon."

We were like very young children who have discovered a moderately naughty word and feel compelled to say it every few minutes.

"Poop."

"You're the poop."

"You're a big poop."

"You're an even bigger poop."

Garry and I were five years old, going on four. We were laughing so hard we might have been in a state of infant ecstasy.

"We are," Garry said, "on a roto run."

"In our roto wagon."

He passed a line of three lumbering trucks. "Roto one, roto two, roto three . . ."

"Roto-ed 'em."

"Roto-ed 'em good."

We were laughing and shouting and not making any sense at all. I realized, at that moment, that Garry and I fully understood each other. We could handle anything the Pan-American Highway had to throw at us. We were roto and men who descend into rotohood at the same time in the same place, only inches away from each other, are forever brothers.

Roto.

Garry horsed the big truck through central Lima and parked outside the Hotel Gran Bolívar at 5:00 P.M. on the dot, precisely as we had promised. Joe Skorupa was not there.

PSALM 91 VERSUS THE GASOLINE BANDITS

October 4–5, 1987

GARRY GUARDED THE TRUCK while I ran into one of Peru's most venerable hotels—*in my condition*—and inquired, hysterically, after the whereabouts of a guest named Joe Skorupa. He was registered, I was told, but was now out having a late lunch with . . .

Late lunch?

The desk clerk found the concierge for me, and together we sat at the man's desk and made phone calls to restaurants inquiring after Mr. Skorupa. Lima is a town of five million souls: how many restaurants could there be? Skorupa was supposed to be packed and ready to go at five.

The concierge, an elderly gentleman with a dignified air, was dialing frantically, caught up in a quick burst of contagious Zippy's, when he looked at his own watch and informed me that it was not yet five. It was, in fact, four in the afternoon.

It can't be, I told the man. Here, look at my watch. 5:00. On the nose. See? See! I couldn't be an hour fast because I had set the watch in southern Argentina and . . .

Oh. . . .

I had neglected to consider the fact that Lima is one time zone west of Ushuaia.

We were an hour early.

Garry walked into the carpeted lobby and stood under the chandelier, looking for me. Well-dressed guests glanced at him, surreptitiously, and adjusted their paths so they didn't have to walk near this apparition. His eyes, in a civilized setting, were frightening: they seemed to be sunk deeply into his skull and surrounded by bruiselike circles, which set off the blue of his irises so that he appeared to be staring in a kind of fixed madness. His movements were jerky.

Skorupa, he said, had arrived. He was outside with the truck. Garry looked at me strangely. I wondered if I looked as bad to him as he looked to me.

Joe Skorupa, a handsome young man sporting a dark mustache, wore neatly pressed slacks and a clean polo shirt. He was staring into the cab of the truck where there were mounds of jerky wrappers and milk shake cartons and a note on the suckerboard that read, WE ARE NOT MEN, WE ARE ROTO.

The last time he had seen the truck, in Moncton, it was shiny clean, with logos all over. Now it was caked in filth. The last time Garry and I had seen Joe, we were men, not roto. Joe looked a little shocked about the situation. Were filth and insanity part of the adventure of a lifetime?

Worse, Garry and I were jabbering at each other in our own mad language: what the hell, Skorupa must have wondered, did it mean to go with the Zippy's, forget Zorro, and just roto the damn gasoline bandits. Was *Popular Mechanics* paying him nearly enough to deal with this situation?

Joe, who is nothing if not a reporter, made a perceptive observation. "You guys," he said, "look like shit."

He regarded us with a combination of shock and pity.

Enrique Viale, the director of a Lima auto-service center and Stanadyne representative in Peru, was standing with Joe. He concurred with the reporter's thoughts. It was a long haul to Ecuador and by the time we got there, the border would be closed anyway. We'd have to sleep somewhere. It seemed to him that we needed sleep here and now. Viale had a garage with a security guard where we could safely park the truck.

Garry considered the idea. The wiring on our console was shorting out anyway. On the last run into Lima, the pump that fed diesel from the big auxiliary tank into the factory tank had shorted out. Garry had crawled into the back, crushing milk shakes on the way, and filled the factory tank through some combination of skill and magic that required the use of a jumper cable. Maybe we could get the short fixed at Viale's garage.

Garry and I excused ourselves and talked.

"Tim," he said, "maybe they're right. When I saw you in that hotel lobby, it was strange. People looked like they were afraid of you."

"You mean, I looked bad."

"As compared to normal people."

"The normal people," I pointed out, "avoided you, too."

"I'm afraid," Garry said, "that we look like dangerous crazies."

"Rotos."

And so we decided to sleep that night in Lima.

WE GOT SEPARATE ROOMS and I took a shower, slept for three hours, and snapped wide awake. I was on that kind of schedule. Garry was at Viale's garage, dealing with the short in the console. He also needed to telex Jane: where's the letter of recommendation from the tourism ministry in Honduras? Would we have an escort through customs at the southern Nicaraguan border? Or had our trip to Managua earned us a pocketful of empty promises?

It was just after dark and I strolled around the Plaza San Martin, outside the hotel, where Garry had met Graham Maddocks and learned the dirt-on-the-shoulder pickpocket trick. I bought a paper at a news kiosk and walked off through the teeming crowd. When I felt the tap on my shoulder, from behind, I was slow and didn't clap my hand on my wallet or grab behind for the pickpocket's wrists.

Which was good, because it was the handsome young woman who had sold me my newspapers. She had left her kiosk unguarded and chased me half a block. I had forgotten my change. It amounted to about four cents.

Another shower. We had dinner together—Enrique Viale, Joe, Garry, and I—and it was a real dinner in a real dining room with real food. Somehow it made me feel guilty.

Another shower. The more news-oriented of the papers I had bought, *El Comercio,* reported that there had been over twenty-five armed assaults on interprovincial buses in northern Peru in the last thirty days. As we would be in northern Peru presently, the article was of uncommon interest. Last week, an Expresso Sudamericano bus had been stopped by nine machine-gun-toting assailants who had stripped all the passengers of their belongings, money, and jewelry. Two hours later another group of assailants got another bus.

The other newspaper was a tabloid with a three-page picture spread about a woman boxer. In this age of equality, she dressed for the sport in Everlast trunks and gloves. Though I had a sense that the pictures weren't the essence of accurate reporting or journalistic verisimilitude, I did admire one shot of the woman standing in mid-ring, her arms in the air, as in victory. She was bathed in something that looked like sweat and she had terrific breasts.

EVERYONE WAS UP at five-thirty the next morning. We did not lock Joe Skorupa in the camper shell. He rode in the extended cab. The new freeway out of town took us past an area of abject slums and it seemed a cruel joke that these people's misery was on such public display. On the hillside above, where affluent drivers could see it, there was a political poster, a full-face illustration of a thin-faced stern-looking man wearing glasses. The artist had evidently thought to make the politician appear to be a man of the future, willing to take harsh but necessary measures. Set as it was above a tangle of hard poverty, the billboard seemed badly placed. I thought: Big Brother is watching you.

SOME MILES OUT OF LIMA, along the drear coastal desert, we dropped into a relatively fertile valley. There were orchards along a river, and the town was bustling with Sunday-morning activities. The houses were small, perhaps fifteen feet by fifteen feet, with dirt floors and low ceilings. They fronted the Pan-American Highway, and the sidewalks were only two or three feet wide. A man could step out of his house and be run over by a tourist from Des Moines.

The streets were alive with strange bicycles: they had a single back wheel and a wooden basket on the front supported by two wheels. The bicycles could carry three people in the basket, or a load of firewood, or thatch.

Bicycles were racing down the graveled side streets to a parade on the Pan-American. We passed a float—a jeep covered over in a white cloth—and there were dozens of little girls in clean white first-communion dresses riding and hanging on to the vehicle. They waved at us and to the townspeople who lined the street.

In a less-affluent area of small mud houses, a beautiful dark-haired little girl of about seven was sitting in the basket of a bicycle and being pedaled frantically to the parade by a man I took to be her father. She wore a brilliant white dress, a kind of pointy witch's cap covered over in rhinestones, and carried a wand with an aluminum-foil star on the end. She was holding tight to her hat and her eyes were wide with a kind of full-blown happiness you seldom see along the Pan-American Highway in Peru.

*   *   *

THE PAN-AMERICAN HIGHWAY is just not a viable way to see the best Peru has to offer. In Chimbote, the houses that lined the road were constructed of woven straw mats on poles. A port city, Chimbote smelled of rotten fish. It had a population of 185,000, and an earthquake in 1970 had terminally damaged its sewage system, so the place stunk of human waste and sickness.

There was a rock tunnel outside Chimbote, and in the cool darkness Garry said, "Maybe when we come through, we'll be back in Kansas and it will all be a horrible dream. We'll wake up and realize that there is no place on earth where everything stinks and people die because nobody thought to fix the sewage system."

I sought to defend Peru. I had last visited in 1977, and had spent little time in Lima or on the Pan-American Highway. The road, I said, is a major artery, a way out, and it attracts poverty and hopelessness in the same way that the U.S. border with Mexico does.

No, the Peru I loved was a couple of hundred miles inland, over one of the sixteen-thousand-foot passes through the Andes, and in the forested slopes above the Amazon jungle, the land the local people call "the eyebrow of the jungle." It is humbling to walk the steep trails of the eyebrow. An elderly Peruvian woman, bent double under a load of firewood, can outwalk any gringo marathon runner.

The mountains of the eyebrow rise to ten thousand feet, and in those high cloud forests can be found the remains of the Inca civilization, and, farther north, pre-Inca cultures, like the Chachapoyas. Most Peruvian archaeology is performed on the Pacific side of the Andes, in the desert, where logistics are not such a headache, where access is easier.

When I brought back maps and schematic drawings of cities my friends and I found in the eyebrow, professional archaeologists dismissed them with a wave of the hand. These pre-Columbian cities included hundreds of circular stone houses, covered over in jungle. There were larger habitations, probably civic centers or fortifications, located nearby, on commanding ridges.

But there are ruins everywhere in Peru, one distinguished archaeologist pointed out.

Yes, of course, it's part of the country's charm, but had the professor ever visited these ruins in the eyebrow?

No need to, nothing significant there.

It seems suspicious to me that every single archaeological site in

Peru that academics consider to be significant is located in the coastal
desert or on the western slope of the Andes, accessible from the Pan-
American Highway.

And I suppose that if I were an academic archaeologist nearing
retirement, I wouldn't want to hear about discoveries that could invali-
date my scholarly papers, my theories, my years of teaching.

So there are ancient stone cities, covered in cloud-forest vegetation,
dreaming, undiscovered, on the peaks that drop down into the vastness
of the Amazon.

The eyebrow is a forbidding land, virtually roadless, relentlessly
steep, and not particularly providential. Local Indians may never have
seen a white man before, and they speak Quechua, not Spanish. It's
hard to get around.

That has always been the case in the eyebrow. In 1541 Gonzalo
Pizarro, half brother of Francisco Pizarro, the conqueror of the Incas,
set out to find cities of gold rumored to exist on the eastern slopes of
the mountains. The expedition included two hundred Spaniards and
four thousand Indians. The local Indians directed him to the groves of
spice trees and the wealthy cities he sought: sure, you bet, Gonzalo, the
city of gold is a mere ten days march over a dozen ten-thousand-foot-
high ridges. There were no groves of spice trees or cities of gold, of
course, but the Spaniards never came back to discuss the matter.
Which, in essence, is what the Indians had in mind.

One of Gonzalo's lieutenants, Francisco de Orellana, left the expedition and pushed down one of the rivers in a search for provisions which
didn't exist. Rather than try to make it back up the steep forested
slopes of the eyebrow, de Orellana chose to build a raft and float to the
sea down the great river he named Amazon.

Gonzalo and his men were forced to eat their horses and dogs. A
year later, he stumbled back into Quito, with a handful of men. Over
four thousand of his people had died.

These days, the eyebrow may be a somewhat more dangerous place
than when I visited it. Our walk from the nearest road had taken us
several days over a well-trod trail. One day, from a slope far away, we
heard whistles and shouts. Several hours later, we encountered a mule
train headed out to the road. Twenty mules, each of them carrying 150
pounds of dull gray coca leaves, were being driven through the mountains by a group of ten men.

The leaves were grown on slopes leading down to the Marañón
River, one of the source tributaries of the Amazon. It was a perfectly
legal procession. The coca leaf—not the cocaine that is made from it—is

a legal stimulant in Peru, and there are some who insist that no work would ever get done east of the Andes if it was outlawed. The drug helps workers endure cold, hunger, and exhaustion. A chew of coca, in eastern Peru, is the Indian equivalent to a coffee break.

And the effects, I found, were somewhat similar. Unrefined coca leaves are not a particularly strong drug. I first chewed some with a Peruvian police officer. He had been dispatched from a frontier town to check on my party. We had been asking around about ruins; the word was that we were trekking the ridges, making maps. It was possible that we were grave robbers, that we were in the business of stealing priceless pre-Columbian artifacts.

The officer had trekked two days, over three sets of five-thousand-foot ridges to find us. He found no digging at our campsites, but offered to "accompany" us for a few days. The man wore a poncho and a .38 revolver on his belt. He also carried a woven shoulder bag full of coca leaves.

At the base of every ridge, the officer would tell us that the walk ahead was "very easy." Sometimes the hills were steep and endless. It was wiser not to listen to the officer regarding the relative difficulty of climbing the hills. Better to simply see how many coca leaves he wadded into his mouth at the base of the ridge. Lots of coca meant a long hard climb.

The officer offered my party some of the leaves—people always find it difficult to believe that I was offered my first taste of raw coca by a police officer—and I found the effect not entirely negligible. Still—this was 1977, remember—I didn't think you'd be able to sell a single leaf outside a disco in Queens. Coca leaves turn your teeth and lips green. Chewing them involves a lot of gloppy spitting.

It helped on the long climbs, though. Most people have felt something of what coca leaves do. Imagine that you have had a hard day: up before dawn, no time for breakfast, errands all morning, nothing for lunch, and now it's two in the afternoon. You stop at a diner, exhausted, and order coffee and a piece of pie. Half an hour later you're ready to go again: that's pretty much the lift you get from a mouthful of coca leaves.

In the decade since I had been to Peru, the government, responding to pressure from the United States, has been raiding the coca producers. The plantations—I saw one on the banks of the Marañón—are now heavily defended. It is worth your life, these days, to stumble into the wrong sector of the eyebrow.

My experience in 1977 was somewhat happier. The Indian people,

I found, took me into their homes and fed me eggs and the meat of
guinea pigs they raise as a source of protein. They sat with me around
a fire and offered their sugarcane beer. One man introduced me to his
family and friends, and to their friends' families until I was surrounded
by hundreds of polite, curious people, anxious to see a real gringo. They
wanted to hear me sing (poor fools), see me dance (they were disappointed), but my talentless audition was, finally, a roaring success. One
by one people dropped off the homemade wooden benches and fell onto
the dirt floor where they rolled about, men and women alike, all of
them laughing helplessly. I have, I told myself at the time, this gift for
comedy.

The Peru I visited a decade ago, I told Joe and Garry, was a land
of mystery and hospitality and discovery. It had nothing to do with the
filth and despair and astoundingly bad driving we were seeing along
the Pan-American.

ABOUT TWO THAT AFTERNOON, in an agricultural valley, a truck driver
began blasting his air horn at us. Garry let him pass and the driver
pointed urgently toward the back of the Sierra. We stopped and didn't
have to examine the truck for leaks. Diesel was literally pouring out
of the back. It was dripping thickly from both sides and out of the
tailgate. The auxiliary tank, we discovered, had ruptured at a seam.

We pulled off the highway, into some tall grasses beside fields of
fernlike young palms. An elderly woman, dressed in black, tended a
flock of sheep. A dozen children, who seemed to have simply erupted
out of the ground, watched us unload gear and curse the tank. Since
the boxes were already out on the ground, the kids all got several milk
shakes. They stood watching with big curious eyes above the straws in
their mouths.

We had a full tank, ninety gallons, about seven hundred pounds of
diesel, and it took an hour for it to drain. I was sitting in the shade,
contemplating the future. The big tank fed into the factory tank. Okay.
We would just have to use the thirty-five-gallon factory tank, buy some
jerricans for extra diesel, and be careful about filling up frequently.

Garry, mindful of his sponsors, explained to Joe that the auxiliary
tank was not GMC equipment. It was an after-market addition to the
truck.

"One good thing," I said. "We don't have to worry about the pump
shorting out anymore."

Garry did not see this as a blessing. He was examining the welds,
trying to find where the worst ruptures were, and he shouted at me to

"go clean up the cab or something." I didn't like his tone of voice, and I didn't like being ordered around in front of a reporter. No reason to lose my temper, though. I had the formula for dealing with this situation. Although I knew it would never happen, not now, not after the roto run below Lima, I envisioned myself slapping Garry Sowerby in Alaska. Or maybe I'd just knee him in the groin.

I DROVE THROUGH A HAZY SUNSET doing seventy-five on a new road over the desert. There was a fierce wind from the west that drove a sandstorm before it. The sand was heavy and the wind lifted it no more than a foot off the ground, but it swirled over the pavement in odd serpentine tongues that sometimes created dunes two or three feet high.

There was a small hut ahead, the first we had seen in this northern desert. Three big trucks were parked nearby, and, as we passed, a man and a woman stood in the doorway, kissing passionately. The western sky was a reddish bruise. The lovers were silhouetted in the warm light of a kerosene lantern.

"Cathouse," I said.

But we didn't stop.

We were not men.

We were roto.

TRUJILLO is an oasis town of 750,000 and, on this Sunday evening, everyone in the world was going to a party somewhere in Trujillo. There were trees lining the outlying highway, but no streetlights, so it was dark and dangerous. I was driving, following a truck with no taillights, going about twenty miles an hour. Young men on small motorcycles were screaming out of town, on their way, I supposed, to pick up their dates.

Joe Skorupa was charmed by the vitality of the people, their evident good humor, but wondered about my driving.

"You could," he suggested, "probably pass this guy."

I would have at any other time in my life.

"Too many people," I said. There were all over the road, standing on the shoulder and chatting with friends, walking, yelling for rides. The people on the roadside were shadows under the trees, and any little miscalculation—a swerve to avoid a motorbike without a light—would send the five-ton Sierra crunching over some laughing innocent. I pictured a little girl in a rhinestone witch's hat holding a wand that ended in a tin-foil star.

The irony of adventure driving is that it is the least adventurous driving anyone will ever do. There is absolutely no room for error.

I felt Joe was disappointed in my skills. Garry, on the other hand, was sleeping peacefully. I was doing the job.

There was a central plaza arranged around an immense traffic circle where delivery bicycles, motorcycles, overloaded pickups, and semis bound for Ecuador or Lima all whirled around to pounding Latin rhythms booming out of every portable sound system on the face of the earth. I took the circle twice, slowly, then guessed on the proper turnoff.

The road seemed to end in a pile of sand. Garry was awake, and a couple of flat-out rotos holding bottles of liquor shouted to us. They stumbled toward the truck, yelling and offering us drinks. Their faces were shiny with perspiration, and between the two of them they had enough teeth to fill a single human mouth. One man had large yellow eyes, like a pair of fried eggs.

"Let's get out of here," Garry said. We sensed that we were in gasoline-bandit city.

I asked another group on another corner for the Pan-American north, and their directions led to another dead end. I needed to back up, then pull forward in order to turn around, and now dozens of people surrounded the truck.

"Move," Garry said. We were both very tense.

Several more sets of directions given by several more friendly people, both drunk and sober, resulted in disappointment. Mostly we found ourselves on dirt side streets facing some adobe wall that featured a faded advertisement for Inca Kola. Directions, in South America, are not meant to be taken seriously.

Perhaps local people feel it is rude to simply say, "I don't know." It is possible they may concoct false directions out of a sense of hospitality rather than any desire to mislead. Or it may be a macho trait: how embarrassing to have to admit to a stranger that you do not know your way in your own hometown. Then again, it may be the Gonzalo Pizarro effect. It was almost two hundred years after the ill-fated Pizarro expedition until the Indians of the eyebrow felt the lash of the Spanish.

At any rate, in South America, it is always best to ask directions several times, then triangulate a route based on what appears to be the best information tendered. We stopped half a dozen times until we found the road north out of town.

Garry took the wheel. This was bandit country and he had the evasive driving skills. The road ran straight through the sand and darkness.

No lights, no traffic. . . .

And there they were, half a dozen men with guns, waving us over. They didn't seem to be wearing uniforms. On the other hand—and these calculations were made in the space of about twenty seconds— there were two buildings on either side of the road and both were lit. It was close to the border with Ecuador and hence a good spot for a military or customs checkpoint.

"What do you think?" Garry asked.

"Military. I think."

It was, in fact, a military checkpoint. The tallest of the men, the officer who seemed to be in charge, wore a khaki safari suit and a foot-long knife in a leather sheath on his belt. He had a Spanish face, a crew cut, and pockmarked skin. The men serving under him were mestizos and looked like teenagers. They wore the black silky T-shirts of the Peruvian military which are emblazoned with the motto HONOR, DISCIPLINE, LOYALTY. We were motioned out of the truck, and one of the teenagers held an automatic rifle at my neck. I could see that he had been trying, without much success, to grow a moustache. The safety on the rifle appeared to be off, and he had his finger on the trigger.

I smiled brilliantly, as if happy to see new friends and exchange stories. I thought: put your safety on, bozo.

Our papers were in order, and the soldiers lowered their guns, cautiously. We began handing out the flyers in Spanish, but the man with the knife simply dropped his on the ground, unread. It was a contemptuous gesture. He had the knife out of the sheath, and motioned at Garry to open the tailgate for a search.

The lights across the street came from a small bar that had apparently sprung up to serve the checkpoint. Several drunken men wandered over to watch the fun. Two of them held communal bottles of the fiery pale brandy called Pisco. They looked into the cab of the truck and muttered solemnly among themselves as Garry unlocked the camper shell. There was an anticipatory hush among the assembled drunks.

Garry fiddled with the twin padlocks, then pulled both doors open at once. A fetid smell of bad sour milk and diesel flooded out of the truck in a cloud that was almost visible. There was a loud murmuring among the drunks.

The officer thought about climbing into the back, looked at the diesel-smeared tailgate he'd have to kneel upon, regarded his spiffy safari suit, and pointed the knife at a box that, for once, did not contain milk shakes. Garry opened it for him. It was filled with cans of Argentine hashed beef.

"Bad food," I told a soldier. "I wouldn't feed Argentine hash to a dog." Peruvian food was much better, I said. Especially the seafood. And a Pisco sour was the best drink in the world.

The teenaged soldiers were warming up a bit, and several of them came over to listen to me blather on about the virtues of Peru and Peruvians. Our trip would take us through thirteen countries. We would always remember Peru. It was so beautiful. Did they want to see some letters of recommendation from the Peruvian auto club? In Spanish? Look here where it says that our trip perfectly expresses the ideal of Pan-American unity. Hey, did anyone want to ride with us to Alaska? Huh? How about you?

Meanwhile, Garry was dealing with the officer who, having decided against a search of the reeking camper shell, now wanted us to drive the truck back behind the building. Garry looked at me. We didn't like the idea of being pulled off the road, out of sight, where anything could happen. I motioned for Joe to follow me as I walked behind the truck. We didn't want them to split us up.

The drunks followed in a merry band. I hated them.

In back there was a narrow pit dug into the ground and Garry, as instructed, drove the truck over it. The officer lowered himself under the truck, and Garry followed him down so no contraband could be planted. The pit, it seemed, wasn't used much. It was filled, calf-deep, with garbage. Using a flashlight and flexible file, the officer poked around for ten minutes.

I was in full joke mode with the drunks and teenagers. What a pleasure it was to talk with such honorable and witty men. Would anyone like a lapel pin? This is a maple leaf; this one is a replica of the truck. Well, yes, the truck is very dirty now, so it's hard to see the markings, and the pin isn't exactly the same, but who would want a very dirty lapel pin? Ho ho, it was to laugh, such a joke of humor.

Oh, and had anyone ever drunk sweet milk from a box? Here, try a couple of these. Take a dozen for the wife and kids.

The officer came out of the pit and walked into the ramshackle checkpoint shack without a word. One of the teenagers followed him in, then came out a second later and said we could pass.

It had all taken an hour and had been a very bad search, a Psalm-91 stop all the way.

Joe Skorupa was impressed. "It was grim at first," he said, "but by the time you left, they were all laughing."

"What we try to do," Garry said, "is sell them on the trip itself.

Make them feel that they're part of it, that they're helping set the record. We're dream merchants. And these guys were a hard sell."

"Tim," Joe said, "was going back and forth with this guy, and I don't know Spanish, but all of a sudden he says, 'You need to wear a jacket,' in English. It sounded funny."

"And you laughed out loud there," I said, "which was good, because we want them to see us as funny, happy guys. I think I was trying to tell the guy what the weather was like on Tierra del Fuego, and I kept looking down and seeing that he had the safety off on his rifle. It affected my ability to speak Spanish."

The road ahead was mostly gravel, but other roads, equally well traveled, led out into the black desert night where praying mantis–type oil rigs bobbed moronically. These distant rigs were illuminated with security lights and looked like ships afloat on a dark sea.

It was ambush country, according to the Lima papers. Garry wondered if the military might be in league with bandits. Stop us for an hour, let a bunch of civilians from the bar across the way case the truck, then delay us until the ambush party could get into position, probably under one of the washed-out bridges over a dry riverbed.

"They were drinking Pisco," I said.

Garry had noticed. Pisco is expensive. Where would a desert drunk get the money to buy Pisco?

It was a long dark drive through Psalm-91 country.

BUS-PLUNGE
FOLLIES

October 5–8, 1987

THE BORDER with Ecuador was closed and we slept for six hours in a hotel at Tumbes, the most northerly Peruvian town. We were the first in line at the customs shed at Aguas Verde, a squalid, bustling border town with a bad reputation for thievery. A handsome man with curly blond hair saw the truck and introduced himself. Alejandro Peñaherrera, who worked with service and repairs for General Motors Ecuador, had been sent to meet us, help us through customs, and would escort us to the capital of Quito, where the truck would be serviced.

Aguas Verde was jammed with people. There were makeshift wooden stands lining the street and people sold Capris vegetable oil, sunglasses, canned milk, and T-shirts. One man sold nothing but spoons of all sizes. An Indian woman presided over a pile of men's jockey sorts, all of which had a banana stenciled over the fly. People sold watermelons, shoes, chickens, and guinea pigs.

Men wore sunglasses and baseball-type hats with HONDA or FIAT written on them, and they carried sacks of oranges on their backs. A fat man, very drunk at eight in the morning, pedaled a bicycle unsteadily through the throng of vendors and shoppers. His shirt was too short and his belly bulged over his pants. When he passed the church (Our Lady of Everlasting Customs?), he tried to cross himself, lost control of the bicycle, and crashed into an umbrella stand. There was much yelling and confusion.

The Peruvian customs building featured a large poster that read, SAY NO TO DRUGS, SAY YES TO LIFE. Below the poster, a cloud of flies was buzzing around a large burlap sack full of confiscated bananas. The Ecuadorian side had a poster of a young man taken through a series of about ten pictures. In the first, the man looks clean-cut and eager.

He becomes sad. Then depressed. His hair gets longer. Then it gets messy and dirty. Finally he's unwashed, there are great dark circles around his eyes, and it's plain that his life is consigned to the scrap heap of society.

The caption read, DRUGS DESTROY YOUR MIND.

Garry and I stared at that last picture and said, in unison: "Roto."

THE ECUADORIAN MAPS were different than the Peruvian ones. In 1942, after a short war, the Rio de Janeiro Protocol of Peace, Friendship, and Boundaries awarded Peru a fifty-mile stretch of land which consisted mostly of Amazon forest and certain areas of the eastern foothills of the Andes. One of Ecuador's essential foreign policy objectives is to redraw the border and obtain possession of the Marañón River.

In 1981 there were border skirmishes over this issue. In order to thwart any planned Peruvian invasion, Ecuador has let the Pan-American Highway out of Aguas Verde fall into something close to ruin. Every ten miles or so there was another military checkpoint, five of them in fifty miles. These were usually placed in a canyon and we could see gun emplacements above. Fifty-caliber machine guns were trained on the road. These weapons have a range of about one mile and can knock out an armored personnel carrier.

When we left the checkpoints, papers stamped and authorized, we did so slowly, waving at the officers and crawling along at about ten miles an hour for half a mile or more. It is bad form to go squealing out of any military checkpoint. We did not want to look as if we were escaping.

On the other hand, if we were to be captured by terrorists anywhere, Ecuador was the place. The previous month, during a wildly vitriolic campaign for president, one candidate, Abdala Bucaram, claimed he had been abducted by terrorists for a time. Bucaram, who opposed the government's ties with the United States, had made his reputation as mayor of Guayaquil, where he campaigned vigorously against pornography.

Bucaram, in fact, claimed that he had been abducted secretly, and he had told no one of the kidnapping. The videotape released by his opponents, Bucaram said, had been filmed during his captivity. He had been forced, at gunpoint, to have sex with the three women in the video. The evil terrorists who had subjected him to this appalling torture intended to destroy his campaign. And, okay, sure, he appeared to enjoy it, but you had to understand, his life was at stake.

"Never a dull moment," Garry offered.

"From gasoline bandits to pornography terrorists," I said.

"Frying pan into the fire," Garry agreed.

WE WERE FOLLOWING ALEJANDRO, who was driving a Chevrolet Aska, which looked like a version of the North American Chevy Monza. About fifty miles into the country, the desert gave way to a lush, flat land of banana groves and waist-high grasses. The dirty-gray fog that had deviled us since the Atacama was gone. The Pan-American Highway here was in good repair and wider than anything we had seen in Peru. It was, in fact, so wide that traffic often formed a third lane, in the middle of the road, which was populated by adventuresome souls traveling at high speeds in both directions. The width of the highway provided drivers the opportunity to pull out into the middle lane, evaluate their chances of success or death, then swerve back into their own lane, cutting off other drivers who leaned bitterly on their horns.

It was like a video-arcade car-crash game.

Worse, the electrical short in the auxiliary-tank fuel pump had reasserted itself. Since we had no auxiliary tank, this would not have been a problem at all, except that the people who had put in the tank had rewired the truck. Our windshield wipers were connected into the short. Which wouldn't have been a problem if it weren't raining. But it was and because we were doing seventy-five miles an hour, a moving shimmer of water on the wiperless windshield distorted the highway ahead. Looking through the glass in front of my face made me feel as if we were driving underwater.

Garry, who was at the wheel, stopped to find his motorcycle goggles. We had purchased a pair for each of us after Graham Maddocks had asked us what we'd do if someone broke the windscreen. Dropped a rock from a bridge, for instance.

So Garry was doing seventy-five on the crowded highway, with his head stuck out the driver's window in a tropical rainstorm. Alejandro, in the light gasoline-powered vehicle ahead, fancied himself a race-car driver and he pushed the Chevy at top speed through a moving braid of traffic. "The Pan-American," Alejandro had said, "is war."

For some reason that wasn't immediately apparent, Alejandro wanted to push on at top speed for Quito.

"He doesn't brake for oncoming cars," Joe observed.

Out in the middle lane, it was a game of chicken, with a new opponent every two minutes.

Garry was staying right with Alejandro in a virtuoso exhibition of

Third World driving. He used the horn more than the brakes. Running down the middle lane, with a bus headed directly for us, Garry would just keep pushing for the pass, then pull in at the last moment.

He seldom used the brakes because he felt there was a greater danger of being back ended than in suffering a head-on crash. In his opinion, drivers on the Pan-American were very good indeed, and he thought that most of them possessed better skills than the typical North American driver.

Joe and I objected to this. Drivers would consistently pull out to pass in the face of an oncoming car or truck. Sometimes both vehicles pulled back into their own lane simultaneously, inches away from death. Bumpers missed bumpers by feet, sometimes inches.

"People grew up driving like this," Garry shouted. It seemed strange to carry on a high-volume conversation with a man wearing goggles and driving a truck through the rain with his head out the window. "It's what they know," he bellowed, "this kind of driving is all they know, and they're good at it. North American rules don't apply. They've got people driving vehicles at twenty miles an hour here, and if they passed safely—what we'd call safely—they'd never get anywhere. So everyone passes everyone, at any time. That bus back there? When we were coming at each other? He saw that I needed more room than he did and feathered back on the throttle. He was good. Different rules here, and if you know the rules, you can see how good the drivers are."

Garry, I could see, was in a kind of esctasy, his teeth bared against the sting of rain on his face.

"Yeah," I shouted, "but how do you know that someone isn't drunk, or crazy macho, or suicidal?"

"Well," Garry screamed, "you usually have about ten seconds to decide."

Through the inch or so of moving water on the glass in front of me I could see the looming grill of a large truck as it peeled off into its own lane.

"These people," Garry howled, "are either good drivers or they're dead."

LATE THAT AFTERNOON we turned out of the banana plantations of the coastal lowlands and headed east, into the mountains and Quito. Ecuador's capital city is set in a mountain basin 9,350 feet high. The city is only about twenty miles south of the equator.

The road into the city wound its way upward through a lush moun-

tainous jungle. The highway was a narrow black ribbon of asphalt, in
very good repair, but the logistics of the mountains sent it spinning into
loops and switchbacks and various Möbius strip variations that would
have been dizzying if we hadn't been crawling along behind creeping
diesel belchers at four miles an hour for most of the way.

There was no passing and depending on the other guy to feather
back on the throttle here. Trucks and buses, barreling downhill, could
literally not stop, even using their brakes, because the road was steep
and slick with rain.

The thick columns of trees that lined the road were alive with
parasitic flowers. A waterfall four or five hundred feet high poured
through the greenery above. At the bottom, near the road, the waters
fell as a fine mist which glittered in a strange lunar manner. Green
hanging vines brushed the windshield and roof of the truck.

There were thick pockets of silvery fog hanging in the hollows, the
kind of ethereal mists that inspire German philosophers and Japanese
Zen masters. We were, I thought, ascending into realms of the spirit.
Ahead, through the purely spiritual fog, I could see a looming, giant
form. A revelation, no doubt.

It was, of course, a large truck doing five miles an hour, and,
through the fog, I could barely make out some markings on this erstwhile celestial apparition: the markings read, COCA-COLA. The truck
was belching diesel and we were nearing the ten-thousand-foot mark
on the hump that would take us into Quito.

Garry said that the road was well engineered, but the mountains
and the wet asphalt were treacherous. He thought that the wives of the
drivers who plied this road probably worried about their husbands in
the same way wives of fighter pilots worried about theirs.

Off to our left there was a stupendous drop-off that would take a
truck rolling through some steep greenery, then send it out into the
sky, where it would plunge through a layer of clouds and land, in a
burst of fire, in some banana grove next to a wooden shack on stilts. The
people in the shack would have to suppose that the truck had simply
fallen out of the sky.

It was 5:30 P.M., and here, near the equator, the sun sets promptly
at 6:00. It rises at 6:00. There is none of the lazy, lingering light of more
northerly or southerly climes in Quito, no such thing as twilight. The
sun rises and sets at 6:00 sharp, all year long. Twelve hours of light and
twelve hours of darkness.

It was no longer possible to see to the bottom of the roadside drop-offs. They were shrouded in shadow, and the impossible depths seemed to purple down into an absolute and final blackness.

We pushed through a pewtery pocket of silver-gray fog, then rose above the cloud bank itself into a final explosion of dying sunlight. I could see a triangle of sky between green hummocky hills and spires. Streaks of crimson ran across the western sky, and that light fell on the cloud just below us so that I felt I was looking down onto a pastel cushion. It was a stupefying vision of cartoon heaven where people in white robes sit on clouds and play harps.

And then, bam, it was dark and we were running over a wet, black highway, through the fog, in the dead of night.

And coming down the hill, careening toward us at crazy speed, was a vehicle decorated with rows of blinking lights arranged at the rectangular periphery of its front end. It looked like a Forty-second Street adult bookstore on wheels, but it was a bus, decorated as buses are in Ecuador, and the driver was speeding, heedlessly I thought, over the wet, slippery asphalt and into the cloudy darkness below.

Buses, in Argentina and Chile, are not necessarily objects of dread. There, drivers wear white shirts and ties. They are relatively courteous at the wheel, and are treated with the respect accorded airline pilots in the U.S. In Peru, Ecuador, and Colombia, by contrast, buses are hurtling projectiles of terror.

Gringo travelers generally find bus trips in the mountainous regions of Latin America occasions of mind-expanding tumult. Lawrence Millman, in his book *Last Places,* pretty much hits the note:

> . . . those infamous Latin American bus rides where the bus—actually a hodgepodge of cast-off tractor and automotive parts mounted on bald tires—bashes its way through mountains, swivels along precipitous gorges, straightens out hairpin curves, and generally avails itself of scenery to which no bus should have a right. Meanwhile the driver pulls off at every roadside shrine and leaves a bribe for the Virgin Mary; Mexican drivers leave iron washers in lieu of pesos, whereas Ecuadorians are more diligent and leave a certain number of sucres per wheel. But it wouldn't matter if they left Her cassettes of salsa music. Sooner or later the bus will justify everybody's worst fears by plunging (Latin American buses never crash, they plunge) into a deep gorge, ravine, gulch, coulee, or canyon, the only survivor being a three-year-old child muffled by its mother's breasts.

Tom Miller, in *The Panama Hat Trail,* advises his readers that the driver's sobriety "isn't a factor. The presence of his wife or girlfriend is. If she's along, she will usually sit immediately behind him, next to him, or on his lap. He will want to impress her with his daring at the wheel, but he will also go to great lengths not to injure her. If he has no girlfriend or wife, the chances of a gorge-dive increase."

On the other hand, Miller quotes a *New York Times* editor who finds bus-plunge stories useful as fillers. "We can count on one every couple of days or so," the editor told Miller, "they're always ready when we need them."

In Miller's experience, the stories are generally no more than two sentences long and invariably feature the word *plunge* in the headline. The text will include such facts as the number feared dead, the identity of any group aboard—a soccer team, church choir, or children from a certain school—and the distance of the plunge from the capital city.

Moritz Thomsen, a Peace Corps volunteer in Ecuador who stayed to farm the land, listened well to neighbors when they told bus-plunge stories. In *Living Poor,* he writes:

> One of the stories they tell about the Ecuadorian bus driver is that whenever he runs off the road and kills a few of the passengers without killing himself, he immediately goes into hiding in some distant part of the country so the bereaved can't even up the score. There are rumors of whole villages down in the far reaches of the Amazon basin populated almost entirely by retired bus drivers.

WE CAME UP over a final rise and drove into a mass of lights arranged in a series of neat grids. Although Quito is only a few miles from the equator, it is high enough that the climate is wonderfully temperate: a spring day in England. The skies had cleared and lights were strung out along wide boulevards.

Alejandro led us to a locked gate at some kind of garage. He honked his horn, a pair of metal gates swung open, and we were looking into a bank of incredibly bright otherworldly lights, white hot, like something out of a Spielberg film. We drove slowly into them as people on all sides yelled at one another and at us.

The truck was to be serviced in here, but no one had told GM Ecuador that we did not want to be interviewed. There were two sets of video cameras from an evening news program, and a few print reporters were present along with half a dozen mechanics and a man in a white lab coat, like a doctor's, who was to supervise the service.

This, I realized, was the reason Alejandro had been in such a hurry. Everyone was waiting for us. Garry worked with the mechanics and I tried to tell the assembled press that, as much as we would like to, we couldn't do interviews. They filmed me telling them that. I realized that they would use this snippet of film no matter what I said.

"A team rushing through Quito today on their way to a world record," I heard an imaginary newscaster on an imaginary newscast say, "will be pulling into Colombia tomorrow and will be available to those contemplating armed robbery and/or kidnap."

We were going to get some publicity whatever happened, and it seemed to me that it would be better to get good publicity than to disappoint these reporters who had spent a couple of hours waiting for us to crest bus-plunge hill. So I spoke with the press.

"Why do you want to do this?" they asked, and "Do you think of yourself as a romantic adventurer?"

I told them the drive had been a dream of ours for some time. We were now making that dream come true, and maybe when people saw us, they would think of their own dreams, and they would work to make those dreams come true.

At the service bay, mechanics were changing the oil and the fuel filter. One of the mechanics, a man with a reputation as a crackerjack electrician, was working on the short in the console. He would attempt to rewire the windshield wipers back into their original circuit. Garry was watching the electrician work. Together, they pulled the console off and saw a tangled bird's nest of multicolored wires running every which way to every device that we had added to the truck. Why someone thought a nonessential system, like an auxiliary fuel pump, should be wired into the same circuit as an essential system, like windshield wipers, has never been satisfactorily explained.

I was telling the press that our trip was an expression of Pan-American unity and friendship.

"It's the dog's goddamn breakfast in here," I heard Garry scream. He and the mechanic were tearing at the wiring.

Our South American friends were helping make our dreams come true, I told the press. Ecuador was the most beautiful place we had seen, and our friends here were the most helpful. The Pan-American Highway was a ribbon of friendship connecting all of the Americas . . .

"Someone dies when we get back!" Garry shouted. He had a handful of wires and did, indeed, look homicidal.

*   *   *

WE STORED THE TRUCK at the garage, slept a few hours, and drove out of Quito before dawn. It was a beautiful, gracious city but Indian people in threadbare clothes slept on the wide boulevards under the glowing streetlights.

Our windshield wipers were working. People were living on the street in poverty, but by God, we had windshield wipers that worked. That thought tugged at my conciousness, but I refused to entertain it. I wanted to feel good and felt bad about feeling that.

JOE SKORUPA, who lives at sea level, had a fierce headache generated by the altitude. We were driving through an area of fertile farms. Indian women in colorful ponchos, lime-green slacks, and porkpie hats were already out hoeing in the potato fields. The houses were white-washed adobe affairs with red-tile roofs and flowers in the front yard.

As we rounded a sharp corner, Garry had to brake for a cow that was standing in the middle of the road. We drove around the beast and it regarded us with bovine indifference.

"That'd be pretty hard to explain," I said, "hitting a cow."

"You couldn't exactly say that it *darted* out in front of you," Garry agreed.

And we started in on that idea, letting it get silly and stupid and all roto around the edges.

"Cows don't dart."

"It's one thing you can say about cows all right. They're piss poor in the darting department."

"Don't dart worth shit."

This imbecilic conversation, punctuated by idiotic guffaws, continued for at least fifteen minutes until we heard Joe, in the back, moan loudly. It was a piteous sound meant to be heard over the roar of diesel engine and it meant, Guys, for the love of God, please.

Garry and I were struck silent. We had been inconsiderate. Still, we hadn't really finished laughing about those darting cows and occasionally the bottled-up emotion came snorting up out of our noses. We were like children in church who can't stop laughing.

"Shhh," I said, "Joe has a hiddach."

Garry fell into a phoney coughing fit, but Joe saw through him. "We get back to sea level," he said, "and you guys are dead meat."

BY THE TIME WE CROSSED the equator, Joe was feeling better. Garry and I were elated.

"We're in the Northern Hemisphere," I shouted. "Nothing can go wrong now."

"Don't say that," Garry pleaded.

Stamp this document, then that one. Stamp. Stamp, stamp, stamp, stamp. Uh, señor, this says that your truck is from 1988.

Yes, brand-new.

How can that be? This is 1987.

Well, it's what we call a model year. . . .

Did you go into the future and bring this truck back? Ha, I made a joke.

And a very good one. But no, you see, in the United States . . .

There is a mistake on your carnet, no?

A mistake?

It says 1988 but it is 1987.

Oh, right. Very good you caught that: a stupid mistake. This is clearly a 1987 truck.

Just as I thought. Very good.

Stamp. Stamp, stamp, stamp.

Across the border into Colombia. Stamp, stamp, stamp. Occupation? Mother's maiden name. Marital status? Stamp. Stamp, stamp, stamp. Carnet? Rip, stamp, stamp. Stamp, stamp, stamp. . . .

A mere four hours of this and we were in Colombia where we were met by two men from GM Colombia, called Col Motors or Colmotores. Santiago Camacho wore a blue jacket, jeans, loafers, and wore his black hair moderately long. He had the quick smile of a ladies' man and walked with a confident swagger.

The other man, Luis Nieto, stood by the truck while we spoke with Santiago. He had close-cropped dark hair, a nose that had been broken at least once, and he carried a small black suitcase in one hand. People passing by would look at the truck, as they always did, everywhere, and Luis would look at the people and then they wouldn't look at the truck anymore.

Santiago said we were to follow him to the port of Cartagena and that the drive would cost us two days.

"Two days," I said, amazed. It didn't look that far on the map.

Well, we would stop at night between about midnight and five in the morning, Santiago explained.

"Because it's dangerous to drive at night?" I asked.

"Not at all," Santiago said.

*   *   *

BUT OF COURSE it is dangerous to drive at night in Colombia. A travel
advisory from the U.S. State Department in my clip files read, "Because
of sporadic guerrilla activity, travel in certain areas may be hazardous.
Before venturing into rural areas, check with the nearest U.S. Consul-
ate. . . ."

The clip file was bulging with newspaper articles which indicated
that Colombia was either a vigorous country of extremely high-spirited
adventurers or a nation on the verge of anarchy. "Ranchers and peasants in rural Colombia are arming themselves with more and better
weapons to resist attacks from leftist guerrillas," *The Miami Herald*
said. The guerrillas kidnap ranchers, engage in extortion, and harass
rural business people. The ranchers were buying Uzi submachine guns.
A government official thought this sort of thing could escalate the
spiral of violence.

Which seemed to be true: members of the Patriotic Union—a political party representing the leftists and born out of a 1984 guerrilla-
government effort to reintegrate armed rebels into civic life—were
being assassinated at an alarming rate. In the last two years, 375
members of the party had been shot to death by unidentified gunmen.

There were three groups of rebels: ELP, M-19, and FARC. M-19 had,
for a time, been at war with the Medellín drug cartel, but the drug lords
had taken to disemboweling the leftists and hanging the corpses in
trees outside the homes of the victims' families. There was an uneasy
truce at present.

FARC, previously on good terms with the cartel, was now engaged
in a miniwar with drug traffickers for control of plantations in the
eastern jungles.

The previous week, one clipping read, a rebel land mine killed three
government soldiers and wounded eleven others. Meanwhile, rival
gangs of emerald traffickers killed twenty-three people and injured
twenty-four during a war for control of the precious stones.

And last year eleven thousand Colombians were murdered, making
homicide the country's leading cause of death among males aged fifteen
to forty-four.

In the area of the country we were presently driving, a lot of trucks
were being hijacked. It was easy to see why.

The road was a good two-lane blacktop with ample shoulders, but
the pitches were steep through mountains rising to seven thousand
feet. Along the sheer hillsides, there were scars where the mud and
rock had simply given up to gravity and fallen away from the land. The
roads writhed painfully through this wounded land. The turns were

sharp and continuous. Our tires screamed through them: Garry was pushing hard and we were doing no more than thirty miles an hour.

Santiago and Luis were out ahead in another Chevy that looked like a Monza but was called a Classic. It was red and had an automatic transmission. Santiago was driving, pushing the gutsy little gasoline engine hard, and when he passed a truck, he'd hold beside it for a while and then we'd see his arm shoot out the window and make a graceful circle: come ahead, come now.

If there was a car coming, he'd make a motion like patting a dog on the head: stay back.

"The guy," Garry said, "is a great driver."

Sometimes Santiago would circle us forward, then quickly pat the dog on the head: come ahead, ahh, sorry, not now boys, we got certain death up here.

The trucks, even the best of them, were moving ponderously on this serpentine roller coaster of a road. We followed one semi down a pretty perpendicular hill and he was going so slowly that our speedometer didn't even register. The driver, certainly in his lowest gear, was tapping his brakes every thirty seconds, holding them for perhaps five seconds and then letting go. The truck was probably overloaded—I imagined the driver was carrying at least twenty tons—and if the vehicle got away from him on a grade this steep, he would go screaming to the bottom of the hill and be horribly crushed by his own cargo. The grind of the brake pad against the wheel echoed off the scarred hillsides. It sounded like the moaning of a large wounded animal.

The truck, I couldn't help but notice, was going no faster than a man could walk. An ambush could be a one-man affair: jump up on the running board with a gun and discuss the matter with a man who couldn't take his eyes off the road or his hands off the wheel.

JUST AFTER SUNSET, we came screaming around a corner that led into yet another blind curve, but in the middle of this one there was a disabled truck carrying a load of logs. There were no lights or flares, and we didn't see it in the dark. Santiago slammed on his brakes and the little Chevy stopped about two feet from a projecting log.

Both Joe Skorupa and I knew that, on a steep downhill grade, our four- or five-ton vehicle was never going to be able to stop. We were going to smash into the back of the Chevy, drive it into the logs, and kill Santiago and Luis. But Garry hit the brakes full on and he stopped with inches to spare.

Garry was delighted and talked with Joe about GMC antilock

brakes and real-world capabilities and the wonders of this Sierra, which wasn't just a truck anymore. It gave me a hiddach.

We passed through too many military checkpoints to count. In the darkness, we'd switch on the dome lights so the soldiers could see us. Coast up to the guns with our hands where everyone could see them. Sometimes the soldiers simply waved us through. Sometimes they spoke with us for less than a minute. Sometimes they pulled us over.

"God, I hope they don't have a pit," Garry said, "anything but the pit."

When we were stopped, Santiago and Luis came back and talked to the soldiers. Luis showed them some sort of identification that seemed to impress them.

The road took us through a few towns and the streets were narrow, just wide enough for two trucks to pass. The sound of music boomed out of the open doorways of the crowded bars, and couples walked the streets, hand in hand. Everyone, it seemed, was socializing in the cool of the evening.

I saw a black woman with a rather astonishing figure standing in the doorway of a pool hall. There was a bright yellow light behind her, and I could see the shape of her legs through a thin bright-red skirt. A man standing beside her whispered in her ear, and she raised her fingertips to her lips to cover an involuntary smile.

I was contemplating this charming scene when a white Jeep carrying four municipal policemen in green military uniforms cut us off, forcing Garry to stop. I stood there with my hands in the air, smiling happily, while yet another teenager held an automatic rifle at my neck. I was getting awfully sick of this scene.

One of the officers searched the cab while Santiago and Luis talked with the man who seemed to be in charge. The guns came down after a tense few minutes and the officers began checking documents. They seemed especially impressed by a letter we had from the Colombian ambassador to Ecuador: "Please afford all possible cooperation to Garry Sowerby and Tim Cahill . . ."

"Good," the officer said. "Go."

He saluted us.

But it had been another Psalm-91 situation: a fast stop and lots of guns.

I pulled the map off the suckerboard.

"You know what the name of that town was?" I asked. I was probably shouting. Bad stops always made us loud and giddy. "Buga!"

"Buga?"

"BUGA!"

"Then," Joe Skorupa suggested, "those guys were the Buga men."

Joe, it seemed, was becoming slightly *roto*.

"They checked under the front seat again," I said.

"They always look under the front seat," Garry replied.

"They see those jerky wrappers."

"Figure us for jerky junkies right off."

Joe Skorupa, newly *roto*, thought that we could kick the habit. "Just go cold jerky," he said.

He was taking brutal revenge for those darting cows.

WE PULLED INTO THE TOWN of Pereira about midnight and were promptly stopped by two motorcycle policemen who listened to our story and took us directly to our hotel. They rode little dirt bikes with small engines that sounded like the buzz of mosquitoes against the throaty roar of our big diesel. Last night a press conference, I thought, today a motorcycle escort.

We went to sleep at twelve-thirty and were back on the road in four hours. On the way out of town, we were stopped by two more teams of police on dirt bikes: the mosquito patrol.

"I had a good time last night in town," Garry said. "Rode an elevator up one floor. Locked my door. And this morning was great. I brushed my teeth. There's a lot to do in that little town, especially when you schedule enough time to really enjoy yourself."

WE ROSE through lush mountains, alive with flowers, and watched as banks of clean fog rolled down the green coffee-growing hillsides in the distance. We rose up over a series of classic bus-plunge curves and, at the most obvious places—here, here is where the bus is going to go over—there was usually a shrine about the size of a doghouse with a statue of the Virgin inside. Sometimes there was just a metal plaque with an inscription: Humberto Díaz. Just that name and the date poor Humberto went spinning out into the abyss.

Everywhere in the country, on every mountain, we saw sweating cyclists in high-tech gear pushing expensive ten-speeds up impossible slopes. Colombian cyclists are the best hill climbers in the world. It is a known fact and a great source of pride to Colombians. Santiago always leaned out the window and cheered them on. Animals, he called them.

"Ahhh-knee-maul."

At the top of each summit there were always two establishments:

a coffee stand and a brake shop. We stopped now and again for coffee, which was better than any coffee I had ever had in my life. It was served in small ceramic cups, and rough-looking truck drivers drank it daintily, with a pinkie in the air.

We had a chance to talk with Santiago and Luis a bit. Santiago was the supervisor of the testing grounds at Col Motors, which, I suppose, meant he was one of Colombia's best test drivers. He had four children: the oldest was eighteen, the youngest was seven. Santiago had no English, and he couldn't speak with Garry, but he made it clear: Santiago Camacho thought Garry Sowerby was a hell of a driver. Garry returned the wordless compliment and showed Santiago pictures of Lucy and Natalie.

Luis was one of the senior security executives at Col Motors. He had four children. His oldest was fifteen. He was a friendly man with a slow, lazy smile, but somehow I didn't feel that I could ask him what he carried in his black suitcase.

"IT'S AN UZI," Garry said. We were running over another summit with puffy white clouds below us.

"Probably."

The road wound through a typical bus-plunge abyss, complete with three shrines, and Garry geared up to pass a truck on a blind curve. Santiago had already passed and all Garry could see was an arm, a circling hand gesture.

"It's funny," Garry said as we pulled in front of the truck. "There's three of us in here. Think about our families and everyone who knows us, and what they'd feel if we went over this cliff. I mean, we come into a blind corner on the edge of a cliff and there's a huge truck in front of us and here's some guy I can't even talk to and I'm looking at his hand and he's saying come ahead. And I do. That's trust."

"Am I wrong," I asked, "or do you get the feeling these guys really sort of like us?"

"It's because we're putting our lives in their hands."

"You know what Luis told me? He said that the Chevy they're driving belongs to the president of Col Motors. It's his personal car."

"Oh Jesus," Garry said. "We're beating the crap out of it."

Ahead of us, Santiago swerved to miss a large dog running across the road.

"You see that," Garry said.

"Big dog."

"You wouldn't think a dog along the Pan-American Highway would live long enough to get that big."

"A rule," I said. "There are no old dogs on the Pan-American Highway."

We were coming into Medellín and I was thinking about the dogs I had read about in my clip file. A week ago, an avalanche of red mud and rock killed at least 175 when it thundered down a mountainside and covered a neighborhood of tar-paper shacks to a depth of twenty feet. According to *The Miami Herald*, "rescue workers said they were guided in recovering many bodies by dogs howling at the spots where their owners were buried."

THE U.S. STATE DEPARTMENT has issued an advisory: "Travel to Medellín is potentially dangerous and if travel is necessary it should be undertaken with great care." The State Department would seem to have a point.

In 1981, Drug Enforcement Agency (DEA) officials, noting the markings on drug seizures, began to realize that much of the cocaine sold in the United States was supplied by a group of men working out of the Colombian city of Medellín.

In 1984, a small-time Colombian importer-exporter named Francisco Torres purchased seventy thousand gallons of ether from a New Jersey chemical wholesaler. Ether is used to refine cocaine from the coca leaf. Torres paid cash, $300,000; the ether was to be shipped to Colombia. It all seemed a bit suspicious: the salesman Torres spoke with called the DEA.

Chemical drums were bugged and the shipment was tracked to a huge complex of cocaine labs in the Amazon basin, not far from the border of Peru, where coca leaves are easily obtained. Some of those leaves, no doubt, came from the same plantation I saw on the banks of the Marañón in 1977.

The jungle city built on cocaine—it was called Tranquilandia—was raided by Colombian police in March of 1985. They seized fourteen tons of cocaine. It was the world's largest seizure ever, but records at the site showed that the lab had produced nearly twenty-five tons of cocaine in the previous seven months.

The records—a series of ledgers—showed links between the top drug lords of Medellín. For the first time, the DEA realized that the world's cocaine trade was a near monopoly run by the Medellín cartel.

The above information is taken from an informative six-part series in *The Miami Herald.* It was ground-breaking reporting, but there were no bylines on the front-page stories. That would be too dangerous, the editors agreed. The cartel was perhaps the largest criminal conspiracy on the face of the earth, and murder was a favored tool of the drug lords. In Medellín, the morgue processes an average of nine homicides a day. Drug lords have taken credit for the violent deaths of dozens of judges and police officers in Colombia, and they even gunned down a federal witness in Louisiana.

One of these drug lords was a handsome charismatic man named Carlos Lehder, a country boy who liked John Lennon and Adolf Hitler. Lehder's peculiar genius involved transportation of drugs from Colombia to the United States. Using early profits, he bought an island in the Bahamas for the purpose of shipping drugs into the States.

Eventually he was chased from the island and returned to his hometown of Armenia, in Colombia, where he bought eighteen apartment buildings and fifteen cars. He built a resort where the disco featured a huge statue of John Lennon, complete with bullet holes in the chest.

The provincial police chief told *The Miami Herald* that, "his influence was such that some youths were dressing like he was and talking like he was." Townspeople addressed him as "boss" or "doctor."

Lehder was indicted for drug trafficking in the U.S. and his extradition was sought in 1983. The Colombian Supreme Court approved Lehder's extradition. For the next three years, he hid in the jungle. Once Colombian police followed his girlfriend to one of his hideaways, but Lehder escaped in his underwear. He left behind a cardboard box containing over a million and a half dollars, mostly in American twenties.

On February 4, 1987, he was finally captured and flown to Florida in a DEA plane.

In June of 1987, the Colombian Supreme Court, under a death threat from the cartel—many judges were, in fact, assassinated— struck down its extradition treaty with the U.S. Lehder had been extradited under the terms of the old treaty. His trial was set to begin next month, in November 1987.

Now, in October 1987, we were approaching Medellín in the aftermath of a visit from John Lawn, America's top drug enforcement official, who called on the government of Colombia to resurrect the extradition treaty. He said the arrest of Lehder in Colombia and his upcoming trial in the United States proved that the old treaty had worked. Lawn had said these things only three days ago. He had, I guess, been allowed to leave the city. We were rolling downhill, closing fast on Medellín, a place where angry, dangerous men had had three days to think about what needed to be done with (or to) United States citizens.

The drug lords of Medellín, these instant millionaires, are known in Colombia as "the magic ones." Cocaine is seen, in Medellín, as a North American problem. The traffic grows out of demand in the United States.

And the traffickers have been wise to spend large amounts of their money on public-works programs. The majority of the big-time soccer teams in soccer-mad Colombia are said to be owned by drug lords who can afford astronomical salaries for the best players.

Traffickers have subsidized schools, bought soccer fields for children, built parks, and given away food to the poor. They have organized programs like "Medellín Without Slums" and built small villages of homes with plumbing for people who once lived in cardboard shacks. Carlos Lehder funded a fire department for his hometown and renovated major buildings.

Now, a few weeks before the start of his trial in the U.S., poor people all over Armenia and Medellín were praying for him at candle-lit vigils.

So a number of Colombians had reason to dislike North Americans, and we might expect some hostility. But I had done a press conference in Quito two nights before, and felt that gangs of *sicarios,* paid assassins, would be the most immediate threat. The assassins, according to a story in *Rolling Stone* by Howard Kohn, are actively recruited between the ages of fourteen and twenty-one. They go to one of seventeen different schools, where they sit through lectures, run obstacle courses, and learn to shoot during marathon sessions on the firing range.

Solely for training purposes, Kohn states, a prospective assassin must engage in a "murder of proof." Usually, an innocent stranger is selected, unless the trainers feel that a more difficult test is needed, in which case the victim may be a neighbor or a relative. Becoming a certified *sicario* "depends on shooting the unsuspecting person in a public place with witnesses and at point-blank range, eyes meeting eyes."

The assassins are sometimes organized into gangs like the Terminators, who stitch their victims up with bullets in the shape of a "T." The Black Flag gang leaves little black flags in the bullet holes. I don't know what the Devils, Rambos, Crazies, or Cockroaches do.

I did know that, a week before the start of Carlos Lehder's trial in the United States, it was a bad time for an American citizen to be passing through Medellín.

*   *   *

WE RAN down a double highway toward some modest mirrored sky-scrapers, and the city of Medellín. There was time to notice a haze of pollution in the city which was set in a basin below steep slopes. Medellín is just under a mile high, a temperate but frenetic city where flowers bloom in green parks, and men in expensive suits dine in elegant-looking restaurants.

We entered the city in an industrial section and stopped for diesel. Luis stood close by, watching everything, his suitcase in hand.

I asked Santiago if this was a dangerous city.

No, no. Not so bad. About like Lima or Caracas. Still, it wasn't a place you wanted to go to alone. It was best to have Colombian friends along.

You mean, I suggested, as guides. Like somebody might want a guide to Disneyland. Because of all the wonders?

Santiago smiled, all goodwill and charm.

I saw a newsstand across the street and decided to go buy a paper.

"Teem!" It was Luis.

"I'm going for a newspaper."

"No."

THE STREETS OF MEDELLÍN wound through a factory district alive with bustling workers, all of whom turned to regard the truck with what Garry took to be hungry eyes. He felt he was in a den of thieves.

"Taking the truck down this street," Garry said, "is like taking a naked woman through death row."

"The truck's filthy dirty."

"It's like taking a filthy-dirty naked woman through death row."

Hard-looking men did seem to be staring at the Sierra with a kind of lust in their eyes.

ON OUR WAY out of town, we passed an area of recent mud slides. Everything on all sides was green and fragrant, except for a half-mile-wide swath, like an avalanche chute, where the earth was naked. In that half-mile section of slope, rain had loosened the earth, and its face had melted off the bone. There were poor homes—made of cardboard and tin and tar paper—to either side of the rock-and-gravel scar.

I saw a mound of dirt several feet high and a mile long where the debris from the mud slide had been plowed off of the Pan-American Highway. I could see bits of cardboard and tin and tar paper in the dry red dirt. It made me think of those dogs, howling over the places where their owners had been buried.

WE WERE DOING SOME HARD DRIVING and the car that belonged to the president of Col Motors was not faring well. It had suffered two flat tires, and its brakes were fried. Santiago was using the emergency brake. Happily, we were out of the mountains, running through the northern rice-growing flatland that was veined with rivers, swollen red with the jungle mud that had been washed down the hillsides in the recent rains.

It was pleasant to follow Santiago and not have to ask directions in my bad Spanish. Because I didn't have to concentrate, I could observe, more closely, the delightful intricacies of the South American direction dance. It often involves making a quarter turn and extending the arm straight out from the shoulder, a stiff arm. Sometimes the wrist is held limp and the hand is flicked upward. This is a motion a person might make shooing flies off a cake on a table. It means, go straight. Another less common but more ebullient gesture is the simple basketball hook shot which is meant to take you around a corner and send you speeding down a straightaway.

Because Santiago was no fool and used the triangulation method of asking directions, we stopped many times and were treated to a dozen different styles.

Garry, Joe, and I began awarding points and arguing the merits of various performers.

"Oh, man, I'm telling you, that was a 9.6."

"Naw. 9.1, maybe. I thought he was a little slow on the stiff arm."

"Yeah, but did you see his shoofly? Absolutely superb shoofly. Followed by a double-hook shot. *Double* hook, man. 9.6 for sure."

THE PRESIDENT of Col Motors's car was running on one patched tire, and was now badly out of alignment. It was night, along a rural stretch of the lush flatlands, and Santiago hit a pothole that popped off a hubcap. He stopped to retrieve the hubcap that belonged to his boss, and suddenly out of the darkness, a huge screaming vehicle with one dim light in front shot past us at about eighty miles an hour, narrowly missing Santiago, who all but dove into the ditch. There was a man sitting atop some kind of strange frame, about ten feet in the air, and he was howling drunkenly.

"What the hell was that monster?" I wanted to know.

"Dune buggy from hell," Garry said.

"Looked like something out of *The Road Warrior*. Monster roaring out of the night with one bad eye. Somebody up there screaming curses."

"It was just a frame and a steering wheel up there."

"Why," I wondered, "would something like that exist?"

"It looked like a truck," Garry said. "The guy must have stripped it. No cab, no box, just an engine and a frame."

Santiago was standing in the middle of the road sadly regarding the hubcap that belonged to the president of Col Motors. It had been squashed flat by the dune buggy from hell.

WE SLEPT THAT NIGHT in Sincelejo, and made Cartagena the next afternoon. It was an easy day, with a mere half dozen military checkpoints, and two moving stops, only one of which required a gun at my neck.

Garry and I checked into a beachfront hotel on the Caribbean. There were telephones that actually worked in the rooms, real air-conditioning, and an in-room bar. We were sitting on the balcony of my room, looking out at the sea, and drinking a beer. We had one business day to complete the paperwork necessary to ship the truck to Panama.

"Nothing," I said, "can go wrong now."

DOCUMENT
HELL

October 9–12, 1987

I CANNOT PRODUCE a list, an orderly list, of the things one must do to load a one-ton four-wheel-drive pickup truck onto a containerized cargo ship out of Cartagena. The suffocating blizzard of paper generated in the process, when finally assembled, stacks up like the manuscript pages of *War and Peace*. It takes two or more people to cart the paper around, and all the documents must be allowed to visit many different buildings in all areas of the city.

The boat was leaving sometime in the evening or early morning hours. It was Friday, October 9, and we had one business day—until five o'clock—to write War and Peace. If we failed, it would be a week or more before we could book passage on an appropriate ship. It was a make-or-break day.

Luis and Santiago met us at the hotel in the battered Chevy. They introduced us to a tall clever-looking man, Jaime López, who had some experience in expediting these matters. Jaime, I saw with dismay, was not at all sure we could complete the work in one day, and especially not on this day. The coming Monday, October 12, was a national holiday, Discovery of America Day, and Colombians were looking forward to a three-day weekend. Latin Americans are little different from North Americans in such a situation. Not a lot of work gets done on Friday afternoon. People were looking forward to family outings, parties, binges at the disco.

My stomach felt fluttery, a sensation symptomatic of incipient Zippy's.

THE SHIPPING AGENT took our money and told us that our ship was called the *Stella Lykes*. He said they did not have twenty-four-foot containers: if our truck was twenty-one feet long, we'd have to shell out for a forty-footer. We paid cash, and got a few hundred receipts for our money. The shipping agent said we'd have to come back to this downtown office later with certain official forms obtainable only at the port.

There was a parking lot at the port where a crowd of people saw fit to surround the Sierra and the Chevy. Luis looked at them and they went away. A black man with a crutch and a withered left leg wandered into the sudden void and said he'd watch the car for us. His upper arms were huge. He said his name was Danny and that he had been in twenty-seven countries and he was wondering whether we'd like to buy any cocaine.

A few of us stayed by the truck until we were cleared to drive it into the port area. We gave Danny $5 to watch the Chevy. In point of fact, we had all noticed that Danny's crutch would be useful for wreaking havoc upon automobiles owned by penny-pinchers. It was the president's Chevy and, for that reason, we wanted Danny to like us. The car had suffered enough.

After an interminable conversation with a number of friendly but uninformed officials, it became clear that we couldn't put the truck in the cargo container and obtain the documents we needed to give to the shipping agent until we secured yet another set of documents at the customs office, which was not at the port but conveniently located a mile away.

The customs office looked like a junior college in Bakersfield and a man wearing muted-green slacks and a bright-green shirt came out to examine the truck. He looked like the late comedian Andy Kaufman: he had that same expression of eager bewilderment. It was, he said, impossible to examine the truck because it was raining. Did we have an umbrella? No? This is true? He seemed to be staggered by the information. He appealed to Jaime López: these men had driven the length of South America without an umbrella? Yes. But it was unthinkable!

A compromise was reached. Kaufman would ride down to the port, where a soldier could examine the truck in the rain and report to him, and then we could all ride back to the customs building and sign the proper documents.

Back at the port a tall soldier in a crisply pressed uniform opened the camper shell and reeled back, assaulted by the putrescent odor of rotting organic substances and the reek of diesel. This was, by far, the worst the truck had ever smelled. Everything had been baking in the tropical sun. Garry and I were very proud.

The fastidious soldier fingered an extra pair of shoes I had—they were covered over in what must have seemed a strange, vaguely strawberry-colored crust—then took a clean handkerchief from his pocket and wiped his hands.

He could, it seemed, sign one of the necessary documents himself if Andy Kaufman cosigned.

Luis stayed with the truck. Santiago, Jaime López, Garry, and I piled into the Chevy and drove back to the customs office. Kaufman noticed that Santiago was drifting into intersections at stoplights because he was using the hand brake to stop.

"Don't you have any brakes?" he asked.

"No," Santiago said, "I don't."

Once inside the customs building, we were subjected to a cruel psychology experiment involving a maze of offices. A man sitting behind a desk and wearing a big gold chain around his neck looked at the carnet, stamped it, and gave it back. In an office fifty feet down the hall, a large lady in a red skirt with tightly curled black hair put another stamp on top of the stamp the man with the gold chain awarded us. We visited five more offices where we secured various stamps or where previous stamps were initialed. After an official initialed a preexisting stamp, he usually stamped it himself, bam, for good measure.

The group of us had scattered throughout the maze, working independently but for the same goal. Jaime López appeared in the lobby, looking disproportionately forlorn. He motioned us back through a maze of corridors into a corner office where Andy Kaufman sat behind a large empty desk, looking morose in his eagerly bewildered way.

The carnet was written in French and though he didn't speak the language himself, he knew what information went where. All except for item number twelve. He didn't know what it said and couldn't sign the document.

The desk was covered with a glass plate, and under the glass was a large picture of Jesus, His Sacred Heart glowing in His chest. Garry looked at the picture. It was huge, about twice the size of a record album.

Garry explained, through Jaime López, that he was from Canada and that French was a national language there, taught in all the schools.

"Ahh, well then you could . . ."

"Of course."

Garry can't read a lick of French. He stared down at the picture of

Jesus, took a deep breath, and lied. "Item twelve is the number of your badge."

And so, with another flourish of the pen, we had cleared customs. Back at the port Danny offered us the services of attractive women who might help us enjoy the use of illegal drugs, and we gave him $5 to watch the car. There was, it seemed, the need for another search by another soldier. Buffeted by an unspeakable stench, he motioned for me to close the camper shell, hurry up, right now. Another document was signed.

Garry could now drive the truck into the container, which was a large rust-colored metal box with iron hooks protruding out of the floor to secure the load. We had to fold back the wire side mirrors to fit the truck into the container, and it was necessary to position the vehicle in the middle of the box, for balance. We couldn't however, lock the container until we had certain other necessary documents. Santiago smiled at the soldier, put an arm around his shoulders, and walked him a little way down one of the piers. There seemed to be an exchange made, hands touching hands. They came back laughing together and the soldier said that, for us, he would lock the container. Not only that, he'd personally stand guard over it until we came back.

Then we were speeding through the crowded streets of Cartagena, on our way to collect documents from the immigration service, when Santiago had to pull up hard on the emergency brake. We slid halfway out into a street where a parade was in progress. Attractive young women in abbreviated black dresses were doing hoochi-coo dances in the back seats of old Chevy convertibles. We backed out of the festivities and waited. It was maddening: how many 1966 Chevys could there be in Cartagena?

"What did you say to that soldier back at the port?" I asked Santiago. "How did you get him to do that?"

"Do what?"

"Get him to watch the truck?"

"He's my cousin," Santiago said.

WE WERE PARKED next to the Fortress of San Felipe. It had thick brick walls that sloped inward as they got higher. There were gun ports scattered over the great expanse of leaning brick that rose perhaps forty feet above us. It was a historic old fort, built around 1600, and, from my position at the bottom, it seemed impossible that any number of men, armed only with muskets, could overrun these massive and intimidating fortifications.

The central part of Cartagena itself, the old city, was surrounded by walls about ten feet high and fifteen feet thick. The walls were built by the Spanish between the years 1634 and 1735. There were two more forts defending the city and one that guarded the sea approach.

Cartagena was in need of walls because it was a collection point for all of the gold and silver the Spanish conquistadores collected from the conquered Aztecs, the Incas, the remnant Maya. Gold was shipped out of Peru and taken north up the Pacific coast to Panama, where it was ferried across the narrowest part of the isthmus by man and mule. It was then collected at a port on the eastern coast of Panama, Portobelo, and shipped down to Cartagena, where it was stored, sometimes for as long as a year, until a flotilla of cargo-carrying galleons and warships could be assembled to take the treasures back to Spain.

The amount of gold that the Spaniards took out of Peru alone is staggering: billions of dollars worth of it. The Incas used gold ornamentally. There were hammered golden plates representing the sun, which was sacred to the Incas. There were whole temples containing ornamental gardens made of gold: golden stalks of corn, for instance. Piles of golden potatoes.

All these riches poured into Cartagena, and the city was a tempting target for privateers, as the English pirates preferred to call themselves. They were only doing their patriotic duty, harassing Spain in the interest of England. Sir Francis Drake and 1,300 men sacked the city in 1586. A Frenchman, Baron de Pointis, took Cartagena with 10,000 men in 1697. In 1741, the great walls were in place, the fortifications strengthened and improved. An English force of 27,000 men laid seige to the city for fifty-six days but were finally turned back.

The walls of Cartagena are monuments to an officially sanctioned thievery that the culprits called glory. The English could steal from the Spanish for the glory of England. The Spanish could steal from the indigenous peoples of the Americas for the glory of Spain.

As in any large and successful criminal enterprise, greed expands and infects the entire chain of command. It is thought that many of the Spanish treasure ships that sunk on the way back to the Old World did so because they were dangerously overweighted with undeclared treasure that returning conquistadores had hoarded for themselves.

And, in Spain, there was a growing sense that not all of the gold and silver stolen in the New World was reaching its "proper owners." Officials wanted records to trace the path of the treasure. Intense documentation of every phase of the plunder business was implemented. How much gold from the Inca mine? Fill out some documents and make copies for the viceroy, for the accountants in Seville. The captains of the ships that ferried the treasure up the west coast of the Americas filled out documents. Wherever gold and silver changed hands, there were documents to be filled out and signed and stamped and initialed and signed and stamped again.

Men whose duty it was to process these documents felt left out of the process. They had to stamp this or that piece of paper and watch an unimaginable fortune pass by under their noses, untouched.

Officials found that they could delay work on the newly required documents, they could "misplace" essential papers, they could cause no end of trouble. It became easier for those moving the treasure to simply pay for the documents. Everyone, all down the line, got a little bit of the take. Things went smoother that way. It was only fair.

And that, I thought, sitting under the walls of the fort as an interminable line of 1966 Chevys and hoochi-coo dancers passed by, is the reason that the simplest business procedures in Latin America must be built upon a mountain of paperwork. It's a time-honored tradition.

Even today, public officials, customs officers for instance, are very poorly paid. On the other hand, everyone knows that they are entitled to a little bite of all business that passes their way: a kind of informal tax.

Whole villages can still be fed on the proceeds derived from one official document. In Latin America, every time a new official document is created, more families eat. No other area on the face of the earth is so dazed by documentation.

THE PARADE KILLED US. It was noon, and every official office would be closed until two. Jaime López groaned in despair: it had now become impossible.

Santiago dropped Garry and I at the hotel, where we said good-bye to Joe Skorupa who was flying back to New York. He said he'd check with Jane to see where we were and promised to meet us in Prudhoe Bay with a bottle of champagne. I said I didn't know if we would make it to Alaska. Maybe I'd just stay in Cartagena and sign documents for the rest of my life. I could die happy then; hell would hold no terrors for me.

Santiago went off to get the brakes fixed. He figured the last three hours of the impossible paper chase would be frantic and thought he'd be able to drive faster through the growing tangle of traffic if he felt himself able to stop.

The brake job took until two-fifteen and Santiago was afflicted with a severe and perhaps irremediable case of Zippy's when he picked us up. He tore through traffic, violated stop signs, and parked in the only available spaces, all of which were under clearly visible signs that read, NO PARKING. If there was a police officer present, all the better. Santiago would leap out of the car, throw his arms around the officer, hands would touch hands, they would laugh together for a moment, and then the officer would stand and watch our car until we had completed our business. Once, when the five of us came running out of a building, we saw one of these policemen waving away a tow truck.

Santiago, it seemed, had a lot of cousins in Cartagena.

We got the very last document we needed, the bill of lading from the shipping agency, at exactly 4:59. Jaime López didn't care about the Pan-American Highway: he thought we had set an unbreakable record on this very day.

THE *STELLA LYKES* was a Constellation Class cargo carrier, 665 feet long with a 75-foot beam. A steam turbine engine generated fifteen thousand horsepower from a single four-bladed screw. Registered in the United States, the ship has a normal cruising range of twenty thousand nautical miles and is manned by a crew of thirty-six. She cruises at a maximum of twenty-eight miles an hour and uses $200 worth of fuel per mile.

There were accommodations for eight passengers in four double cabins. Passengers on board for the duration pay $3,000 per person for a voyage of approximately thirty-five days with stops at Cartagena, Balboa, Buenaventura: working ports. There are two Panama Canal transits.

Garry and I shared a stateroom which was set amidships and might have been a room in a motel called the Economy Eight Travel Rhode Inn. There were four such staterooms, but we were the only passengers. Across the hall was a huge lounge with three couches, two card tables, a coffee table, a TV, a VCR, and a small galley.

We had said good-bye to Santiago and Luis only a few minutes before, and it had been a surprisingly emotional scene. They had come up to the stateroom, and when we were safely ensconced in the lap of economy, there was nothing left to do but say good-bye. Garry took Santiago's hand: the two of them looked each other in the eye, and then it was time for the big Latin embrace. Everybody hugged everybody, and we all did it again, on the deck, as Luis and Santiago were leaving.

"Those guys," Garry said, "were pros."

When had we ever even talked to them? Once, over coffee, on the road. A little bit in the Chevy as we were assembling War and Peace. I suppose Garry and I were impressed with the way Santiago and Luis carried themselves, their confidence and skill.

"We put our lives in their hands," I said.

"Sometimes, on those blind curves, all I could see was Santiago's hand, circling or patting the dog," Garry said. "I put our lives in Santiago's hand. His left hand."

"And they were beat. Did you notice that? Big circles under their eyes, running around half roto."

"I think they figured we'd been driving like that from Tierra del Fuego and would keep doing it on to Alaska. There was some mutual respect going on."

"And then Luis grabs your arm," Garry said. He imitated Luis's voice: " 'Teem, don't get off the boat.' "

These two pros had gotten us on the *Stella Lykes* after three days of hectic mayhem and didn't think it would be a good idea for us to go into town for any reason whatsoever. Something could happen: a fight, an arrest, a misunderstanding. No, it was safer to stay on the *Stella Lykes*.

"I think," Garry said, "I was sadder saying good-bye to those two guys than I was when I said good-bye to Jane and the girls. Because I knew I was going to see my family at the end of the trip. I don't know when or if I'll ever see Santiago and Luis again."

We sat for a while on our respective beds.

"Good guys," Garry said.

Time went by.

"This is strange," I said.

"The boat is supposed to set sail early this morning."

The whole day had been a hundred-yard dash, a frustrating, exhilarating race. Now we had nothing to do. Nothing at all. Run as fast as you can for a hundred yards but don't cross the finish line. That's what it felt like.

"Teem," Garry said, "don't get off the boat."

WE WENT DOWN four flights of stairs to the officers' mess in the *Stella Lykes*. Stacked near the door were compressed air tanks, very tightly secured, and above them was a big sign informing passersby that such tanks can fall over and that compressed air can escape through a hole the size of a pencil, which would cause the heavy tanks to rocket around and ricochet off the walls and kill people.

We had a good diner-quality U.S. meal, nothing gourmet, and our waiter was a man who looked like the entire front line of the Washington Redskins. We were tempted to call him "sir" rather than "waiter" but mustered up the courage to ask if there was any liquor available.

The front line of the Washington Redskins approached another gentleman, a tall black fellow with a way of standing that suggested his bones had a great deal of elasticity to them. The front line said: "These boys ain't had a taste for some time."

The rubber man—his name was Frank—told us to go up to our stateroom, and he arrived a short time later with a bottle of vodka and a bucket of ice. It was his own personal bottle but he wouldn't allow us to tip him. "Worth about, I suppose, eight bucks," he said.

A few drinks later, Captain Juergen Steinebach, the head of the stevedore company, stopped in for a visit. He was a burly man who had been around the world and done some rally driving. He had heard about our project and knew we would be concerned about our vehicle. He wanted to talk about what we were doing.

I said that the record run had two aspects: driving and documentation. The captain had worked in ports all over the world and agreed with me that the countries of Latin America had produced the most document-intensive set of cultures on the face of the earth.

It was now after midnight. The longshoremen were supposed to stop working at one-thirty. The captain took us for a stroll down the pier. We walked past a ship called the *Encouragement* and Captain Steinebach said that there was more to a cargo ship than one that will carry a lot of weight at good speed. He was most interested in the loading gear. "A cargo ship," he said, "becomes obsolete not because of her hull or engine, but because of her capacity to load and unload quickly."

The night was hot, the air heavy with humidity, and the pier was still wet with the morning's rain. Light from working ships fell across the damp pavement in sheets and patches. All else was darkness. It occurred to me that here, in a major Colombian port, there was a possibility that persons currently pursuing a career in international crime might be hard at work, and that such individuals could resent an accidental intrusion.

Still, we needed to be sure that the truck was loaded onto the *Stella Lykes*. In the utter darkness behind warehouse number 7 was the large rust-colored container that carried our truck. The longshoremen loaded it onto a towing trailer, hooked the *Stella Lykes*'s crane into it with a spreader device (most of the other containers were twenty-footers) and loaded it atop the other four forty-foot containers on the port bow.

We went back to the stateroom and tried to sleep. I was up three hours later. We were on that kind of schedule. I went into the lounge, then wandered back to the room where I lay in bed, on my back, staring up into the darkness. All Zipped up and nowhere to go.

THERE WERE SOME BOOKS in the lounge. One was about a man who killed people and kept a diary detailing his foul deeds. His wife found the diary. There was a confrontation and the wife was in jeopardy for some time but the bad guy got his in the end. I read the book while lying in the sun on a lawn chair on the gray metal deck in a deep canyon formed by towering stacks of rusty-orange containers.

It was an absolutely clear day. The water was a brilliant deep-water blue and there wasn't a whitecap in sight. We had a 260-mile voyage to the Panama Canal and Panama City. To the west, I could see a bit of the jungle: the roadless Darien Gap.

The Panamanians say that completing the road would be difficult: there are a lot of bridges to build, a lot of grading to be done. The official explanation for the eighty miles of roadless wilderness is that South American cattle have hoof-and-mouth disease. A road would allow infected cattle to wander into Panama and introduce the disease to Central America. (Which is why Roberto Raffo, the Argentine who was organizing the horseback traverse of the Americas, was having such a hard time getting permission for the trip into Panama.)

There are other reasons for the gap. On my previous visits to Panama, I had the distinct impression that Panamanians hate and fear Colombians on the basis of the sort of news that I had in my clip file. Why build a road for the convenience of paid assassins? That seemed to be the attitude.

Finally, everyone everywhere agreed that General Manuel Noriega, the Panamanian strongman, was involved in the drug trade. Specifically, it was alleged that he allowed traffickers to land and refuel planes in Panama in return for a percentage of the profits. Given a road from Colombia through Panama, Colombian freelancers could simply drive through the general's territory, thus depriving him of a major source of income.

So the gap was there because the Panamanian people didn't want a road. General Noriega didn't want a road.

I made the mistake of finishing the book in about an hour. Why was I speed-reading? Now what was I going to do?

There was a momentary shadow, a patter of rain, then it was clear again. The sun touched the clouds on the horizon and they burst into flame, burned out spectacularly, then darkened down into the color of a deep bruise. Below these damaged clouds there was the occasional flash and streak of lightning. Then it was dark.

ABOUT TWO the next afternoon, we were in Gatún Lake, the huge artificial lake in the center of Panama, eighty-five feet above sea level. We had passed through the first set of locks, Gatún Locks, and had risen into the lake at two in the morning. The water was greenish and there were strange circular islands, tufts of tangled emerald jungle that dotted the lake. The islands generated a slight misting fog that rose out of the greenery in drifting silver pillars.

The large freighter was hugging a meandering curve of red buoys, carving a wide sinuous wake around the jewel-like islands.

The *Stella Lykes* passed close to the southern shore and I could see areas where the waters of the lake had eroded the banks. The land was the deep red of jungle clay. Creeks that emptied out into the lake flowed red: the color of diluted blood or bad catsup. There was something feverish and malarial about the color of these sluggish rivers against the impossible greenery of the jungle and the more muted palette of the lake.

The channel winds twenty-four miles through Gatún Lake before it enters the Gaillard Cut, an eight-mile-long canyon blasted through the rock of the continental divide. In places, the freighter seemed a stone's throw from shore and the land looked vaguely prehistoric with ferny grasses and large-leafed plants. Frank, the rubber man, said that before the cut was widened, about twenty-five years ago, a man on the deck of a ship had to duck overhanging branches.

"Snakes on those branches," Frank said.

The jungle seemed to close in on the ship, and the odor of the land, rather than the sea, freshened the air. Birdcalls burst out of the jungle with increasing urgency just at dusk: the whistles and melodic songs of jungle life and not the shriek of seabirds.

The last set of locks—Pedro Miguel, a thirty-one-foot drop, and Miraflores, a fifty-four-foot drop in two steps—would lower the *Stella Lykes* back to sea level. Lines connected to four small locomotives pulled us into the narrow lock. The engines were called mules.

"They used to really use mules," Frank said.

Beside us, a large cargo ship, painted bright-yellow, was rising in the adjacent lock as we sank. The lights of the lock complex, set on high poles, were blinding, and the night seemed exceptionally dark behind them.

"Ought to be tying up in Panama City in a couple of hours," Frank said.

At nine that evening, the *Stella Lykes* was in port. Longshoremen began working immediately, and we waited for them to off-load the truck. Frank, who hadn't been around for some time, emerged from the crew's quarters wearing an iridescent gold suit, gold boots, and a wide-brimmed gold hat. He carried a polished wooden walking stick with a gold handle. On board, Frank was a man who wore T-shirts and faded jeans.

"You boys ought to come along," Frank said.

"We need to be sure they off-load the truck."

"Be a shame," Frank said, "to miss the flatback factory here."

"Next time, buddy."

An hour later the container carrying the truck was unloaded and trucked over to a large customs shed. Garry and I stood on the pier, shaking hands, and I assured him that nothing could go wrong now. We could clear customs in a couple of hours tomorrow, head north, and have the record in our pocket inside of two weeks. About that time, Frank appeared out of the darkness, flanked by two Panamanian policemen. He seemed to be under arrest.

"Forget my shore pass," he explained.

We followed him back onto the *Stella Lykes*. "Maybe you boys want to go into the lounge, have a drink," Frank said.

"We're driving tomorrow," Garry said.

Frank shook his head: negative on that.

"What?" I asked.

"See, you boys shoulda come with me. I met this girl. She was a master of tongue fu."

"Frank, what are you saying about driving tomorrow?"

"I'm saying you ain't gonna be doing any. This girl, she could . . ."

"Frank!"

"Well," Frank said, "it seems that, uh, tomorrow is, well, it's a national holiday here. National Revolution Day. They tell me customs don't work for sure, not on National Revolution Day."

NATIONAL REVOLUTION DAY, I suppose, is an occasion of great merrymaking in Panama. I can tell you that customs officers do not work on National Revolution Day.

We were staying in a hotel in Panama City, just off a major road flanked almost entirely by bank buildings, twenty and thirty stories high. Swiss bank. Bank of this country, bank of that. In the distance, down the empty streets, I could see a pair of golden arches. It could have been a street in any major North American city—indeed, the official currency in Panama is the U.S. dollar—but everything was closed and there was no one on the streets. It was like an Ingmar Bergman film, with ceiling fans.

My room had a TV and I watched CNN for a while. Bork would not be confirmed for the Supreme Court, the Minnesota Twins had won the American League pennant, there was a hurricane approaching Florida. I lay there in bed and the same news kept happening: Bork, Twins, hurricane.

Garry called from his room, which was next to mine.

"Wouldn't it be terrible," he said, "to be in jail?"

Bork, Twins, hurricane, Bork, Twins . . .

Our rooms were on the third floor. Across the street was a three-story pink apartment building badly in need of paint. There were no windows in the building: balconies, which could be closed off by a curtain, opened up into a combination kitchen and living room. I could see women cooking dinner and men sitting shirtless on the balconies, drinking beer. The walls of the building were covered with graffiti: CHANGE NOW, the words read, and ENOUGH!

I assumed that these messages had reference to General Manuel Noriega, head of the Panamanian Defense Forces, the man who ran the country.

Just outside my room, sitting on the sill of the hallway window, were two men in their thirties wearing white polo shirts with alligators on them. They had been there all day, sitting beside the kind of white suitcase used to carry a computer. The suitcase was open, and some sort of electronic listening gear was arranged to pick up conversations from the "change now" apartments. The men were sitting out in the open, in a public hallway, and didn't seem to care who saw them.

Sure, we listen in on the conversations of private citizens. So what?

IT WAS A HOLIDAY, and there wouldn't even be a riot. Riots only happen on workdays. This is a rule.

On our last trip to Panama, there had been the electric threat of riots in the streets. The middle class wanted badly to get rid of Noriega who they saw as increasingly bad for business. The fact that he had had political opponents murdered and dismembered did not endear him to the people I met, and his reputation as a drug profiteer was an embarrassment.

"He makes fifty thousand dollars a year as head of the Defense

Forces," one executive told me. We were having lunch at an exclusive
club overlooking the Pacific. "So how come he owns at least three
houses worth a million dollars each?"

The executive had picked us up at our hotel in an expensive four-
wheel-drive vehicle. He apologized for being late, but he felt there
would be a riot that afternoon—perhaps the government would fall—
and he thought that it would be wise to take his money out of the bank.
Just in case. The cash was stashed in the back of the vehicle, in a large
leather suitcase.

As we drove to the club, past the row of banks, I saw hundreds of
people standing in line to make similar withdrawals. Workers were
putting plywood boards over the plate-glass windows of the banks in
preparation for the afternoon's riot.

Did the executive expect to participate?

Sure. He'd stand behind barricades and wave a white flag, the symbol of opposition. He'd pound pots and pans like everyone else. That is,
if a riot developed.

Were there a lot of wealthy executives rioting in the street?

Yes.

That afternoon, there had been a heavy tropical downpour and the
riot was postponed. It was to erupt several days later, after I left. There
had been a sense, then, that the general could not survive.

Now, two months later, the opposition seemed dispirited. Noriega
was too cunning, too clever. He was entrenched.

FOR WANT OF ANYTHING BETTER to do, Garry and I went to the hotel
restaurant for an early dinner. It had been an excruciating afternoon.

"This," Garry said, "is the worst day of my life."

We discussed the possibility of going out. There were any number
of enterprising nightclubs all over the city. On our last trip, we had
been to an art deco bar where women on stage, dressed in crossed
bandoliers and little else, did a close-order drill with toy rifles to the
music of the "Colonel Bogey March." All the customers in the place
were men in suits who seemed to consider the drill the apogee of classy
eroticism. Forever afterward, whenever I wanted to make Garry laugh,
all I had to do was whistle the opening bars to the "Colonel Bogie
March."

Which is what I did at dinner. Da-da, da da da dat dat dada.

"We can't," Garry said.

"I know."

"I can't stand this," Garry said. He was actually suffering.

Which is the final irony of the adventure-driving business: on a down day, it is wise to sit in the hotel room, alone—Bork, Twins, hurricane—on the off chance that you could get into some kind of unexpected trouble just walking around. The essence of our adventure was to avoid adventure at all costs.

Garry called from his room.

"I just threw up," he said.

ON THE MOUNTAIN
OF DEATH

October 13–14, 1987

THE PHONES in Panama City worked just fine. You could dial an international call from the hotel room. At five-thirty the next morning, Garry was speaking to Jane in Moncton. Could she please get in touch with the Canadian embassy in Costa Rica? Find out if there was any word from Honduras? The director-general of the Institute of Tourism there, Melissa Valenzuela-Treffot, had promised us a letter of recommendation to smooth our passage through customs. It had been three months since we talked to her. Where was the letter?

We were waiting on another letter from Mayda Denueda, the director of international promotion for the Nicaraguan Institute of Tourism, called Intourismo. (Yes, the Nicaraguan Institute of Tourism.) Another woman, Chistita Caldera, who worked for Intourismo, had made a vague promise to meet us at the southern border of that country. Could that be confirmed?

Jane had been working on these matters but there had been no one at the Canadian embassy in Costa Rica yesterday. It had been a national holiday there as well: Columbus Day.

One other thing: Jane said that GMC expected us in Dallas at nine next Monday morning for a press conference. The public-relations firm organizing the event was adamant. If there were a bunch of reporters waiting for us and we didn't arrive on time, or at all, it would look very bad indeed. Our absence could be blamed on the truck and not on the fact that, for instance, we were enjoying a few carefree days in some Central American jail. Or that we had been shot and were hiding in the jungle, bleeding and without food.

No, the public-relations firm's thought was that our absence at the press conference might be attributed to mechanical failings in the Sierra. "In its first real-world test," the nightmare AP wire copy might read, "a GMC Sierra driven by a team seeking a world speed record on the Pan-American Highway failed to appear as scheduled today in Dallas. Spokesmen for the automotive giant could not explain why the Sierra, newly redesigned at a cost of 2.8 billion dollars, could not be present at the press conference that had been scheduled for almost a week. 'We don't know where the truck is,' one obviously bitter executive said, 'but one of the drivers has kids, and we know where they are.' "

Jane was being pressured: could we promise, absolutely, to be in Dallas six days from now?

Well, let's see: all we had to do was endure an unspecified amount of time in Panama City's document hell getting the truck out of a locked metal box in the port. Once on the road, we had to whip through six borders and twelve sets of formalities. One of those borders—the one between Nicaragua and Honduras—was a war zone.

The public-relations firm wanted a definite yes or no, today.

Hey, no problem. We'd be there, nine Monday morning, sharp.

Jane said she'd call the Canadian embassy in Costa Rica and tell them we'd be there sometime in the middle of the night. Garry said he would call her back from the hotel once the truck had cleared customs.

LUIS PAZ CÁRDENAS, the director of Industrial Equipment and Motors in Panama, took us on our tour of document hell in Panama. He was a calm, dignified man who expected to retire in nine months. There was a statue of the Virgin Mary on the dashboard of his car, and he drove slowly, carefully, to the various buildings housing various officials who needed to stamp, initial, and restamp our documents. Luis did everything slowly and carefully: there was not a germ of Zippy's disease in the man and he may have been the most cheerfully efficient individual we met on the whole trip.

The document that we had to have attesting to our good character? Could we have that now, on the spot?

Ahh, no, never, señor. It was an important and complex document that generally took two days to validate.

Two days?

With the help of Luis, we got the document in two hours.

"You know," Luis told us as we drove through Panama City at about fifteen miles an hour, "I once went to Japan on business. I had never been out of Panama, not even to the United States. I arrived in Tokyo on a Sunday morning, and my Japanese associates were supposed to pick me up that afternoon.

"I wanted to go to Mass. I looked in the phone book in my hotel room and found something that looked like a Catholic church. Then I checked the address against a subway map of the city. I took the subway, then asked a policeman to direct me to the church. I used sign language. I folded my hands in prayer, and the policeman thought I was looking for a temple, so I made the sign of the cross. He understood that. I asked how long it would take to walk there. I made a walking motion with my fingers and pointed to my watch. The policeman took my arm and indicated a fifteen-minute segment on the face of my watch.

"When the Japanese picked me up at the hotel that afternoon, they were amazed that I had traveled halfway across the city, gone to Mass, and gotten back to the hotel without any help at all. That was the one big foreign adventure of my life."

He paused and said, "Of course, it's nothing like what you're doing."

"No," I said, "it's exactly like what we're doing."

"Anyway," Luis said, "I understand what it means to have someone help you in a foreign country."

WITH THE SEEMINGLY UNHURRIED HELP of Luis, we cleared customs and assembled a Russian novel's worth of paperwork in the hours between six in the morning and noon. Six hours to write War and Peace.

Back at the hotel there was good news from Moncton. Chistita Caldera would be waiting for us at the southern border of Nicaragua. The letters from Nicaragua and Honduras had arrived at the Canadian embassy in San José, Costa Rica.

Garry said that it looked like we'd arrive at the embassy in Costa Rica sometime between midnight and four in the morning. How would we pick up the letter? Jane had thought of that. There was a night guard at the embassy gate. He would have the documents in hand.

WE PULLED OUT of the port and I stopped at a large North American–style supermarket to buy more bottled water. Then we drove over the bridge across the Panama Canal and headed for the border, 220 miles to the north.

Garry said, "Let's see what this baby'll do."

"Part two."

* * *

PANAMA, for all its trouble, is not a dirt-poor country. Along with Costa Rica, it shares one of the highest standards of living in Central America. This was reflected in the roads, which were straight, well graded, and very fast. Panama's population is comparatively small and there was very little traffic, which was good for us because it was now one in the afternoon and our information was that the border closed at five. Either that or eight. No one knew for sure. It seemed a good idea to get there before five. If the border was closed and we had to stay overnight, we'd lose our escort through Nicaraguan customs. Chistita would be waiting for us there at eight the next morning.

Our information was that customs formalities at the southern border of Nicaragua could take up to ten hours. Some people had waited two days to enter the country. Others had simply been turned back with no explanation. We needed Chistita and there was no way to contact her at the border. Telephones in Nicaragua most often don't work.

Garry pushed the Sierra to eighty and eighty-five. He was sweating profusely, flushed with heat and concentration. The road rose over some low green mountains and a cooling rain began to fall. The temperature dropped fifteen degrees, and the air was thick with the fragrance of tropical grasses and flowers. There was a roadside shrine to some forgotten bus plunge, but the drop below was only a few hundred feet. If the road through the Darien Gap were ever completed, Colombians would view this shrine as a tourist attraction: the world's shallowest, most laughable bus plunge.

The grasses alongside the road were knee- and thigh-high. Rocky spires, spaced at odd intervals, rose several hundred feet above the lower, more rounded green hillsides. The ridges above us held trees that grew in groves of twenty or thirty along the drainages. The trees had thin trunks and they only branched out at the top, like parasols.

Russell Chatham, the great landscape painter, once said that painting such land was like painting nudes. He would, I thought, love the mountains of Panama. From a distance, the hillsides seemed smooth, like rich green velvet, and the rounded rolling shapes were explicitly erotic. Trees only grew in the folds and pocketed groins of these mountains.

We dropped out of the mountains and a stupendous rainbow formed behind us. Wet pavement ahead steamed in the sudden sun. A roadside billboard informed us that SAN JUAN BEER IS FOR MEN. Garry slowed for a small town that a large sign identified as COCA-COLA. Further study showed that, under the corporate logo, in letters only a quarter as high, there was another name: SAN LORENZO.

Panamanians—the white population, the black, the mestizo—are enterprising people. Every mountain village, it seemed, was either a Pepsi or a Coke town. I envisioned hardworking salesmen dealing with shrewd village officials. Say there were three Pepsi towns in a row; the Coke salesman is going to have to cut the next village in line a very good deal. Some towns, the bigger ones, were both Coke and Pepsi towns.

In the large northern town of David we asked a policeman when the border closed. Five, he said. We were thirty miles from the border. Garry pushed it hard and we arrived at 4:50.

The formalities took until well after five, but people still seemed to be passing. Okay. But maybe what people meant was that the Costa Rican border, across the way, closed at five. This uncertainty made the usual stamping and initialing process infuriating. The last soldier was very young and it was clearly his first day on the job. He wanted to do everything right and had to fill out a short form, then sign his name to it. He drew every letter, one at a time, concentrating fiercely and biting his lip. It was physically painful to watch him.

He handed us the completed form and said we should take it to another official in a building a quarter of a mile back into Panama. That gentleman, an efficient older man, said the document was in order. We took it back to the soldier. He stared at it for some time, turning it this way and that. His face was crumpled in cheerless concentration and he was squinting in the manner of a man staring into a very bright light. Would we take it back one more time and get an informal note from the older man? Just to be sure that everything had been done correctly?

Oh hell, sure.

The older man said that no such note was necessary and that we should tell the young soldier to stop being such a blockhead and let us through. Everything was in order. He did not want to see us again, he said.

The soldier still wasn't sure. We argued for fifteen minutes and were interrupted now and again by other people who rolled through the border with no trouble at all.

"Let's just go," I told Garry.

We got into the truck and drove very slowly past the guardstand where the soldier stood. He yelled something and we smiled happily.

"Thank you," we called back, "thanks very much. Thank you for your help. . . ."

THE COSTA RICAN border was open. A crowd of young children gathered around us at the parking lot fronting the customs building. They were not beggars, but reasonably polite, rambunctious children curious about foreigners. When the word got out on the kid hotline that we were giving out lapel pins, dozens more of the children materialized. We were mobbed and Garry blew up.

"No more!" he shouted in Spanish and pushed his way into the customs building.

It was the first time I had ever seen Garry lose his temper with any of the children who constantly surrounded us whenever we stopped. True, he had just spent four tense hours driving at top speed in what we had assumed was a make-or-break run for the border. But we had endured some tough drives in South America, and Garry was just never short with children. Never.

He was sweating out of proportion to the heat, and his skin was flushed. There was something wrong. Something, I thought, that had to do with Nicaragua. Garry had always hated Nicaragua.

AS BORDERS GO, Costa Rica was almost pleasant. All the officials were young, most of them no more than thirty years old, and they dressed like students. In one room, dozens of officials crowded around a black-and-white television set: it had just been announced that Costa Rican president Oscar Arias would be awarded the Nobel Peace Prize. Arias and five other Central American leaders had signed a peace plan two months ago. It called for regional cease-fire, amnesty, an end to foreign support for insurgents, and government dialogues with the armed opposition.

Arias, at forty-five, was the youngest man ever elected to the presidency in Costa Rica. A lawyer and economist, with degrees from the University of Essex and the London School of Economics, Arias pointed out that in six years of armed strife, the region's trade had declined from about a billion dollars a year to $400 million. There had been a corresponding decline in investments. Not only would peace save lives, Arias seemed to be saying, it was also good for business.

The Arias plan was well received. On the television, Nicaraguan president Daniel Ortega was saying that he was willing to meet with the contras fighting his government.

Before we got the final stamp, we were treated to the televised comments of Ronald Reagan. President Arias, Reagan said, was a world leader of great stature who richly deserved the Nobel Peace Prize. Reagan did not say that he approved of the Arias plan, but that detail was lost on the Costa Rican customs officials who broke into cheers at various times during the broadcast.

There was a sense of great things about to happen in the region, a feeling of hope. I also sensed a wave of great pride among the Costa Rican people, who saw Oscar Arias as a figure comparable to John F. Kennedy.

IT IS SAFE to drive at night in Costa Rica. There are no armed insurgencies, and the country long ago abolished its army. According to Oscar Arias, "in my homeland, you will not find a single tank, a single artillery piece, a single warship, or a single military helicopter." Costa Ricans are forever telling visitors that there are more teachers in the country than policemen; they point out that the country has the highest literacy rate in Central America and the best health-care system in the region.

The government attempts to remain neutral politically, though it has strong ties with the United States. It has been a democracy for over a hundred years, making it the oldest democracy in Latin America, and one of the oldest in the world.

In the 1850s, the government offered free land to those who would grow coffee. The crop brought near-instant prosperity, and the peasant class became landowners. Except for the town of Limón, where the people are primarily black, most of the people are white or mestizo. In recent years, Costa Rica has established several remarkable national parks, which are responsibly administered. (Many areas in South and Central America are designated national parks. These are usually remote, underpopulated areas where life goes on as always. People living on the land often do not know they are living in a national park. Mining, timbering, and petro development are all generally allowed, but the government can always point to national parks on its maps and talk about concern for the environment.)

Costa Rica is sometimes described as the Switzerland of Central America. On this day, when the president had been honored, we expected to see dancing in the streets when we hit the capital city of San José.

What could possibly go wrong?

The road to San José runs along the top of a ridge, through orchid-growing country, on a mountain called Buena Vista: good-view mountain. We would, of course, be driving through the orchids on good-view mountain in the middle of the night.

The road crosses the continental divide at about ten thousand feet. They say from that point, on a rare clear day, you can look in one direction and see the Atlantic Ocean, then turn 180 degrees and see the Pacific.

There is another, informal name for Buena Vista.

"Why," I asked a Costa Rican gas-station attendant, "do they call it the Mountain of Death?"

He was a short man of Italian ancestry and he wore the sleeves of his T-shirt rolled up to reveal bulging biceps.

"Why?"

He stared at me. "The road to San José," he said slowly, as if to a very young child, "is very steep, very narrow, very foggy, and very dangerous. Many have died."

We were used to people dying from gunshot wounds and I wanted to be sure about this: "They die in automobile accidents?"

The man jerked back, as if dumb questions were punches, like left jabs.

"In automobile accidents," he said very slowly, "many have died."

So GARRY, who was still jittery and tense from the run to the Panamanian border, felt he should drive the Mountain of Death.

There was no one walking on the shoulder because there was no shoulder. Trees and foliage lined the road, and it was very dark. It had rained earlier, and the cooling mountain air was heavy with the sensual fragrance of orchids. A short time later, it was too cold to drive with the windows open. At six thousand feet, there was a customs check and the young officer was wearing a parka and wool cap.

We were rolling through long uphill climbs followed by short stretches of flatland that invariably led to another steep pitch. Pockets of thick fog sulked in the drainages of the rivers, on the mountain curves, in the flats.

It was slow, torturous driving through these areas the yellow road signs identified as ZONAS DE NEBLINA. I liked the word *neblina* for fog. Every time we saw one of these signs, we were plunged into a thick pewter-gray fog that limited our visibility to no more than ten feet.

"Another nebulous area," I'd tell Garry.

We were crawling through a fog as thick as porridge on an uphill stretch. There were three big trucks ahead of us and we were probably making all of six or seven miles an hour when a new Toyota pickup truck pulled out and passed all four of us on a blind uphill curve, in the fog. It had been a white truck, its side panels barely visible through the fog. Trees and foliage lined the road, but I had a sense that, just beyond the greenery, there were drop-offs everywhere. It felt like bus-plunge country.

"That guy must be drunk," I said.

"Either that or suicidal."

I was playing word games in my mind—*nebulous, neblina*—when we rounded another corner on a high ridge that was clear of the hellish fog. Two trucks and a car were pulled up on the side of the road. Men with flashlights were standing by a break in the foliage. A truck, they said, had come speeding around the corner, didn't make the turn, and had gone off the road here. It had just happened.

We were somewhere near the ten-thousand-foot level. Four or five of the thin trunked trees were broken off near the ground, the jagged stumps very white in the light of our flashlights.

I followed the beam of one of the lights down until the darkness swallowed it. There was no fire, nothing. I imagined this was one of the places where you could see both the Atlantic and Pacific oceans. The vehicle had sailed off the ridge on the Atlantic side.

"Was it a truck?" I asked one of the men.

"A white Toyota," he said.

So the driver who had passed on a blind uphill curve in the fog had taken a ten-thousand-foot dive into the Atlantic from the top of the Mountain of Death. There was a strange absence of emotion about this. I looked down into the black void and felt insubstantial, nebulous.

WE PULLED INTO SAN JOSE, which was set in a mountain basin, like Quito. The weather was cool enough for a light jacket, and a woman who sold diesel at a convenience store that might have been an American 7-Eleven used her only phrase of English about a dozen times. "Welcome to Costa Rica, my friends," she said.

It was just after midnight, but people were indeed dancing in the streets, celebrating the honor their young president had brought to the country. We stopped on a corner to ask directions. People wanted to banter, to joke, to ask us what we thought of Costa Rica and Oscar Arias. It was a very good-natured crowd and we were handing out lapel pins, pledging eternal friendship and Pan-American unity when a flashy red Toyota truck pulled up in front of us and everyone disappeared. The truck was jacked up on monster tires and carried a lot of shiny chrome.

There were three men in the Toyota. All at once they were crouched behind the open doors of their vehicle like men expecting a gunfight.

Garry put his hands, both of them, on the wheel at eleven and one. I put mine flat on the dash. When the men saw we were unarmed, they moved out from behind their doors. One of them—a big man with a scar that ran from his ear to the tip of his chin—came at us from the passenger's side. Another approached from our left. He had a ponytail, a furious untrimmed beard, and wore a faded denim jacket which was open to the waist so you could see expensive gold chains against a black T-shirt. You tended to focus, however, on the gun tucked in the front of his pants. It was a big automatic, a nine millimeter that might carry a fourteen-shot clip.

Here we were in a country with no insurgencies; a country that had more teachers than policemen.

So who were these guys with the guns? Teachers?

The third man—younger than the other two—stood by the red truck. He wore a blue short-sleeved polo shirt that set off his brown leather shoulder holster and the wooden handle of a large revolver. Probably a forty-four. He never moved, and his eyes never left mine.

The man with the scar wore a light-beige rain jacket and there was a gun-sized bulge just under his left arm. He approached Garry, put his right hand into his jacket, and flashed a badge that was in his wallet along with a picture of the scar-faced man and some official-looking stamps. "Police," he said.

The man checked our papers. A few minutes later, he handed everything back and apologized for the inconvenience. The officers said they were looking for drug dealers. We had aroused their suspicions: two bearded strangers in a big truck talking with people after midnight in an unsavory section of town. There had been objects passed back and forth: the seemingly surreptitious exchange of what the officers now knew were lapel pins and milk shakes.

The big man with the scar spoke good English and suggested that we not park our truck on the street. We told him that we were pushing on for Nicaragua anyway. Well, he said, that was going to be a problem. "If you take the Pan-American, you'll drive for three hours and then be turned back."

The highway to the north, he explained, was blocked by a rock slide that would take several days to clear. There was however, a back road.

It was gravel and dirt, very bad, but if we wanted to get to Nicaragua by eight the next morning, it was our only chance.

The man took our map from the suckerboard and, in consultation with the bearded man, traced a new route over a spiderweb of back roads.

"But look," he said, "even here in Costa Rica, if you're driving at night, don't ever stop for someone in an unmarked car."

"But you guys have an unmarked car," Garry pointed out.

"We're looking for drug dealers," the man explained. "It helps," he said, "not to look like a police officer."

"But what would you have done if we tried to run?" I asked.

The man shook his head slowly, and in a negative manner.

"SCARFACE," Garry said. "Guy tells us not to stop for unmarked cars. Don't stop for anybody unless he's driving a red pickup and has a badge. How are you supposed to know?"

We had found the Canadian embassy and picked up a manila envelope containing the letter from Honduras and the one from Nicaragua. I had opened the big three-ring binder that contained all our letters for all the countries we were driving through. Customs officers seemed to like to look through it, and the sheer volume of official correspondence, festooned with the great seals of various countries, often impressed them favorably. On the other hand, the Sandinista government in Nicaragua accused Honduras of harboring contra camps. If a Nicaraguan official saw a letter of recommendation from Honduras, we might be denied entry into the country. No friend of Honduras, the man might feel, is a friend of Nicaragua.

The letters were inside clear envelopes, one on one side, one on the other. I placed our letter from Honduras in one of the envelopes, between two letters from Argentina, so that it was reasonably well hidden.

We made coffee, but it turned out that I had not bought drinking water in Panama City. It was sparkling water. When you tried to make coffee with it, it foamed up like an experiment in the mad scientist's lab.

It was beginning to get roto on the down side of the Mountain of Death, and we drank our furiously foaming coffee cold, without pleasure, for the caffeine. It was the essence of roto.

THE ROADS WERE BAD and Garry was driving, as he had been since noon. It was now two in the morning.

"The road sign says eleven," Garry said. "Aren't we supposed to be on three?"

"I looked at the other map, the colored one. Three is marked eleven."

"What's the next town?"

"San Mateo. If we hit San Mateo, it doesn't matter what the road is called, we're going the right way."

There was an unmarked crossing and both roads plunged steeply downhill.

"These maps," I said, "say the road we want will run north."

We checked the compass. The road to the left looked to run more generally north. We drove for half an hour and the road jigged east for a time, then jagged west, but it never turned south, which was mildly encouraging.

"If the Pan-American is closed," Garry reasoned, "why don't we see any traffic? Wouldn't truck drivers know about this route?"

"Good point."

"Navi nightmare time."

"No, wait. There's a sign for San Mateo up there."

"Yeah," Garry said, "but where are the trucks?"

THEY WERE STACKED UP where the narrow winding road—all mud and loose gravel—dove through thick jungle foliage into the lowlands and Nicaragua. The drivers had set out flares: branches that they had broken off trees, doused in diesel, and set afire. We stopped in the back of a line of perhaps fifty semis.

Two of the big trucks, we were told, had had a mishap and were blocking the road. A small car could squeeze between them, but our Sierra was too big. We would have to wait. It would take twelve hours, at a minimum, before the road could be cleared.

We had to meet Chistita Caldera at the border in a little over five hours.

Garry fumed in silence. In the dashboard lights, his face looked feverish and, though it was cool enough for a jacket, he had begun to sweat copiously.

Suddenly he got out of the truck and walked down half a mile to the accident, carrying a flashlight. I made myself a cup of foaming roto coffee and when I had just about finished it, I saw Garry walking back uphill. He was moving fast, like an angry, determined man and I knew that we were going to go for it.

Garry folded our wide side mirrors into the truck. "We have," he said, "about five inches of clearance between those trucks."

"You measured it?"

"Eyeballed it."

He put the truck into four-wheel drive, low. "The problem is," he said, "that there are sheep guts all over the road. The stuff looks fresh and it's slippery as hell. I don't know why someone would do that, but there must have been a lot of animals. The road is ankle-deep in blood and intestines."

Garry drove past the line of trucks, and the drivers, who had nothing better to do, followed us down to the metal narrows that Garry had eyeballed. Two trucks blocked the road and were sitting back-to-back, one on the uphill side, one on the downhill. It was a very steep section there, and we'd have to try to drive across the road, at a right angle to its direction of travel, in order to squeeze between the back ends of both trucks. It looked too narrow to me. Worse, we would be traveling across the hillside, over a slippery carpet of gore.

The truck drivers stamped around in the foliage and found an area where Garry could back up to get in position. A very large crowd had gathered to watch the show.

"You'll never make it," one man called.

Another bet we would. Money began to change hands in the light of burning branches. Garry took it pretty fast, afraid that the truck might begin to slide where the sheep guts were thickest.

We were through in twenty seconds. There were three inches to spare on my side and two on Garry's. The truck drivers cheered: loud whistles and shouts in the jungle night.

WE WERE IN LOWLANDS. After sixteen hard hours at the wheel, Garry crawled into the back and tried to sleep. I was driving a fine, straight asphalt road that looked red in the headlights.

We stopped for diesel not far from the border. We wouldn't be able to buy any in Nicaragua, where it was rationed.

Garry looked terrible.

"You know what we could do," I said. "We could market this drive as a board game. Shake the dice to see if you can get to the border on time. Pick cards that give you all sorts of contradictory information. Drive over the Mountain of Death, dodge the Costa Rican drug police, and slide through sheep guts in order to, ta-da, enter the war zone."

"I'm sick," Garry said. "I have a fever."

I felt his forehead. He was a little hot but his eyes were fever bright.

"You have a little fever," I said.

"I wonder if it's malaria?"

"No. It's not malaria," I said.

"I feel strange. Bad."

He spoke in a strained whisper and his eyes were burning, wild things trapped inside his head. They moved in a way that had no relation to anything he was saying.

WE ARRIVED at the border early and had to wait two hours until it opened at eight. I spoke with some truck drivers who said that things were very good through Nicaragua. People all over were celebrating the Arias peace plan. It was a fine time to drive through Central America, a very good time, the best.

Garry couldn't talk with anyone. He was walking back and forth, in the growing tropical heat, propelled by some internal demons that he wouldn't tell me about.

A grandmotherly Costa Rican lady placed herself in front of him and struck up a conversation. I saw her try to give him something, but he waved her off.

Back at the truck, he told me what had happened.

"This lady," he said, "had the world's kindest face. Did you see her?"

"Yeah. She did have a kind face."

"She asked what we were doing and I told her. Well, she looked at me. I'm standing there, I haven't changed my shirt since Panama, I'm sick, I can't talk. She figures I need money. She tries to give me a five-dollar bill. It was all crumpled up in her hand."

Garry was very shaky and his eyes glistened.

"Jesus," he said.

The small act of kindness had hit him like a blow and he was still reeling from it.

"I thanked her," he said. "I told her I didn't need any money and showed her pictures of my kids. It was all I could think of to do."

He ran his hand through his hair and said, "The basket case shows pictures of his family."

Garry looked north, into Nicaragua.

"Goddamn it," he said.

NICARAGUA

October 14, 1987

GARRY'S ANTIPATHY toward Nicaragua and Nicaraguans was puzzling. Our reconnaissance trip to Managua had been difficult, to be sure. The city, a graceless lowland steambath that is all of fifty feet above sea level, was a mosaic of empty lots and rubble piles interspersed, now and again, by habitations and office buildings. It was hard to get around. Managua had been decimated in the earthquake of 1972 and had never been rebuilt, though ruling General Anastasio Somoza and his family profited hugely from relief efforts.

In Managua, trees and grasses grew out of piles of debris and rubbish, and the concept of numbered addresses had little meaning. Letters to people in Managua are labeled with reference to various landmarks, like this:

> In the old Little Rocks section
> Below the hospital
> One block south
> One block west

The telephones generally didn't work. Sometimes, I dialed twenty or thirty times over the space of an hour to get another party in Managua itself. A single page of telex cost an outrageous $36, U.S.

We stayed at the Intercontinental, one of the centers of social life in Managua. There were sometimes Sandinista officials in the bar. It did not seem to be a bar in a war-torn country where drinking and coupling and laughing are matters of some serious import. In the Intercontinental bar, there was a sense of serious import, and nothing else. No one laughed, ever. It seemed the most joyless place on the face of the earth.

Inflation was running at 1,200 percent. Nicaragua's money was useless outside the country and not much good inside. The government needed valid currency to purchase foreign goods, so anyone visiting the country was required to cough up $60, U.S., upon entry. This bought 240,000 córdobas, which you got in hundreds. You could always tell the American citizens who had just flown in. They had huge córdoba bulges in their pockets and they wore skulking looks of guilt.

They had, doubtless, just read a little pamphlet in English that every American was handed sooner rather than later. It was a history of U.S. involvement in Nicaragua. The United States marines had occupied the country and propped up a corrupt government, on and off, from 1912 to 1933. In the last five years of the occupation, General César Augusto Sandino had fought the Americans, who were in the process of installing General Anastasio Somoza, father of the earthquake profiteer, as supreme commander of the Nicaraguan National Guard.

Sandino was captured by the guard and killed in 1934. The Somoza family, supported by the United States, used the national guard as a personal army. By 1978, the family owned over half the land in the country and had a hand in most of the larger businesses.

In 1978–79, there was fighting in the streets. Anastasio Somoza, the second son of the U.S.-installed general of the same name, was ousted by a coalition of groups calling themselves Sandinistas, after Augusto Sandino, who, pictures in the Nicaraguan embassy in Argentina suggest, had been somewhat cross-eyed.

The U.S. had occupied the country and supported the corrupt Somoza regime. So there was plenty to feel guilty about standing there drinking a beer in the Intercontinental bar with a pocketful of córdobas that you couldn't spend because the hotel wouldn't take them. Hotel bills had to be paid in dollars.

I met a Catholic priest visiting from San Francisco. He was, he said, on a fact-finding mission. He wore civilian clothes and was full of compassion for the poor and dispossessed but I thought he lacked the reporter's instinct. The fact finders, I learned, a dozen of them, were ferried around in a government-owned van. They could ask the driver to stop anywhere.

"Some of the houses," the priest told me, "are very poor. And our translator will ask the people in them any question we have. Just anything at all."

I imagined the scene: a man is sitting in his house and a government representative herds twelve grim-faced gringos inside. The man can see them all noting the dirt floor, the shabby bed, the cooking fire. What does he think of the Sandinista government? He tells the government translator that he thinks the Sandinistas are doing fine. He thinks they're swell.

Nicaragua, the priest said, is a largely Catholic country, and there had been some talk in the United States that the Marxist Sandinistas were suppressing freedom of religion. But the priest told me that his translator had pointed out graffiti that read, THERE IS NO CONTRADIC-TION BETWEEN THE CHURCH AND THE REVOLUTION.

It was not a message that I saw someone scrawling on a wall in a burst of anger or inspiration. Still, I was willing to entertain the concept. There was a stifling solemnity to life in Managua that reminded me of the Catholic grade school I had attended. Managua was like a city run by nuns.

"There will be no laughing in this classroom. No comic books. Puberty is strictly forbidden. We will keep our thoughts pure and our minds on God."

Instead of God, however, people in Nicaragua were forever being told to keep their minds on the New Man, the proud and free Nicaraguan who would grow out of the revolution.

All over Nicaragua, reading material was strictly censored. The opposition newspaper had been shut down but someone had climbed to the second story of the closed building and hung out a large black cardboard skeleton. It was labeled THE NEW MAN.

The only books available, anywhere, were inspirational tracts about Karl Marx and the New Man. Even at the Intercontinental, the revolving bookrack had nothing but thin paperback volumes with black covers printed on bad stock. They had titles like *Fidel Castro Presents Three Ways You Can Improve Your Village*.

I FINALLY DID FIND something apolitical to read. It was a full-color brochure, in English, that I found on a table in the lobby of the Nicaraguan Institute of Tourism, Intourismo.

> You can visit Nicaragua at any time of the year and will always find an excellent weather. . . . At the central highlands of Nicaragua . . . temperature is cool the whole year long, with a dry atmosphere and during the rainy season between October and November turns out to be one of the most delicious climates in the country.

There's a lot of this sort of thing in the brochure. Weather is an inoffensive proposition. Garry and I were killing time, waiting for an interview with someone from Intourismo. Finally, after some hours, we talked with a zaftig, fashionable young woman named Chistita Caldera. It had to be a hard job, working for the Institute of Tourism in a country at war, and Chistita, who was called Chepy, could barely endure my bad Spanish. She broke into English in the middle of one of my excruciating sentences.

"They don't pay me to translate."

I continued to explain the project in Tarzan Spanish and memorized phrases: nonpolitical . . . mission of peace . . . unity of the Americas . . . Pan-American Highway, a ribbon of hope . . . *Guinness Book of World Records* . . . worldwide attention.

And—these sentences specially polished for the interview—"what a shame if we were stopped in Nicaragua." It would be in all the papers all over the world and could even—*¡caramba!—negatively affect the tourism industry in the country.*

Chepy listened, and, as she did, her face brightened by degrees. She began speaking English which they didn't pay her for but which was easier for both of us.

"Ahh," she said. "This is good. This is not what I had thought. Not at all."

What had she thought?

Nothing. Nothing. How could she help us?

We asked her if there was a way of smoothing things over at the southern border. Chepy said she would think about it. If it could be arranged, she would come herself to meet us.

CHEPY WAS, in fact, there at the border. She was wearing jeans, a flowered blouse, and an appropriately Latin amount of lipstick. She eased us through the formalities in only three hours and we didn't even have to buy córdobas or demonstrate that we had been taking the malaria pills that Rich Cox had brought to the end of the earth for us.

Garry had not completely shaken off the fever—his bad case of jitters—but he needed to drive through Nicaragua. It seemed to be a matter of principle. Driving would also relieve him of the necessity to talk. He was, he told me privately, afraid of what he might say.

Chepy said that it had been tough for her to get a car from the government, to get the gasoline, to get a photographer who could drive the car back while she rode with us. In the end, the Sandinista government had agreed to assist us in clearing customs because they "are interested in attracting tourists to the country." Chepy said that there were plenty of "internationals" in Nicaragua, people from the United

States or Germany or Sweden who come to see what the revolution had wrought. They came out of curiosity or idealism. They were very sincere and they lived cheaply, in solidarity with the people. Which is not what the Institute of Tourism had in mind.

Officially, the government said it was "interested in classical tourism, not sociopolitical tourism." The Institute of Tourism, for instance, had turned deposed dictator Anastasio Somoza's seaside estate into the Olaf Palme Convention Center. The government hopes the golf course, casino, and private airstrips will be attractive to conventioning dentists.

The photographer took our picture for the Institute of Tourism newsletter. He took our picture because we were real apolitical visitors and a potential inspiration to dentists worldwide.

Chepy told us that she had thought Garry and I were internationals when she first met us in Managua. She had expected us to express solidarity with the revolution and do nothing whatever to foster the cause of classical tourism or in any way help her attract dentists to Nicaragua.

It had taken her half an hour of my bad Spanish before she realized that we were Institute of Tourism kinda guys.

THE ROAD was exceptionally bad and there were huge potholes all over. It was like the road into Ecuador from Peru and it was a bad road for all the same reasons. There would be no high-speed invasion over this cratered pavement.

Chepy, sitting in the back of the cab, said she wanted to interview us for the Intourismo newsletter. How did I like Nicaraguans and Nicaragua? We were fifteen miles into the country, driving along the shore of Lake Nicaragua. On the far shore was a huge volcano looming over the blue-gray waters of the lake. It was a perfectly shaped cone, rounded and green and inordinately sensual.

I said that Nicaragua was beautiful, as anyone could see, and all Nicaraguans were imbued with the spirit of friendship. Nicaragua was the friendliest, most beautiful . . .

Chepy cut me off.

"I would like you to comment on the political situation."

"We are apolitical visitors," I said. "That's the point."

"But you must say something about the political situation."

Garry muttered under his breath and shot me a murderous look. I was going to have to take this one. Chepy didn't want to hear what Garry had to say.

I thought about it for a while. Telling the whole truth was out of the question. I thought the Sandinistas were heavy-handed ideologues who had succeeded in squeezing every ounce of joy out of the country.

On the other hand, the contra insurgents were terrorists, funded by my own government. I had seen pictures of women and children who had suffered at the hands of the contras. The pictures were taken by my friend Paul Dix, who lives in my hometown in Montana. He had spent two years in Nicaragua, working for the quasireligious organization Witness for Peace. He was interested in documenting the effects of the conflict on civilians. He would document atrocities on both sides, he said.

Paul tried to get out to the scene of the fighting as soon as it was reported. More often than not he found a house burned to the ground, most of a large family dead, and one or two survivors wandering around in a daze. The contras often targeted health-care workers and teachers.

Paul thought the Sandinista leaders had some poetry in their souls and didn't find life in Managua completely oppressive. He would admit that, under the Sandinistas, Nicaragua wasn't exactly an ideal society. There were some things that irritated him.

"But so what?" he had argued. "What if the whole country is a totalitarian dungeon? Does that give us the right to pay a bunch of terrorists to basically go around and cut the throats of four or five people a night?"

Paul often talked at length with the children who had survived various attacks. He gave them crayons and asked them to draw pictures of what had happened.

One of the pictures I saw showed a bright red house. A stick man standing outside, a contra, was throwing a little round ball through a window into the red house. The little round ball was meant to represent a grenade. Because this was a child's drawing, the contra was smiling. Small children don't know how to draw a face that isn't smiling.

In another drawing, there was a bodyless smiling circle on a stick stuck into the ground. The girl who drew the picture said that contras had decapitated her nineteen-year-old brother and put his head on a fence pole. The head was drawn like a bright, round, happy face.

And now Chepy wanted me to talk about politics, for the record. I had had half an hour of sleep in thirty hours and didn't want to have to think at all. I said that I hoped the Arias peace plan would be fully implemented.

"You are against the interference of foreign governments in Central American affairs?"

"Yes." I sensed that this was what Chepy needed to hear me say, for the sake of her job. It had, for me, the benefit of being my actual opinion.

"Would you write this down so I can translate exactly?"

And so I wrote that down and drew a happy face under the place where I signed my name.

LATER, CHEPY SHOWED US a picture of her daughter, a blond six-year-old cutie dressed in a clown suit for her birthday party. Chepy and her husband were separated, she said, and she had to raise her daughter alone. He didn't support the child at all.

She had thought about going to the U.S.—one of her sisters was attending college in Seattle—but she imagined that she'd end up being a waitress. "And here," she said, "I work in"—Chepy made an expansive gesture that encompassed the filthy cramped cab of the truck—"international relations."

We dropped her at her home in Masaya and exchanged addresses. Chepy said that her home address would be the best place to reach her. "I don't know what will happen," she said. She might have been referring to the political situation or to her personal life. It seemed best not to inquire more closely.

Garry tried to give her $100 but Chepy said she couldn't take it. "Yes you can," Garry said, "you have a daughter."

"Then," Chepy said, "I will spend it all on her."

THE ROADS IN THE INTERIOR were good and fast. There was little traffic because gasoline was rationed, but we did see several large Bulgarian-made trucks full of people being ferried somewhere for some reason. The people wore civilian clothes and were jammed tightly into the back of these trucks. They weren't shouting or singing or laughing. They didn't look like they were on their way to concentration camps, either. They looked like everyone in Managua: people who weren't having a good time at all.

We were never stopped, not once.

The road to the border with Honduras rose into a series of rounded green hills. The trees were more sparse than in the lowland, but the heat was less oppressive. It was not the great weight upon the land that it had been in Managua. We had found, as the tourist brochure promised, "an excellent weather." When I looked down from the summit of one of the higher mountains, I could see groves of trees separated by meadows of thigh-high grasses. The ridges were closely spaced. It was beautiful country where, I thought, small groups of armed men could maneuver for months and never be detected.

A brisk wind had sprung up and was blowing the petals of some bright red flowers across the road. There were brick houses along the highway, and all of them had flowers growing in the yard. We passed a school. Dozens of children were walking back toward the houses, carrying books and laughing.

We saw several billboards that looked like advertisements for a *Rambo* movie, but the words below the noble-looking armed men and woman read, DEFEND YOUR LAND, DEFEND YOUR CITY, DEFEAT THE ENEMY.

Not far down a slope near the road, there was a pond fringed with green algae that was so bright the color seemed bogus, a kind of artificial Day-Glo green set against the lighter green of the grass and the darker, more brooding cast of the forecast.

The hills were steeper near the border and there were rocky cliffs. A man in patched jeans, a yellow T-shirt, and sandals was pushing a homemade wheelbarrow full of wood. He had an automatic rifle slung over his back.

And then we were at the border, only four hours after we had entered the country. The customs building was located in a small settlement with an indoor market where the produce looked better than anything I had seen in Managua. A group of boys, ranging in age from about ten to eighteen, surrounded the truck and clamored for our attention. They would take us to the right offices, in the right order, and we would clear customs in a flash. We were given to understand that we needed their help, which, they assured us, would be very inexpensive.

Some of the boys looked too young to hire for this purpose, some looked devious. One, an older boy, was a tall gawky fellow with a loony, toothless smile who appeared to be happily insane. We chose the oldest of the border hustlers. This responsible individual promptly turned our papers over to the toothless loon, who gave out with a mighty shout and ran off down the street. He waved our documents over his head and whooped and laughed and staggered as he ran.

All of the other boys were laughing.

"We gave your papers," one of these evil ten-year-olds said, "to the craziest person in all of Nicaragua."

"What did that kid just tell you?" Garry asked.

"He said they gave our papers to a lunatic."

The fever flush bloomed in Garry's face. He took off at a dead run and caught the boy with our documents at the entrance to a building.

Inside, I was amazed to discover that there were, in fact, customs offices. The officers seemed to know the boy with our papers, and when he didn't get things right, they gently corrected him and sometimes actually guided him by the arm to the next stamping station.

Garry worked on the act—smile, laugh, hand out lapel pins—but he was flat and unconvincing. We suffered through a pit search and were cleared for immigration.

The officers instructed us to drive a few miles and check in at the immigration trailer on the left side of the road. We gave our guide a five-dollar bill and he ran back down the road, waving it over his head, whooping and laughing, as was his way.

"Shitheads," Garry said.

"I don't know," I said. "Maybe they were giving the kid a chance. Couple of strange-looking gringos. Let the crazy kid have a little fun. Maybe he wasn't crazy. He could have been retarded."

"Those papers," Garry said, "are the key to this whole thing." He was very angry. "They were playing around with us."

"I don't think so."

"Nicaraguans," Garry said. He made the word sound like a curse.

The border was a war zone and the old immigration building didn't look so good. There were bullet holes in the adobe. The roof, what there was of it, consisted of twisted girders. It had apparently taken a direct mortar hit.

So the government was checking passports out of an old airstream trailer home. Soldiers drove it down to the relative safety of town every night. A wooden set of stairs led up to a window in the trailer. There was a thin cloth over the window and we understood that we were to hand our passports through, one at a time. You couldn't see inside. It was like a confessional in a Catholic church. There was no way to know precisely how much disgust the information presented has generated. There could be a big penance to pay.

I don't know what they did with my documents, but I stood on the top stair, alone in the sun, for a full ten minutes. Then a brown hand reached out. I took my passport and saw that I was stamped for exit. No words were exchanged.

When Garry took his passport back, his hands were shaking in fatigue or fury or some combination of more complex emotions.

While Garry drove to the Honduras border station, which was a mile away, over a rocky summit, I quickly hid the letter from the Nicaraguan Institute of Tourism and put the letter from the Honduras Institute of Tourism in its place.

* * *

IN HONDURAS, there was the usual scatter of boys, twenty or twenty-five of them, offering, at top volume, to guide us through customs. I looked out at the customs hustlers, the bustle, the black marketeers sitting on benches, the soft-drink vendors, and I felt myself slide into a bleak depression. Here it was: the border rat race, again. This was the seventh set of formalities we had gone through since starting from Panama thirty hours ago.

Garry did it all, laughing with officials and bargaining with the boys. He had completely shaken off the strange fever that had deviled him for most of the day. It took two hours to clear the vehicle.

Garry had been at the wheel almost continuously since Panama City: twenty-six out of thirty hours. It was Nicaragua that had somehow driven him, kept him awake, and sent the fever flush rushing to his face.

And now that we were out of the country, the tension was gone. Garry sat back in the passenger seat and sang, to the tune of "We're in the Money," a little song of his own. The only lyric was "We're in Honduras, we're in Honduras . . ."

I WANTED TO KNOW what was going on with Garry and Nicaragua. Perhaps he didn't want to talk about it, and I came at him from an angle. I advanced a theory that the Sandinista government, in its attempt to build the New Man, had appropriated some of the least appealing aspects of classical Catholicism, like the squirming agony of confessional. Guilt. Single-minded pursuit of a higher goal. Restricted reading matter . . .

Garry wasn't as willing to generalize about the country on the basis of a curtain over a window in a trailer. He thought there might be a simpler explanation: "Maybe the Elephant Man got a job in Nicaragua."

The comment was encouraging. Eight hours before, my friend's conversation had to do with an imagined case of malaria. .

"Tell me about Nicaragua," I said.

"We made it."

"Something else."

"It was always the biggest obstacle on this . . ."

"There's something else."

Garry paused.

"I lost it there once," he said finally. It was a story he didn't like to tell. "The only time in my life I ever just really lost it."

Back in 1977, Garry had been traveling in Latin America with his girlfriend, a French Canadian named Solange. They were hitchhiking back to Canada. At the southern border of Nicaragua they were detained at customs. Garry was put into a small room. A man who seemed to be the commanding officer came in, and, without a word, took off his cheap digital watch and put it in Garry's shirt pocket. When the man started to walk out of the room, Garry jumped up and gave the watch back.

"The guy was playing around with me," Garry said. "You know. He was showing me he could do anything he wanted to me. A bully kind of deal."

"Yeah, but that was Somoza time."

"You don't understand," Garry said. "It's not politics I'm talking about. I'm talking about losing it."

I thought about the times stress and fatigue gang up on a person; about the swirling mindstorm of dread and anxiety that is panic. It is a kind of insanity, accompanied by profuse sweating, a racing pulse, and the inability to function. And what is more frightening than any outside stimulus is the idea that you are no longer in control of your own life. You think: I can never come back. Not now.

It happens to everyone at some time or another; it happens in business, or in personal relationships. It happens for good reason; or for no reason at all. The context isn't important. When people say they are losing it, they mean they are losing their minds.

Ken Langley, Garry's partner on the around-the-world trip, knew he was "losing it" when he asked to be restrained, tied up, because he couldn't stop seeing himself opening the airplane door and happily stepping to his death.

Garry said: "This customs guy tried to put his watch back in my pocket—I don't know what he was doing or why—and I wouldn't let him. So they wouldn't let us into the country. We had to go back to Costa Rica. The only place to sleep was in that town where we got diesel this morning. What's it, about forty miles from the border?"

A bus came by and Garry flagged it down. The driver would take them to the town for $10. "It was robbery," Garry said, "but we paid it. So we get on the bus and all the women are sitting in front, all the men are in the back. The men started calling out to Solange. She spoke fluent Spanish and didn't like being called what they were calling her. She also had a fiery French-Canadian temper and she said a few things that made the women laugh. The men just shut up and stared at me.

"This all happened in a few seconds. I still hadn't found a seat. The only place for me was in the very back. So I squeezed in there. The guy next to me leans over. I can feel his breath on my neck. He says, in English, 'Twenty bucks or you bleed.' "

"So what did you do?"

"I gave him twenty bucks."

I thought about it for a minute.

"So," I said, "when we came up on that southern border . . ."

"Where it all happened ten years ago . . ."

"You started feeling it again."

"Yeah," Garry said. "And that's probably why I thought I had malaria. I mean, that sounds crazy to me now. And then when they gave our papers to that poor crazy kid, I thought it was starting all over. I thought they were going to start that bully stuff, playing around with us."

"You kind of barked at those kids at the Costa Rican border. I thought there was something wrong then."

"It started before that," Garry said. "I felt it in Panama, but it got worse. And then I'm sitting at the gas station, talking about malaria. I figured you knew I was starting to blow up. But you were calm. You reached out and felt my forehead. I thought, there's another person here. It's going to be all right. I'm going to come through it.

"And then the Costa Rican lady tried to give me five bucks. I looked down at this wadded-up bill in her hand and I felt tears come into my eyes. She saw it. I know she did. And she thought I really needed the money. I don't know . . ."

We hadn't been stopped by police once in Nicaragua. There were no guns and no threats of ambush. The war was on hold until the various parties decided what they wanted to do about the Arias peace plan. It had been a fast, easy drive. And, for Garry Sowerby, it had been terrifying.

"It was never about politics," Garry said. "It wasn't about Nicaragua or Nicaraguans. All that back there: it was about me."

THE HANDSOME
GRINGO MEETS IGOR
AND THE CYCLOPS

October 14–17, 1987

THE MOUNTAINS of Honduras were more lush than those on the Nicaraguan side. There were occasional rocky cliffs, and a few small waterfalls. Men on horseback wearing blue jeans and straw cowboy hats drove cattle across the roads to autumn pastures. There was a billboard for Lee jeans featuring a man who dressed much like these Central American cowboys. The last billboard we had seen was in Nicaragua. It showed a heroic Nicaraguan woman taking a blond-haired man captive near the wreckage of a small plane. This one was about pants, proper fit, and buttocks.

Garry had fallen asleep in the passenger seat, which was something he never did. It was as if he had just run a marathon and collapsed.

The road dropped into a flatland between mountain ranges. There was a perfect Central American sunset in progress. The sky was blood-red and the long shadows cast by the trees were dark scarlet on thick pink grass. Great flocks of small black birds, like starlings, swept across the flatland. They flashed in front of the windshield, one after the other, dozens of blurred black shapes.

The sun was near the horizon, perfectly round, perfectly red, and I could stare directly into it without squinting. Which is what I was doing when something hit the truck with a terrific thud. Bullet, I thought, but it hadn't sounded like a bullet at all.

A voice I had never heard before said: "Wah!"

Garry had snapped bolt upright from his slouching position in the passenger seat. He was holding his belly, as if he had been shot.

"Wah," he said again in his strange, thick, sleep-clogged voice.

He opened his hands. I saw one of the small black birds that had been sweeping past the windshield. Its neck was twisted to one side, and it lay on its back against Garry's stomach, staining his white T-shirt with blood.

He looked at it for what seemed to be a very long time. Nothing made any sense to him. He had been asleep for an hour and then there was a loud noise and now there seemed to be a dead bird in his lap. I reached over, took the bird by one leg, and tossed it out the open window.

"I thought," Garry said, "I had been shot."

"Those birds," I explained, "were flying in flocks across the road. You know how birds fly right across your windshield? I think this one hit the side mirror on your side and flipped right in the window."

"I reached down there," Garry said. "I felt something warm and wet. I was sure I had been shot. I thought I was feeling my own intestines. Then I started wondering why my intestines would have feathers and bird feet on them."

"You were dead asleep. Drooling."

"It's the wide side mirrors," Garry said. "I bet we have the widest side mirrors in Central America." He was beginning to wake up. "I bet the last thing that bird thought was, 'Oh shit, wide side mirror.'"

The road began a long, twisted climb to the capital city of Tegucigalpa, which sits in a cool mountain basin.

An hour later, we saw four Honduran soldiers in camouflage gear with rifles on their backs. They were flagging us down with the hearty handshake wave that means stop when soldiers do it. People in civilian clothes use the same gesture to hitchhike.

"Slow down," Garry said.

I backed it down to fifteen miles an hour while he examined the soldiers. "Doesn't look like a stop," he said. "I think they want a ride."

We turned on the dome light so the soldiers could see us. When we were abreast of them, Garry said, "They don't look sure of themselves. They want a ride and don't know who we are. Just coast on by."

We passed the soldiers at a crawl and Garry waved at them imperiously. One or two of the soldiers saluted, uncertainly. "Don't speed up," Garry said, "we're not escaping."

"What are they doing?" I asked.

"They're talking together. One of them is pointing at us."

Then we turned a corner, and I floored it. We both began laughing for no reason at all. It was just tension and release in rotoville.

"Damn," I said. "I wanted to do that ever since you told me about the soldiers you left on the road in Turkey."

"Just leave 'em standing there," Garry said. "They don't know whether to shoot or salute."

We both had a piece of beef jerky and Garry made himself some cold, foaming roto coffee.

TEGUCIGALPA is located in the highlands, at 3,200 feet. Honduras is the poorest country in Central America, but there were plenty of Mercedes cruising the streets. I thought of the cars as badges of corruption. The town itself was alive with neon signs, and there was a vibrant street life. It was a hilly place, hemmed in by mountains, and it is considered "quainter" than Guatemala City or Mexico City, by which people usually mean that the poverty is more apparent. The people, however, tended to be clean and polite and cheerful.

It was not safe to drive in Honduras at night. It was, according to an American embassy official I had talked to, not safe in Honduras at all. The embassy was located atop a hill and there was little evidence of a military presence. Honduran security guards admit you into the building, and then the marines take over. The man I talked with was blond, about thirty-five, and could not, he said, assist us in any way. He strongly suggested that we forget the entire project. He told me this from behind a pane of bulletproof glass, and from my point of view his features were vaguely distorted. He was a man who was slightly out of focus.

There was a casino at our hotel. A large sign at the entrance to the gambling hall featured the silhouette of a handgun. A thick red line slashed diagonally across the gun. "No pistols in the casino." It was the sort of gay, madcap sight tourists can expect in Honduras.

WE WERE ON THE ROAD at five-thirty the next morning. A man in a yellow Toyota truck saw us studying a map and asked if we wanted directions out of town. If we were going north, we could follow him.

The road was very good, lined on either side by pine trees, and it was too early for traffic. We crested the mountains that surround Tegucigalpa and drove down into a valley where the sun was just burning away an early-morning fog.

Fifty miles later, the man in the Toyota signaled that he was turning down a dirt road. We stopped to thank him for his help. He was, he said, an Israeli, working in Honduras for a year as an agricultural consultant. He wouldn't renew his contract. Honduras, he said, was too dangerous, too bloody.

I thought he was talking about soldiers, guerrillas, violence in the streets, but he was referring to the stretch of highway we had just driven. Almost every day he saw mangled bodies, or blood on the pavement. "Traffic," he said, "is murder."

HONDURAS is a country of mountain ranges. We drove through some cuts in the road where the rocks were a deep, burnished red. There was a large graceful lake called Yojoa, surrounded by green mountains. In the flatlands, between ranges, men on horseback led packstrings of mules. The mules were loaded with bananas to be sold in the markets of the mountains. They would be purchased by men in blue jeans and straw cowboy hats who herded cattle for a living.

THE OFFICIALS at the Guatemalan border were particularly impressed with a letter from their director of immigration. It suggested that people fully cooperate with us. The fact that the director of immigration was the brother of the president of Guatemala was also helpful.

Our destination was Guatemala City, a mere twelve or thirteen hours of driving. We might have pushed on, driven all night, but that would have put us in Dallas a couple of days early, and waiting around in motel rooms made Garry vomit.

The road out of the checkpoint dropped into a reddish sandy-brown desert of scrub brush and stunted trees. Then we rose into the central highlands, climbing up to Guatemala City, another capital set in a mountain basin, this one almost a mile high. We were crawling along behind creeping oil-burning trucks.

I was daydreaming, listlessly, imagining, for some reason, a time in the distant future:

The world is a dismal place. The Amazon forest has been decimated. The trees that once absorbed the carbon dioxide humans pour into the atmosphere by burning fossil fuels are gone. The carbon dioxide now simply floats to a certain level and hangs above the earth, like an encircling pane of glass. The planet is a blistering greenhouse.

Meltwater from the polar ice caps has raised sea level over one hundred feet. There is no more Central America. Instead, there are the Central American islands: the island of Tegucigalpa, the island of Guatemala City, the Costa Rican island of San José.

I see people in the poor sweltering shacks of the Amazon desert.

Many of them believe the past was a golden era of enlightened men. Some of them talk about the Lost Continent of Managua. They study its books of ancient wisdom: *Fidel Castro Presents Three Ways You Can Improve Your Village.*

ON THE HIGH TRAFFIC-CLOGGED ROAD above Guatemala City, we drove by the scene of a bad accident. There was glass on the pavement, sharp knifelike shards of it floating in a tremendous amount of blood. Four or five motorcycle policemen were working the scene, which was under a large billboard that read, CEMENT IS PROGRESS.

We checked into a hotel and had dinner with Ricardo Pennington, a GM dealer who ran a business called Fuertequipo. While Pennington's mechanics swarmed all over the truck like ants on a broken watermelon—they changed the oil, the oil filter, the fuel filter—we ate dinner at Rodeo, a steak house where patrons sit at picnic tables and listen to a live steel-drum band.

Ricardo, who spoke good English, often drove to the United States, and he didn't advise traveling at night through Mexico. Taxis, he said, have lights on the roof and it is easy to mistake one for a police car. The lights on the police vehicles, however, revolved; the ones on the taxis did not. "If someone tries to pull you over at night and his lights don't revolve, don't stop. You're going to get robbed, or worse."

If we were stopped by police and detained for no discernible reason, it was best to tell them that we didn't have much time and ask if it was possible to pay "the fine" on the spot. Ricardo taught me the Spanish word for fine. Five bucks was usually enough.

WE WERE UP before dawn and beat the traffic out of Guatemala City. We were driving on a good fast road, through a lush valley that was lined, on one side, with a spectacular range of perfectly conical volcanoes. It was a brilliant, sunny morning, not too hot, and I found myself rehashing something that had happened in Sincelejo, Colombia.

We had pulled into town late in the evening and driven through traffic-strewn streets. A motorcycle pulled up alongside the truck. Sitting behind the male driver was a young woman wearing a long purple skirt and a white blouse. A breeze blew her skirt high up on her thighs and she pulled it back down. The woman glanced up at the truck, saw me staring at her, and blew me a playful, meaningless kiss. She had wonderfully large, almost Eurasian, eyes. Some congenial confluence of races had blessed her with an olive Polynesian complexion.

I don't know: maybe other people have noble sexual fantasies.

Maybe they don't have them at all. Better men and women than I can probably drive for weeks through various foreign countries without the consolation of a proper companion of the opposite sex. They don't suffer unbidden and undignified sexual fantasies. They contemplate the dialogues of Plato and concentrate on the road.

The woman on the motorcycle and I made love in the most astounding locations, and we did it constantly, without surcease. She was, of course, educated in a convent. She had much to learn about the physical aspects of love and was always eager to learn more about the physics of copulation in, say, a hammock. I am, in my fantasy, a masterful lover.

I felt an obligatory twinge of guilt—a voice from the past; my own personal radical feminist, circa 1972—and told myself that there was a *reason* for meditating on a sexual relationship as it might be conducted in South America, with a South American woman. These were the very countries that gave us the word *macho* after all. I would, yes, examine this strain in myself to better understand my Latin American friends. I was indulging in a kind of contemplative sociology. It would be best, then, if I had some social position, if I were, for instance, rich and powerful. A patron.

I am now married to this woman I first saw on a motorcycle in Sincelejo.

We live in a large white house with flowers all about. I have sired several delightful children. When local people talk about me, they do so in folkloric phrases.

"The handsome gringo is very rich and he has a beautiful wife."

"Do not think of the handsome gringo's wife, Juan. You must never think of the wife of the handsome gringo."

And then the handsome gringo and his beautiful wife were making love underwater, wearing scuba gear.

On the shoulder of the road, a hundred yards ahead, a boy was mounting his bicycle. His dog—I assumed it was his dog—capered alongside. It was a medium-sized black-and-white mutt that I knew would run along beside the boy's bike and give Garry, who was driving, fits. There was a three-quarter-ton pickup truck ahead of us and a bus coming fast in the other lane.

I saw all this, but, in my mind, the handsome revered gringo and his beautiful insatiable wife were experimenting with a rather contorted position under a warm tropical waterfall in a forest alive with birdsong.

"Oh shit," Garry said.

I heard it before I saw it: an obscene crunching of bones. The boy's dog came out from under the back wheels of the three-quarter-ton truck, already dead, its back twisted nearly double. The dog bounced once, four feet into the air, then spun off onto the shoulder of the road.

No one stopped and we didn't either. What could you say to the boy: We're sorry someone ran over your pet.

Traffic is murder.

There are no old dogs on the Pan-American Highway.

My fantasies of sex and power died with the dog, and at the very same moment.

HOURS LATER, in Mexico, the incident was still haunting me. Garry said, "What if it had been a child?" and then we didn't say anything for several more hours.

The border formalities on the Mexican side had gone quickly. We were stopped for a second customs inspection at a roadside checkpoint half an hour into the country. And half an hour after that, two police cars pulled us over for another document check. Ten miles later we stopped for a roadside agricultural inspection and traded jokes with the fruit police.

All the officers accepted lapel pins. All were professional, polite, and there was never a time when I felt a bribe was in order. Mexico was not living up to its reputation as the most corrupt, bribe-ridden society in all of Latin America.

Several hours into the country, traffic died down to a trickle and the road was a two-lane blacktop, as good as any county highway in the United States. The land along the Pacific coast was heavily forested and vultures soared over the highway, looking for road kills.

We turned east, onto a highway that would take us over a range of low mountains to the Atlantic coast. At the intersection, there was a police checkpoint.

The land was bare and sandy. A thirty-mile-an-hour wind drove the heat before it like a blast furnace, and the two officers manning the checkpoint belonged in the Mexican version of *Deliverance*. They were living stereotypes, every gringo's nightmare: two genuine steenking bach Mexican policemen.

The older of the two was a short man with a mean sour face and one gold tooth in the middle of his mouth. His uniform shirt was rumpled, stained with sweat, and was buttoned in such a way that his belly button was visible. He had no holster for his revolver and wore it inside his pants.

The other officer was a tall, stooped man with dull, uncomprehending eyes and a slack face. He wore a sweaty gray T-shirt that had once been white. The officers wanted to see our passports. They wanted to see the lengthy document we had filled out at customs. The short man, who seemed to be in command, reached into his shirt pocket and pulled out a pair of reading glasses. The lens on the left side had been shattered in a starburst pattern.

The tall man leaned over the shorter one's shoulder and together they examined the single sheet of paper.

"You will," the short officer said, "need to show me an inventory of everything you are carrying in the truck."

This, we knew from our reconnaissance trip, was not true. Still, we had the document and gave it to the man.

It must have been infuriating.

The officers already had their lapel pins, but, I saw, they didn't want to settle for mere pin money. Garry and I were well ahead of schedule and pretended not to understand. It was a chance to stand and stretch, to look around a little bit, to torment these officers with shrugs and dumb questions.

"Why can't we go? Everything's in order."

The tall man walked around in a circle, scratching his head and muttering to himself. The short officer stared at us with his one shattered eye. No words were exchanged for at least five minutes. The hot dry wind kicked up a minor sandstorm. It would be much more comfortable inside the checkpoint guardshack.

"Go," the man with the bad eye said finally. "Go now."

We waved and thanked the officers, who were, at that very moment, pulling over a pickup truck carrying three rusty fifty-five-gallon drums.

The land became more fertile as the road rose into the mountains. "The tall guy back there," Garry said, "what do you figure his IQ was?"

"Thirty-four, thirty-five, around there."

"He looked like somebody who ought be called Igor."

"I don't believe they were real policemen," I said. "A guy with a perfect starburst in his glasses? C'mon. I think they're from the Mexican Department of Tourism. Their job is to give visitors something to talk about." I saw, in my mind's eye, a travel documentary featuring these officers. "And so," I said, "as the sun sinks slowly in the west, we bid fond adieu to our new friends . . ."

"Igor and the Cyclops."

*   *   *

THERE WAS A LINGERING golden sunset across the fields and we were following a truck with a large name painted across the back: RENEGADE. The truck was running a straight-through muffler, and it was terribly loud. In all of Latin America, only Mexican truck drivers run these deafening mufflers. Some of the Mexican trucks, however, were no louder than our own.

Garry advanced the theory that noisy trucks belong to bachelors. "When they get married," he hypothesized, "they have to shut their truck up. That way the road hookers and women of the night can tell who's available by the sound of their truck. It's like a sign of virility or something."

We passed a rolled-over truck on a straight stretch of road. There were four or five vehicles stopped nearby, and several people stood over a man who lay in the grass, as if dead.

Traffic was murder, and had been for days. Ever since the Mountain of Death.

WE SLEPT in Veracruz, and were up and out of the city before dawn. We passed through Tampico, and then crossed the Tropic of Cancer.

"We're coming up in the world," Garry said. It looked that way on the map.

"We should," I said, "have a coffee party."

Since one of us was usually trying to drive while the other slept, we seldom drank coffee together. When we did, it was a celebratory occasion.

And now a coffee party seemed particularly appropriate. We had just crossed the Tropic of Capricorn, and in a few hours we'd enter the United States. Matamoros, then Brownsville, Texas. The thought of interstate highways ahead made us giddy. Cruise control! Mindless hours of monotony. Paradise.

"You know those tires we got in Chile," Garry said.

"We didn't need them. We just put them in the back and gave them a ride."

"They're Korean tires," Garry said. "I wonder what they thought?"

During coffee parties, various objects in and on the truck often developed their own personalities.

"They were probably terrified," Garry said. "Get thrown in the back with a couple of old tires that are all beat to hell, punctures all over."

Garry spoke for the voiceless tires: " 'Don't put us on! Don't leave us in Colombia! Take us to the United States!' "

"And our jackets," I said. "Coats that we wore down south, rolling around in the mud, tightening shocks, changing tires. They're all soaked with diesel. Roll 'em up and throw 'em in the back with the old beat-up tires and the quivering Koreans."

"I wonder what they say to one another back there?"

We cogitated on this matter for some time, presenting various conjectures as to the nature of the conversation between our tires and our jackets.

We were only twenty miles from the United States.

WE DROVE OVER a toll bridge on the Rio Grande, checked in with U.S. customs and immigration, got our logbooks stamped, and were back on the road in ten minutes. Garry pulled in at the first convenience store in the U.S. that happened to be on our side of the street. There were two pay phones in front of the place. Garry called Jane. He spoke to Lucy and listened to Natalie gurgle. I called my friend Karen and told her that I was at a convenience store in the United States, not far from an interstate highway. This did not seem as remarkable to her as it did to me.

"Karen," I said.

"Yes?"

I heard my voice rise in excitement. "They have shampoo here!"

A flashy red Camaro driven by a teenaged boy pulled up near the phone. He had his sound system turned up near the level of physical pain.

"This is a place," I screamed, "where you can use the phone and buy shampoo. *In one stop.*"

There was a private home next door. An elderly gentleman was sitting on his lawn in a wooden chair watching a small black-and-white TV that was set up on a card table with a blue cloth over it. A long extension cord snaked its way back to the house. The man had a pad on his lap and was taking notes.

"I'm surrounded," I shouted, "by Americans!"

WE DROVE NORTH on Highway 77, a double highway, two lanes going in each direction, and there was a large grassy strip of land between the lanes. Everything was very clearly marked with big green signs. There were no chickens, burros, or oxcarts on the road. Everyone had lights that worked.

Outside of a town called Raymondville, we were stopped at an immigration checkpoint. The officers chatted with us for all of thirty seconds, then waved the truck through.

"What kind of checkpoint was that?" Garry said.

We were consumed by an entirely feigned anger and shouted at each other fiercely.

"They call that a checkpoint?"

"Wimp!" Garry screamed. "Wimp checkpoint. We should have said, 'Okay, we give up. Take us to the pit. Where's your pit?' You need a pit that doubles as a garbage dump."

"Do we have to teach them how to run a checkpoint? What you do: first you turn off all the lights and then you take people around the corner in the dark."

"To the pit."

"That's full of garbage . . ."

"And you have to put a gun to someone's neck."

We drove for several more hours admiring the flawless monotony of the road. There was an old Aretha Franklin song on the radio and we cranked it up. Somebody named Dick Barkly told us that the song had been brought to us, in part, by Big A Auto Parts. It was, Barkly continued, a solid-gold Saturday night.

Which meant we were going to get into Dallas about a day ahead of schedule.

FULL-TILT
ROTO

-- -- -- -- -- -- -- -- --

October 18–22, 1987

WE SLEPT in Kingsville, drove to Corpus Christi on time for a
Central American–type red-ball sunrise over the Gulf of Mexico, then
stopped in San Antonio to have a celluar phone installed, all of which
put us in Dallas at three on Sunday afternoon. The press conference
was scheduled for Monday, at nine o'clock in the morning.

Garry handled the waiting well. It was his job: the PR payback. We
met with some representatives of the public-relations firm who wanted
to talk about the trip thus far. The PR people cautioned us not to make
the transit of Nicaragua sound "too easy." On the other hand, Chistita
Caldera from Intourismo in Managua wanted us to make the country
sound like a lot of fun for dentists. This, I thought, might require some
tap dancing.

I washed our clothes while Garry watched the mechanics put a new
auxiliary fuel tank in the truck. The Sierra also got new shocks, four
new tires, an oil change, and a new fuel filter. The back of the truck
was cleaned and organized.

I had some time to fill in a pocket calendar with our driving days.
If we left tomorrow at noon, hit it full-tilt roto, all the way to Prudhoe
Bay, we could be there in under twenty-five days, easy.

"Why not," I suggested, "do it in under twenty-four?"

"Let's do it," Garry said.

THE NEXT MORNING, we were standing in the front of the dealership
at nine, ready to lift the veil of secrecy that had shrouded our project
from the very beginning. From here on north, there was no significant
threat of banditry or terrorist activity. Now it could be told.

The media, however, wasn't much interested in what was under the

veil. It was not the kind of slow news day that generates our kind of
story. The stock market had opened badly. We were trying to talk about
places with names like Ushuaia during the Black Monday stock-mar-
ket crash.

Big money is a big story in the United States. So is ongoing human
drama, and there was a potential tragedy in progress just a bit south
of us, in Texas. It seemed that a little girl had fallen into a well. She
was trapped there. The rescue efforts were being televised nationally,
even as we spoke. Every reporter in Texas was there. Which is why so
few of them were in Dallas to see us lift the veil of secrecy.

WE LEFT AT NOON, twenty-one hours after hitting Dallas. Before that,
one of the supervising mechanics in the service department of the
dealership asked if he might speak with us. The man said he was a
born-again Christian and would offer us a blessing. He prayed that we
would have a safe journey. We thanked him for his concern.

"Who was that guy?" I asked Garry. "Did you meet him last night?"

"No."

"Nice guy, though."

"Yeah," Garry said, "Mr. Godwrench."

THE SIGN was a blue shield with a little crown of red: 35. We took the
interstate north into a big, flat, straw-colored grassland that was
patched red with shrubs in their autumn colors. We had had our spring
in Buenos Aires and now we would get to appreciate fall until dark.
When the sun came up, it would be winter.

IN 1910, there was no auto road across America. There were a series
of dusty tracks heading west, but they all ended somewhere in Nebraska. After that, the road was a wandering progression of ruts across
the prairies. Adventurers attempting to drive beyond Nebraska encountered fences and locked gates.

By 1923, a coast-to-coast highway, Route 30, had been built. According to Phil Patton, in his book *Open Road*, there were road signs on
Route 30, but they were not uniform, and interpreting them was a
matter of intuition: did the skull and crossbones mean dangerous intersection, and was it necessary to stop at the painted picture of a raised
palm?

The sudden popularity of the installment plan in the 1920s put
America on wheels. By 1925, over half the families in the country
owned a car. The roads weren't very good, the road signs were some-

times enigmatic, and first-time carowners did not always drive with grace and precision.

Measured in terms of deaths per million miles driven, the 1920s was the deadliest decade in the history of American driving. The road was a festival of blood.

With all the cars on the road, people began to demand convenience. They wanted to be able to drive to the market and park there, a few steps from the door. Roadside business became good business. By the 1930s, American highways were cluttered with shops and clubs and restaurants. One forty-eight-mile stretch of U.S. 1 was found to have nearly three thousand buildings with direct access to the road. There was a gas station every 895 feet.

IN SOUTH AND CENTRAL AMERICA, there are still roadless areas, or places where a cross-country road is nothing more than a path scraped out of the jungle.

There are good drivers on the Pan-American, and bad ones. The rules of the road are informal, and it is assumed that a certain amount of blood will flow. We had not seen a lot of accidents. There was an ambulance screaming away from a wreck in Buenos Aires. We saw trucks off the road here and there; we saw those glittering piles of glass in the Atacama Desert. And then, in Central America, the inherent necrological density of the Pan-American manifested itself on the Mountain of Death, where someone in a white pickup truck took a ten-thousand-foot dive into the Atlantic. There had been blood on the highway near Guatemala City. A man, possibly dead, lay in a field near his wrecked truck in Mexico. These were human tragedies, but it was the dog that died in Guatemala—the sound of crunching bones—that had underscored the bloody nature of the road.

"It seems," Garry said, "darker there."

"It's because there are no cleared shoulders," I guessed. "The forest runs right up to the road." Sometimes the trees were luxuriant and branches formed a canopy over the road, so that, in the day, you were driving through a green tunnel. At night, the headlights did not seem to penetrate the darkness.

Everyone had access to the road. Businesses, rushing to take advantage of traffic on the Pan-American, literally lined the road. Patrons in bars and cantinas could stumble out the front door and onto the Pan-American in a matter of steps.

"And the people," Garry said.

People walked along the shoulderless road because the jungle was thick in places, and, even for those on foot, the highway often the fastest way to go. Sometimes the road was the only clearing, the only flat spot, and if there was little traffic—for instance, on the alternate route over the Mountain of Death out of San José, Costa Rica—people might use the road to work, to slaughter sheep, for instance.

The Pan-American was a form of entertainment. Whole families—men, women, toddlers—stood on the side of the road, watching semis howl by two feet from their faces. Lovers walked hand in hand under the trees, on the pavement, in the darkness. Children dodged traffic for fun and kicked soccer balls to one another across the Pan-American.

It was all very much like the American road of the 1920s, even down to the matter of bandits.

In the U.S., during Prohibition, fast cars were used to run liquor. Later, gangsters—drive-by assassins with tommy guns—operated out of Chicago. Clyde Barrow, of Bonnie and Clyde fame, wrote Henry Ford a letter praising the V-8 engine: for getaways, Clyde thought, a V-8 was the cat's pajamas. The mythology of the road in the 1930s was one of fast cars chasing fast cars over dirt roads through the eroded farmlands of the dust bowl.

There were criminals in cars, and bandits on the road. J. Edgar Hoover called overnight car camps "camps of crime."

ALL THIS is again from *Open Road,* Phil Patton's celebration of the American highway. Patton also examines the genesis of U.S. interstates. They were originally tagged national defense highways and were vigorously championed, in the 1950s, by President Dwight Eisenhower, whose experience in two world wars taught him the military value of a good road.

In 1919, Eisenhower was one of thirty-five officers assigned to a motorized column of seventy-nine vehicles that were to drive from Washington to San Francisco. The trip took fifty-six days.

Twenty-five years later, Eisenhower, as military head of occupied Germany, studied that country's autobahn system, the world's first real system of superhighways. The principles of the modern auto road—division of traffic by a median, the separation of roads at intersections with ramps and bridges, the limitation of access—had all lent themselves to Hitler's theories of mechanized attack and blitzkrieg.

The Eisenhower administration pushed for a system of similar roads called national defense highways. During the late 1950s, at the height of the Cold War, the new system of highways was sold not only as a way to move men and munitions: national defense highways could also be used to evacuate cities in the case of nuclear attack.

The construction of America's interstate highways remains the most expensive and elaborate public-works program of all time. In 1984, near the town of Caldwell, Idaho, reporters and officials watched as "red-eyed Pete, the last stoplight on the interstates," was ceremoniously removed, placed in a coffin, and buried.

WE WERE DOING THE LEGAL LIMIT, which we figured was sixty-five miles an hour, plus five or ten more, depending on the flow of traffic. Canada was only twenty hours away. We would not even have enough time to get bored with the interstates.

Garry worked the cellular phone, chatting with radio talk-show hosts about the drive, working on the payback. Then it was night and there was a fine dusting of dry, powdery snow swirling across the interstate south of Fargo, North Dakota.

At eight-forty the next morning, we crossed into Canada. The officer at the Canadian border station was an attractive woman with strawberry-blond hair who saw the markings on the Sierra—ARGENTINA TO ALASKA IN 25 DAYS OR LESS—and said, "Well, what day is it?"

I checked my calendar. "The morning of the twenty-first day," I said.

"Well," she said, "I guess you boys better get trucking."

She was unarmed.

She was Canadian.

She was nice.

Garry said, "I knew people were going to start asking that question when we got to North America. I'm glad we didn't have to change the sign."

"What do you mean, change the sign?"

"I've got a bunch of sticker numbers in the back. If we were here in thirty days, I could have changed it to read, 'Argentina to Alaska in thirty-five days or less.' "

There was a long silence.

"Why," Garry said finally, "do I wish I hadn't told you that?"

IN WINNIPEG, Manitoba, Garry did a TV interview with the Canadian Broadcasting System. We turned west on Canada 1 and drove into a nasty blizzard. Wet, heavy snow clung to the branches of bare trees but turned to ice on the road. Traffic crawled along at twenty-five miles an hour but winter only lasted fifteen minutes.

It stopped snowing, though the clouds hung low over the land and the sky was a tenebrous misery of gloom. We drove with our lights on, and Garry put the hammer down: there was a press conference in Regina, Saskatchewan, at four o'clock.

We sailed over fields of sandy-brown grain stubble interspersed with patches of snow. It was the kind of land that would convince any reasonable person that the earth was flat. Regina was nowhere in sight, and then, bang, there it was. The city has no outskirts: it simply rises from the prairie in a clumping of ten-story-high buildings. There was a break in the clouds to the west of the city, and the sun fell over the modest high-rises of Regina in a single encompassing pillar.

I felt as if I were on an alien planet. Regina looked like a city in a science-fiction illustration: it was all gleaming towers and celestial illumination set in a monotonous, frightening plain that spread from horizon to horizon.

We did a radio interview, talked with a newspaper reporter, and, a few hours later, spent another half hour doing a press conference in Saskatoon. At midnight, while I tried to sleep, Garry stopped in Edmonton, Alberta, for a television interview. The cameras were waiting for him on the road. I heard him say that Edmonton was the midway point between Dallas and Prudhoe Bay. The reporter thought our sleeping arrangements unique, and there was a time when bright lights filled the cab of the truck. I heard an announcer's voice mention "a great adventure." Piss off, I thought, and pulled the pillow over my head.

About seven-thirty the next morning, I was driving through Grande Prairie, Alberta. The skies were still a bit cloudy and the sunrise—from false dawn to full light—took over two hours. It was like the endless sunrises and sunsets of southern Argentina. We were coming down a long shallow slope into Grande Prairie, and the lights of the town glittered in different colors under the feeble silver glow of the rising sun.

At nine o'clock, the clouds took on the faintest tinge of pink, but to the west, where we were going, I could see clear blue sky. And at Dawson Creek, British Columbia, the sky was, indeed, deep blue. People were walking around in light jackets. They dressed like Hondurans, in cowboy hats and jeans.

DAWSON CREEK is about four thousand miles from Dallas and about two thousand miles from Prudhoe Bay. It is also "mile one" of the

ALCAN or Alaska Highway. During the Second World War, the Japanese attacked Alaska and occupied two islands in the Aleutians, the archipelago that stretches south and west of the mainland.

The ALCAN Highway, a military supply route to Alaska for U.S. forces, was built to defend the mainland, and it was completed in November of 1942. The Canadian portion of the highway was turned over to Canada at the end of the war. The Alaska-Canadian Military Highway was opened to the public in 1948.

Driving the road used to be a survival trip. These days, the road is asphalt all the way to Fairbanks.

I took the wheel out of Fort Nelson and pushed the truck through Stone Mountain Provincial Park. It was the kind of mountain road automobile enthusiasts dream about: moderately challenging, with nicely banked turns winding through staggering scenery. It was, incidentally, entirely free of police. I took the corners hard, listening to the tires scream on the asphalt, and thought that I had never enjoyed driving more.

The sun dropped low in the sky, gathered itself, thought better of setting just yet, made a southward detour, and began to roll along the horizon. A black bear sow and two cubs were wrestling around in the stubbly grass on the shore of a lake. I saw two other black bear on the drive. There was a moose in a small pond, standing belly-deep in the water, grazing on aquatic plants. The slanting light was golden.

IT WAS DARK and our shifts at the wheel now lasted only three or four hours. I was driving and we were somewhere north of Whitehorse, in the Yukon Territory. There was a dream I wanted to have and it was waiting for me every time I closed my eyes. I thought: you should close your eyes. Your eyes hurt and they need rest.

When I blinked for more than a fraction of a second, the dream was there, playing on the inside of my eyelids. I was in an antiseptic room wearing a white coat. I was a doctor or perhaps a scientist.

The road ahead ran straight and there were no lights anywhere.

"Close your eyes. There's no traffic. It's safe now. Close your eyes. It's good to rest your eyes. Close your eyes and see what happens."

I shook my head and a dull ache became a sharp pain.

"Close your eyes and it won't hurt anymore. You'll drive better if your head doesn't hurt. Just close your eyes."

I noticed that I had pencils and pens in the pocket of my white coat. There was someone at the door of the antiseptic room and I didn't know who it was, but I knew for certain that something good was going to happen.

There was a sound that I knew was our engine and another sound that was the hum of our tires on the road. These sounds bothered me. I wanted to open my eyes.

"It's only a short blink. Don't worry. Things happen fast in dreams . . ."

I stopped hard in the middle of the empty road and woke Garry.

"I think I'm tired," I said.

THE DAYS AND NIGHTS began to run together: the beating of a great black wing. At six-fifteen that morning we passed into Alaska at the Tok border station. A few hours later, the morning sky was a light robin's-egg blue, but the sun wasn't up yet. There were some puffy clouds in the east, and the sun, which was still somewhere below the curve of the horizon, lit these clouds from below. There was no red in the light at all. The clouds were a bright golden color, spiritual in aspect, as if they had been sanctified by the light. I studied the clouds for half an hour, and then the sun finally appeared in a sky that had been pale blue for over an hour. It hung on the horizon, in the manner of a harvest moon.

The sky turned a deeper blue but the sun's rays only touched the tops of the fir trees and the uppermost branches of bare aspens and birches. We drove down a shadowed corridor, between the trees, with the golden sunlight trapped in the branches above.

There was a thin cover of snow on the land. We were driving along the banks of the Tanana River, about fifty miles out of Fairbanks. The river was low, not yet completely frozen over, and there were places where great blocks of ice, driven by moving water, had humped up at some obstruction. These great hummocks caught the light of the sun, which was now higher in the sky, and the ice was so bright that looking at it hurt my eyes.

Where there was running water, it flowed in twisted braids through an immense valley. The water was warmer than the air so that a low, thick fog rose off its surface. These narrow banks of fog wound through the valley ahead and they, too, were golden. Everything seemed golden in what we thought would be the final sunrise of the drive.

BY TEN-THIRTY THAT MORNING, we were in Fairbanks, at a GM dealership called Aurora Motors. It had taken exactly half an hour less than three days to drive from Dallas to Fairbanks, even counting the four short press conferences we had done along the way. The GM dealer, Jim Messer, had promised to help us with one last document. We needed a permit to drive the old North Slope Haul Road to Prudhoe Bay.

The 416-mile road, now called the Dalton Highway, was built in 1974 to service the Alaska oil pipeline. The road is about thirty feet wide and took twenty-five million cubic yards of gravel to surface. The gravel insulates the permanently frozen ground. If the permafrost was allowed to melt, the road would deteriorate rapidly. In some spots, the gravel is six feet deep.

In 1978, the road was turned over to the state of Alaska and the first fifty-six miles was opened to the public. In 1981, after a bitter debate in the state legislature, public access was extended another 155 miles, to Disaster Creek.

Disaster Creek is still about 206 miles short of Prudhoe Bay, which is really an oil field, a conglomeration of drilling rigs and pumping stations. Men and women go there to work, to produce oil, and the haul road is Prudhoe's main supply line.

Permits to drive beyond the public portion of the road are issued by the Department of Transportation and are granted for commercial and industrial use only. The haul road is patrolled by a state trooper and the checkpoint, where permits must be shown, operates day and night.

So we needed a permit to complete the last few hours of the drive. The Department of Transportation, when Garry contacted them, had seen no reason to be helpful. There was no appeal.

That left us two choices. We could attempt to run the checkpoint, get arrested, never reach Prudhoe Bay, and watch the days tick by in a jail cell. This choice was unacceptable: I had gotten to the point where the clock inside my head would not stop, not until we completed the race.

The other way was to drive the road legally, on a bona fide commercial or industrial mission. This was not an insoluble problem for experienced *documenteros*.

Jim Messer, the GM dealer at Aurora Motors, bought our truck on the spot, loaned it back, and hired us to deliver a load of spare parts to a garage in Prudhoe Bay. It took an hour to fill out the proper papers, to remove our plates, and to put the temporary plates on the truck. Aurora Motors now owned the Sierra, and we had a valid permit to drive the Dalton Highway all the way to Prudhoe Bay.

*   *   *

IT'S ABOUT SEVENTY-FIVE MILES from Fairbanks to the start of the Dalton Highway. The first half of that is paved, and the pavement was covered over in glare ice so slick that, when we stopped, it was literally impossible to walk on the road. I drove along at a maddening fifteen miles an hour. Near a mountain called Wickersham Dome, the pavement ended, but the gravel was packed over with snow, and a hard layer of ice covered that. I still couldn't take it any faster than fifteen miles an hour.

We were very conscious of the hours ticking by. It was now the twenty-third day and the twelfth hour of the drive. We had about 450 miles to go. At fifteen miles an hour, it would take another day and then some to reach the end of the road. We hadn't taken that long to drive from the tip of Texas to the Canadian border.

The Dalton Highway starts just past Livengood, and, after fifteen more miles and another hour, Garry took over. He drove the ice at nearly thirty-five, feathering off on the throttle rather than braking for curves or for oncoming traffic. Garry's theory regarding glare ice was that you should drive it as if you have no brakes.

"Because," he explained, "you don't."

THE ICE STRETCHED ON for a hundred miles out of Fairbanks, but then it gave way, reluctantly and by degrees, to packed snow. Garry cranked it up to forty-five, the legal limit. He experimented once or twice with the brakes, saw that we had some friction, and pushed the Sierra to sixty.

We came over a steep sanded hill, perhaps two thousand feet high, and found ourselves in a thin winter mist that hunkered over this low summit. The mist was freezing on the branches of stunted fir trees, some of them only six feet high. As we drove down off the summit and out of the cloud, the trees became somewhat more robust but their branches were covered in thick layers of ice. The sky was bright blue and these ice trees glittered in the mid-afternoon sun.

Garry caught sight of a truck in the side mirror. He pulled over and stopped. It was the etiquette of the haul road. The Dalton Highway belongs to the trucks, especially those that are fully loaded, headed north. They take the center of the road and drive with the throttle to the floor. A heavily loaded truck has a lot of purchase on snowpack, and this one blew by us at seventy-five miles an hour. There was a valley below and a steep pitch after that. The trucker was working up speed to attack the next hill.

* * *

THE YUKON RIVER flowed below steep banks, and it was not yet completely frozen over. Blocks of water-driven ice piled up on the sandbars and sparkled under the sun. There was a large hangar-sized building fronting a trailer-park hotel. Garry got diesel and I went into the hangar, which was a café, and ordered some food to go.

There was a radiophone on my table. A sign said it would cost $3 to call Fairbanks and $2 a minute after that. Another sign above the phone cautioned me not to bring any fox carcasses back from above the Arctic Circle due to a rabies scare. I picked up a newspaper, which was, I saw, published by and for Christian truck drivers. There was a picture of a bunch of Christian truck drivers dedicating an orphanage somewhere in Oklahoma.

My bill for two turkey sandwiches, four Pepsis, and a thermos full of coffee was $22. The waitress, I saw, was reading a book about missionaries in Bolivia. The book was in Spanish and entitled *Commandos for Christ.*

The bridge across the Yukon was a sturdy wooden affair, nearly half a mile long. It had been built in 1975. Before that, Hovercraft had been used to ferry goods across the river.

The road began to rise up along shallow slopes and drop into huge and entirely unpopulated valleys, filled with snow. The slopes were labeled for the truckers: Sand Hill, Roller Coaster, Gobblers Knob. Occasionally, we would pull over for another one of the highballing trucks. Some of them were doing eighty over the smooth hard-packed snow.

A hundred miles north of the Yukon, we crossed the Arctic Circle and felt that we had truly come up in the world. The trees were gnomish and twisted. The pipeline, a huge metal monstrosity balanced on six-foot-high metal sawhorse stilts, ran along the right side of the road. From the higher points, I could see it rolling over lower snowy ridges, headed north.

Then, perhaps forty miles later, we had our first views of the Brooks Range. The mountains were shrouded in swirling silver clouds and looked darkly ominous. This range is a northern extension of the Rockies, the last major mountains in the United States to be mapped and explored.

It was four-thirty, and we had been driving with our lights on all day, because that is the law, but now we needed them. The sun, which had not risen very high in the sky anyway, was rolling south along the horizon. In another month, this land north of the Arctic Circle would undergo several weeks of twilight, and then the sun would finally set and darkness would own the land.

A light snow began to fall. The mountains to our right were great stone monoliths, so steep that the snow did not cling to their sheer slopes. The road was white, the land was white, the falling snow was white. Everything was white except for the sheerest rock slopes, which seemed to hover over the road, as if rock could float.

"We are," Garry said, "about halfway to Prudhoe."

We thought about that. It had been a halfway trip. Lima is halfway through South America. Managua is halfway through the total drive. Edmonton is halfway from Dallas to Prudhoe Bay.

"Another hundred miles," Garry pointed out, "and we'll be halfway through this last half."

We passed Disaster Creek and there seemed to be no check station. We were driving through a forest of small, stunted spruce trees. The branches on these trees were short and stubby, so that they looked like bottle washers. And then the forest gave up and we passed the last tree, the most northerly spruce on the Dalton Highway.

It was five o'clock, but the sun was still hovering slightly above the horizon and sometimes I could see it through the lightly falling snow: a dim silvery ball balanced on a snowy ridgetop.

We were making good time, running between two ranges of mountains, and then the road began its long convoluted climb into the Brooks Range. The snowpack was heavily sanded and we didn't need four-wheel drive.

The never-ending twilight was an alabaster glow to the south. Snow, dry and powdery, had been falling for hours, but here, in the mountains, wind sent it howling across the road so that it seemed to be falling horizontally. The peaks above us were white and rolling and rounded: the polar version of desert sand dunes.

There was a danger of vertigo because it was difficult to distinguish the white snow-packed road from the falling snow or the alabaster sky; it was hard to distinguish the mountains above from the drop-offs below. We were closed in on all sides by variations in white. There was a bluish tinge to the snow-sculpted peaks, and a chalky, mother-of-pearl quality to the sky. The world was all a permutation of ice.

There was a check station at the summit of what seemed to be the continental divide. We stopped and a man checked the permit, listened to our story, and came out of the building to take a photograph of the filthy truck parked in the cold silver Arctic twilight.

And then we were plunging down the north slope of the Brooks

Range, running slowly in first gear, past signs that read, unnecessarily I thought, ICY.

IT WAS NEARLY SEVEN and not completely dark. The great plain ahead sloped down toward the frozen sea. The snow was only a foot deep, so that tufts of brown grasses and hummocky red tussocks punctuated the plain. There were no trees at all.

The snowpack had given way to gravel and we could make good time. Even so, every once in a while, a kamikaze trucker blew by us, and the pebbles he threw off pitted our windshield with half a dozen stars.

The mountains formed a vast horseshoe around the plain. We followed the course of the Sagavanirktok River as it fell toward the Beaufort Sea. The road was not nearly so flat as it had looked from the mountains. The land rose and fell like ocean swells.

The snow had ceased to fall, the sky had cleared, but now a heavy wind out of the east sent a low ground blizzard swirling across the Dalton Highway. At seven-forty there was a final streak of light, far to the south, and then it was dark. Directly ahead, to the north, hanging above the highway, a star appeared. I looked up and there were stars all over the sky. They seemed to pulsate with a kind of swirling crystalline clarity that I imagined was unique to the Arctic.

But no, it was fatigue and eyestrain. Every object I looked at—the illuminated compass on the dashboard, the notepad on the suckerboard, everything—seemed to have a small haloed aura around it. In my eyes, the polar night was alive with van Gogh stars.

WE WERE HALFWAY THROUGH the last half of the drive, about one hundred miles from Prudhoe Bay. It was time for a coffee party. I poured us both a cup from the thermos full of Yukon River coffee, then doctored it with an appropriate amount of South American instant. Roto coffee.

"Oh man," Garry said. "The beginning and the end were spectacular."

"Those mountains out of Ushuaia."

"And now that pass over the Brooks Range," Garry said. "What's it called?"

"Atigun Pass."

"That's the most spectacular thing I ever saw in my life."

At 8:06 in the evening of our twenty-third night, a thin pillar of pale green light, like the beam of a colossal spotlight, shot up through the van Gogh stars. It faded, then two more rays fanned out from the north and east. The northern lights—the Inuit people call them Spirit Lights—moved across the sky like luminous smoke.

There was a faint ruby tinge at the periphery of the major displays. Ahead, there was another faint glow on the horizon: the lights of Prudhoe Bay, forty miles in the distance.

"This is nice," Garry said.

"More fun than that fog in southern Peru."

"More fun than a pit search."

We were going to come in, in under twenty-four days. In our minds, we were already there, and we found ourselves throwing out references, words, and names that wouldn't mean much to anyone else in the world at that moment. We owned these words, these images:

Zippy.

Pedro.

The Atacama.

Santiago and Luis.

The dune buggy from hell.

The Mountain of Death.

Igor and the Cyclops.

Atigun Pass.

Spirit Lights over the Arctic plain.

AND THEY ARCHED OVER US like a benediction, the Spirit Lights.

The first building we saw was a guard station that led into Standard's oil fields. It was a small building with windows on all sides because the road ran around it in two lanes. There were four security guards inside. They wore blue pants, blue jackets, light-blue shirts, and blue ties.

We parked off the road and I checked my watch and calendar. We had driven from Dallas to Prudhoe Bay in a little under eighty-five hours. Three and a half days. We jogged stiffly over to the shack. The night was bitterly cold and we were wearing the clothes we had put on for the press conference in Dallas. Over those we wore our filthy diesel-soaked jackets that were sick of talking with Korean tires.

Everything we wore needed to be burned. We probably did not look like good security risks. The guards regarded us with some suspicion until we asked them to, please, sign our logbook.

"Hey," one of the men asked, "are you the guys trying to set that record?"

We admitted that we were.

"There's a guy from *Popular Mechanics* looking for you," the man said. "He flew in yesterday with a photographer. There's a film crew here, too."

"Could you, uh, please sign the logbook?" Garry asked. "Please put the time and date in there. The, uh, the clock is still running."

The guards conferred among themselves and decided that it was precisely 10:13 on the night of October 22. All four signed our logbook.

And the clock stopped.

Factoring in the five-hour time change from our starting point in Ushuaia, it had taken us twenty-three days, twenty-two hours, and forty-three minutes to drive from the tip of South America to the edge of the frozen Beaufort Sea in Alaska.

Garry caught my eye. "Another victory," we said in ragged tandem, "for man and machine against time and the elements."

The men in the blue jackets seemed to be amused by our condition.

"So," one of the guards said, "you guys think you got this record?"

We said that we did.

"Where did you start?"

"Tierra del Fuego, at the tip of South America."

"How many countries did you go through?"

"Thirteen," I said.

"How many miles?"

We hadn't figured it out, but it was somewhere near fifteen thousand.

"And how long," one of the guards asked, "did all that take you?"

"It took," Garry replied (and I could tell that he just purely loved saying these numbers), "twenty-three days, twenty-two hours, and forty-three minutes."

The guard stared at us, as if amazed. "What'd you guys do," he asked, "walk?"

AFTERWORD

JERZY ADAMUSZEK failed to answer any letters and we were never able to locate him. He may have dropped off the face of the earth.

The 1988 *Guinness Book of World Records* accepted Prince Pierre D' Arenberg's documentation. He held the record, fifty-six days, for the drive Garry Sowerby and I made in well under half that time.

The book, however, had gone to press while we were on the road. In 1989, the editors awarded a distinguished international team of endurance drivers that record. There was even a picture of the distinguished team in the 1989 edition: two men in dirty clothes standing by their vehicle and looking, I suppose, reasonably heroic. The caption under the photo was extremely poetic. It read:

"Longest drive south to north: Garry Sowerby and Tim Cahill drove this car from the southern tip of South America to the northern edge of Alaska (with one detour by water) in less than twenty-four days, Sept. 29 to Oct. 22, 1987."

ABOUT THE AUTHOR

Tim Cahill lives in Montana, in the shadow of the Crazy Mountains. Sometimes he lives in the shadow of the Absaroka Mountains. It depends on the time of the year and the position of the sun. A contributing editor for *Outside* magazine and for *Rolling Stone*, Cahill is the author of three previous books, *Buried Dreams, Jaguars Ripped My Flesh,* and *A Wolverine Is Eating My Leg*.